The Conspiracy
Against
Aaron Burr

The Conspiracy Against Aaron Burr

By Oliver Perry Sturm

A Biography of Aaron Burr
with sketches of Alexander Hamilton, Thomas Jefferson,
John Marshall, George Washington, John Vanderlyn,
James Wilkinson, and others

Originally written in 1943 by Oliver Perry Sturm
Published in 2005 and 2019 by the Aaron Burr Association
Edited by Lyman Coddington III, Henry H. Anderson, Jr.,
and Elizabeth Cameron

STORYARTSMEDIA

Published by Story Arts Media
Sonoma, California
www.storyartsmedia.com

ISBN: 978-0-9970672-8-6
Library of Congress Control Number: 2019912573

Cover and Interior Design by Joseph Daniel

Photograph of Sir Robert de Burre brass pg. 16 by Henry H. Anderson, Jr.
Photograph of Aaron Burr bust pg. 79 by Dan Nerney
John Pierre Burr illustration pg. 324 by Deborah Tancik
Photograph of John Pierre Burr headstone pg 333 by Sherri Burr

Photo Credits: Cover & pg. 10 – Dr. John E. Stillwell, pg. 56 – E. D. Hill, pg. 62 – Princeton University, gift of Otis Morse, pg 63 – National Portrait Gallery, pg. 81 – George Washington's Mount Vernon, pg. 161 – Alamy, pg. 168 – White House Historical Association, pg. 178 – Library of Virginia, pg. 238 – New York Historical Society, pg. 239 – Yale University Art Museum, pg 264 – Lewis Walpole Library, pg. 275 – Smithsonian, pg. 316 – Biblioklept, pgs. 330 & 331 – *Wall Street Journal,* Back Cover – Getty Images

POD Edition
Printed in the United States

About the Author

Oliver Perry Sturm was born March 1870 in Missouri and died May 18, 1944, in Fayetteville, Arkansas, where he had resided for one year with his second wife, Elizabeth E. Brown, whom he married circa 1921 in Tulsa, Oklahoma. No record has been found of surviving children or any descendants, nor did he have any children from his previous marriage, to Muriel Elma [Lillard?] circa 1896 in Missouri. He had a brother, George Wesley Sturm, who predeceased him, leaving no children.

Sturm was editor of a family publication, *Sturm's Oklahoma Magazine*, which built an office building in Oklahoma City. He was also assistant editor of the Oklahoma City Times and publisher of Sturm Statehood Magazine from 1905 to 1911.

His early interest in setting the record straight on Aaron Burr appears in the November 1909 issue of *Oklahoma Magazine*:

> *Historians have endeavored always to place upon Burr the entire blame of the duel and unfortunate blot on the country's history, and as a sequence a number of his political enemies afterward succeeded in having him arrested on a charge of treason, which was never proven. . . . To me, Burr is the most maligned man in our history, and yet one of the most brilliant.*

Contents

Contents

Preface

In the early 2000s, I received in the mail, "out of the blue," a wonderful and important manuscript authored by Oliver Perry Sturm in 1943 entitled *The Conspiracy Against Aaron Burr*. Sturm, a journalist, had lived in Missouri, Oklahoma, and Arkansas; he died in 1944. The manuscript was mailed to me by a man in Fort Collins, Colorado.

I turned the manuscript over to Aaron Burr Association (ABA) genealogist Lyman B. Coddington III and to dedicated ABA member Commodore Henry H. "Harry" Anderson, Jr., who, like me, is a collateral descendant of Col. Aaron Burr. Anderson and Coddington not only used their talents to reproduce and publish the manuscript, as *The Conspiracy Against Aaron Burr*, but also collaborated with ABA members Judge Brian Hardison, Phyllis Ann Morales (my sister), and Louella Mitchell Allen—a Philadelphia descendant of Aaron's second wife, Mary Emmons, a lady of color, and their son, John Pierre Burr, who is well known, like his father, as an ardent abolitionist and literary scholar—to author and add an invaluable series of endpapers. Together, this collaboration resulted in the 2005 publication of the soft-cover, 267-paged work *The Conspiracy Against Aaron Burr*, with Endpapers #1, 2, and 3.

First, I wish to recognize, and commend to the public, the scholarly research done by Sturm on this important period of the founding of our great nation. Sturm's writing style is admirable:

concise, lively, directly to the point, and confident in its conclusions. His work is extremely, and justifiably, pro Aaron Burr. As such it fulfills the mission of the Aaron Burr Association: setting straight the historical record on Col. Aaron Burr, our country's third vice president, whom historians have referred to as the most maligned Founding Father.

This new edition of Sturm's work, with our endpapers, deserves to be placed in every library, school, and college in the U.S. The public will love this hard-to-put-down compilation.

The recent Broadway blockbuster musical *Hamilton* has popularized the Burr–Hamilton relationship and is generally favorable to Burr. Nonetheless, it suffers from a deficiency of scholarship in certain aspects important to the ABA. For example, the musical promotes as the gospel truth that Hamilton deliberately chose not to target Burr with his bullet, using the cute phrase "he threw away his shot." This is mere conjecture, but is not recognized as such, in the play's narrative, because the authors of the play portray Hamilton as the charitable good guy in the 1804 duel, and Aaron as the bad guy for deliberately striking Hamilton with his shot.

How the hidden hair-triggers (commonplace in dueling) in both pistols were set will never be known. They are well described in the brochure about the pair by their owner Chase Manhattan Bank explaining with photographs how to set them for a two-down to one-half ounce pull. If the popular misconception that Hamilton did not intend to hit Burr and therefore fired prematurely as he lowered his pistol to get on target were correct, he would have deflected his aim to left or right. A twig, however, from a branch overhead fell on Burr's scalp proving that Hamilton had no such intention. The pistols were owned by Hamilton's brother-in-law and were supplied for the duel by Hamilton.

We, at the ABA, always want to promote the truth concerning our man Aaron.

– Stuart Johnson
President, Aaron Burr Association

Aaron Burr in 1802 portrait by John Vanderlyn, protégé of Burr

Since the noblest life on earth is human life, the literature which deals with human life must always be the noblest literature. And since the individual human life must always have a distinctness and interest which cannot belong to any of the groups of human lives, biography must always have a charm which no other kind of history can rival. . . .

. . . I believe fully that the intrinsic life of any human is so interesting that if it can be simply and sympathetically put in words it will be legitimately interesting to other men.

– Philip Brooks
Biography

Introduction

When President Jefferson charged that Aaron Burr was a traitor, the accusation was believed by most Americans. Although the president failed to furnish evidence that Burr was attempting to divide the Union, his charges took such deep root in the public mind that they still persist, despite the fact that there were seven prosecutions and seven failures to convict. Nevertheless, even today, in the public mind Burr remains condemned as a villain.

Why?

To find the answer to this question, the author has explored the archives of America, England, France, and Spain. From this research new evidence has been uncovered and new explanations formed. These provide the basis for *The Conspiracy Against Aaron Burr*.

The conspiracy united Alexander Hamilton and Thomas Jefferson in a political coalition against Burr. As mastermind of the

Federalists, Hamilton intrigued, persuaded, and bludgeoned the members of that party into supporting Jefferson; not, however, until they had offered the presidency to Burr on terms he refused to consider—terms which Jefferson accepted and paid for.

Hamilton's part in the conspiracy was to attempt to destroy Burr as a candidate for governor in the 1804 New York election. During this campaign Hamilton made charges that, when brought to an accounting, he refused to either affirm or deny. His libel kindled his funeral pyre.

For years, prior to 1790, Hamilton and Burr were friends. At the bar they were the most brilliant lawyers in New York—in fact, in the United States. Hamilton was fond of Burr. He was a frequent visitor at the Burr home, where he often dined—at least until politics and business rendered them political enemies. Then it was that Hamilton displayed spleen and venom of unmitigated malignancy.

Oddly enough, Hamilton's aversion to Burr was not over a woman. Nor was it merely because of political principles, where they differed fundamentally. By instinct and education, Hamilton was an aristocrat, Burr a democrat. It was a combination of political and business differences that brought two of the most brilliant statesmen in America to a parting of the ways. It started when Burr defeated General Schuyler, Hamilton's father-in-law, for the Senate. It was encouraged by Burr having been the principal protagonist in the establishment of the Bank of Manhattan. It was exacerbated by reason of Burr being responsible for the defeat of the Federalists in 1800. By dint of his marvelous faculties, Hamilton attempted to eliminate Burr, his ablest rival, from the political arena.

Jefferson's chief object during his first term was to remove from office the twenty-six federal judges that John Adams had appointed during the closing hours of his administration. This was to be achieved by the repeal of the Judiciary Act and the impeachment of Samuel Chase. As presiding officer of the Senate, Burr declined to assist in this nefarious enterprise, which had, for its chief purpose, the ultimate impeachment of John Marshall.

Burr thereby further incurred the enmity of the president—an antagonism that prompted him to declare that Burr had "formed the no less daring projects than to reduce New Orleans, subjugate Mexico, and divide the Union."

The charge was made while Burr and fifty-five colonists were floating down the Mississippi River on their way to Louisiana, where he had purchased four hundred thousand acres of land (Ouachita Colony, formerly Bastrop property), which he proposed to colonize.

As a trap to catch Burr, James Wilkinson declared martial law in New Orleans. Burr was arrested and taken to Washington Town, the capital of Mississippi Territory. When the grand jury refused to indict him, federal district attorney Thomas Rodney held Burr illegally until Wilkinson sent agents without warrant or authority to kidnap him and deliver him to New Orleans. Wilkinson promised these agents five thousand dollars if they were successful. Realizing that Burr was to be murdered, his friends induced him to flee. This he did, only to be arrested and taken to Richmond, where he was tried for treason.

While Burr was being held, Rodney's son, Caesar A. Rodney, was appointed U.S. attorney general. Burr's prosecution had scarcely begun when the younger Rodney returned to Washington. He advised the president that Wilkinson was a "Pensioner of Spain." Aware of Wilkinson's treachery, the president insisted that this be overlooked until Burr was convicted. Rodney declared that this would exonerate Burr and convict Wilkinson, which so enraged the president that Rodney stepped aside and never again appeared in the trial, although it continued for seven months.

The accusation and trial of Burr constitute the most diabolical political crime in American annals. The president used all the power of the government to convict. He sent a check for ten thousand dollars to William Eaton, a deliberate liar. That was the price of his perfidy. As for Wilkinson, after testimony before the grand jury that was tantamount to self-conviction, he was saved by executive influence. The trial became a tyrannical display. It still stands out as the first instance of overriding the Bill of Rights—a choice bit of irony, for was not the Sage of Monticello the proud father of this very Bill of Rights?

When Jefferson realized that he did not have evidence to convict Burr, he bragged that he could satisfy the public. After seven successive attempts to convict had failed, the president forced another indictment against Burr. This drove him from home and his daughter—drove him to England, to Sweden, to Holland, to Germany, and to France. But in Europe, he continued to be hounded by sleuths so long as Jefferson was president—and even after.

Burr's exile is the strangest on record: one day he was the guest of literati, the next he held long conferences with scientists who found his mind a source of wonderment. Kings and queens were amazed that so compelling a personality should become the object of political destruction by a democratic government.

After four years of wandering, often without food or shelter, and sometimes forced to associate with the scum of the earth, Burr returned to America. There still fell upon him the lash of the political associates of Jefferson, and Burr was all but friendless. So great, however, was his ability that he resumed his position as one of the most successful lawyers in the nation—a place he occupied for a quarter of a century.

Burr's ancestry was distinguished. In college he was a precocious student. His military record was the envy of ranking officers; Burr was the youngest officer in the Revolutionary army to become a colonel. Only Hamilton was compared to him at the bar.

The married life of the Burrs was beautiful and inspiring. The love of husband, wife, and daughter is a poem that no man has ventured to portray because of its superlative beauty. Of this association and its fidelity and graciousness, seven years after her marriage Mrs. Burr wrote, "Love, in all its delirium, hovers about me; like opium, it lulls me to soft repose." Two decades later the daughter penned, "I would rather not live than not to be the daughter of such a man."

Burr cannot in time fail to be classed with the great. In his ability to bear a load of obloquy he rises like a colossus. In ward political organization, in planning the political machinery of the nation, in founding our military intelligence, and in paving the way for the United States Senate to become an open forum, Burr is deserving of enduring fame.

But what of his traducers?

Strangely, a collection of paintings intended as portraits of saints reveal impish figures from which even the canvases appear to shrink. But why uncover skeletons when Burr refused to revile his traducers? In his darkest hour, did he not say, "I never did harm or wished harm to a human being"?

And what about Burr's new portrait?

Shall it be allowed to hang where the lights and shadows will reveal him faithfully? Will it be even thoughtfully examined? Will not partisans of Hamilton and Jefferson refuse to see these three characters in the light of the records? Will they prefer darkness rather than learn the truth, if the truth removes the scales from their eyes? John Heywood wrote, "There are none so blind as those who will not see." Burr said, "Every man likes his own opinion best."

In a personal letter to the author, Walter F. McCaleb wrote:

Aaron Burr typifies the highest type of American. He loved his country, fought for it valiantly. He envisaged its coming greatness and sought with all the energy and intelligence he possessed to lay the foundations for the mightiest republic in the world. He it was who first saw the need of building the walls of the nation upon the margins of the Atlantic and Pacific Oceans. That was the dream that lay at the bottom of his "conspiracy."

Today, with the world shaken through and through by violence, perhaps a wholesome lesson can be drawn from the life of one of our greatest men, who in the hour of his betrayal never lost faith in his country.

– Oliver Perry Sturm

Brass of Aaron Burr's ancestor Sir Robert de Burre, 1302, whose manor house was at Acton in Suffolk, England, and who served under Richard I, II and III. Brasses were effigies in the days before calligraphy in stone was developed. Two companies in London stockpiled them similar to casket makers today. The coat of arms of the deceased was engraved on the shield. The feet crossed on a lamb signified that he had been anointed to join the crusades to the Middle East, but Sir Robert was too busy fighting battles for the Edwards at home to engage.

Never in the History of the United States did so powerful a combination of rival politicians unite to break down a single man, as that which arrayed itself against Burr. For as the hostile circle gathered about him, he could plainly see not only Jefferson, Madison, and the whole Virginia legion . . . but strangest of all companions—Alexander Hamilton himself, joining hands with his own bitterest enemies to complete the ring.

– Henry Adams
The History of the United States of America 1801–1817

1
First the Infant

Just as one of our greatest natural philosophers was lost to the world when Jonathan Edwards became a theologian, and one of our greatest exponents of theology was lost to the ministry when the Reverend Aaron Burr became the leading spirit in founding the College of New Jersey, so, too, the United States was deprived of its natural expansion when Thomas Jefferson prevented Aaron Burr from realizing his dream in Mexico.

Aaron Burr was born while his father, the Reverend Aaron Burr, was constructing Nassau Hall, Princeton's first building. To the great sorrow of the congregation, he had resigned from the pastorate of the Newark church that he had served for twenty years. It was late in the year 1756 when he moved his family to Princeton. Baby Aaron was a mere infant.

Aaron's grandfather, the Reverend Jonathan Edwards, was a name to reckon with. Like John Wesley, whose life was devoted to evangelizing the world, he was born in 1703. A descendant of Jonathan Edwards asserts that he was the most perfect specimen of religious evangelism that existed.

As a boy of ten he and two companions erected a booth in a swamp near his father's home to which they resorted regularly for prayer. At the age of twelve he wrote to one of his sisters, "Through the wonderful goodness and mercy of God there has been in this place a very remarkable outpouring of the spirit of God."

Rare youthful talent for observation of nature was revealed in his twelfth year when this lad wrote an elaborate description of the "wondrous way of the working of a forest spider." At thirteen he was one of thirty-one students comprising Yale College, from which institution he graduated, and to which he returned as a tutor.

Near the close of Jonathan Edwards's college days he wrote, "It pleased God to seize me with pleurisy in which he brought me nigh the grave and shook me over the pit of hell." From childhood he had revolted at the idea of "God's choosing whom he would to eternal life, and rejecting whom he pleased, leaving them eternally to perish and to be everlastingly tormented in hell." However, there came a time when he thought he believed this doctrine.

In Northampton, Massachusetts, as the leader of the clerical profession, this noted "hell-fire" preacher gathered together in twenty-three years the largest Protestant congregation in the world. This pulpit originated the Great Awakening, which was to extend to the remotest hamlet of the Colonies, to England, and to Scotland. While Edwards was still a young man, his sermons were published throughout the English-speaking world. At the height of his fame there arose a dispute between pastor and flock as to who was entitled to the sacrament. The flock argued for saints and sinners alike, but the pastor insisted on excluding the sinners. Dismissal followed this church fight, after which he retired with his large family to a humble post among the Indians at Stockbridge, Massachusetts.

Driven from the most exalted pulpit in America, Reverend Edwards accepted with profound humility his missionary charge among the Indians, where he went about the forest laboring, exhorting, and writing fourteen hours a day. Here he produced his treatise on the "Freedom of the Will." Like Pope's *Homer*, it was written on the backs of letters and the blank pages of pamphlets. Mrs. Edwards and her daughters accepted their primitive environment with rare grace and lost no time in repining; rather, they devoted their talents to making lace and painting fans that they sent to Boston for sale.

After two years of labor with the Indians, Jonathan Edwards received a visit from his intimate friend and co-worker, the Reverend Aaron Burr. From limited information, it appears that Esther Edwards, the third daughter of the family, received practically all of the guest's attention, for she immediately graduated from her art as a painter of fans and maker of laces to become the first lady of Princeton.

Until this short visit of three days to the Edwards family, the thirty-six-year-old college president had apparently shamed the ladies of New Jersey by living a bachelor's life, but his brief courtship resulted in sending to Stockbridge within a fortnight a courier, who was to return with Mrs. Edwards and Esther. They arrived at Newark on Saturday; Monday, June 29, there was a wedding. In the issue of July 20, 1752, the *New York Gazette* observed, "Probably not for some centuries has there occurred a courtship more of the patriarchal mode. Other young men endeavor to restore courtship and marriage to their original simplicity."

The marriage of the Reverend Aaron Burr and Esther Edwards united two of the most distinguished families of New England. The name of Jonathan Edwards comes thundering down the century, while that of the Burr family descends majestically from the intellectually and spiritually minded folk of Connecticut. The Edwardses were Puritans, some of whom appear to have mi-

THE CONSPIRACY AGAINST AARON BURR

grated from Germany, the Burrs from England. They had long occupied prominent places in the Colonies as landholders, members
of the militia, officers of the government, members of the court,
and ministers of the gospel. Matrimonial alliances were with the
first families.

The Reverend Aaron Burr, son of Daniel Burr, was born at
Fairfield, Connecticut, in 1716. A precocious youth, he early revealed a consuming desire for learning. He was graduated from
Yale at nineteen. Having received three scholarships for proficien-
cy in Latin and Greek, he took two years of post-graduate work.
A religious revival turned him to theology, and in 1736 he was
preaching at Greenville, Massachusetts, from where he went to
Hanover, New Jersey. Here increasing fame led to a call to Newark, where he labored for two decades as a teacher of classics, author of a standard Latin grammar, and one of the most thoughtful, inspiring preachers of the Awakening. His fame spread to
Scotland and England; his printed sermons achieved wide sale on
both continents. Like Wakefield and Edwards, he was one of the
chief exponents of the Great Awakening.

During the last ten years at Newark the energies of the Reverend Aaron Burr were largely devoted to education. He taught
mathematics, astronomy, and classical languages. What was originally a class of eight boys outgrew its quarters, and in 1746 the
College of New Jersey was established at Elizabethtown, to be
removed to Newark when he was chosen president.

With the selection of the Reverend Aaron Burr as its president the college took on new life, and plans were made for its
permanent home. Localities entered into competition to secure
the proposed Presbyterian school. Princeton was selected. Nassau
Hall was erected, also a home for the president, from which he
wrote, "The students are well pleased with the situation. I hope
Providence will raise up benefactors for us."

The Burr family was living at Newark in 1752 when the
site for Princeton College was selected. They were living there
May 3, 1754, when Sally was born. They lived in the manse on

February 6, 1756, when Esther wrote to Miss Prince that she was "unexpectedly delivered of a son." This was Aaron Burr, who was not only a son but a grandson, great-grandson, and great-great grandson of a minister of the gospel on both sides of the family. This heritage was enriched by the devotion of Jonathan Edwards to evangelism and by the obsession of the Reverend Aaron Burr for education.

Although this child lived to be an octogenarian, the crowning desire of his life was for the education of all with whom he had personal contact. Not only were his wife and daughter beneficiaries of his ambition for their intellectual improvement, but the obsession extended to every employee and even his Negro servants. What a power for the inculcation and development of youth Aaron Burr would have proven had he devoted his dynamic energies to education. Even so, probably no other man of his day so deeply influenced the education of his associates; none has left examples of better-trained minds.

Why was this rare agency for good destroyed by politics?

Esther Edwards, the mother of Aaron Burr, possessed wit, wrote with a quick pen, and was blessed with physical charm. She was privileged to become the wife of the president of the first outstanding school erected in America by the Presbyterian Church, an institution that has possessed its soul in the stride for education. That Esther was happy is evident from a letter written to Miss Prince, in which she asks, "Do you think I would trade my good Mr. Burr for any person, or anything, or all things on earth? No Sir! Not for a million such worlds."

Then Esther, in her private journals under date of January 3, 1758, gives this picture of her two-year-old son: "Aaron is a little, dirty, noisy boy. He begins to talk a little, is very sly and mischievous. He has more sprightliness than Sally, is handsomer, but not so good tempered. He is very resolute and requires a good governor to bring him to terms." The Burrs were scarcely settled in Princeton when President Burr was stricken with a fever. Before fully regaining health he visited Philadelphia. When New Jersey

Governor Belcher died, the Reverend Mr. Burr was prevailed upon to preach the funeral sermon. The exertion proved too much for his frail constitution, and on September 24, 1757, he died. Four days later the first class of twenty-two students was graduated from this institution—later to become Princeton University.

The memorial was delivered by William Livingston. From it one senses the eminent place in the hearts of all that the youthful president enjoyed. Universal grief permeated the "melancholy occasion":

> *The loss of so valuable a Man diffuses a sorrow among all ranks of People. . . . He was a gentleman of great Judgment, Sagacity, and Erudition. . . . A learned and profound Divine, amiably candid in religious sentiments, and in the pulpit fluent, sublime and persuasive. . . . His sermons were wonderfully adapted to mend the Morals and to warm the heart. In promoting the prosperity of the Seminary over which he presided, he was discouraged by no disappointments.*

Reared among people who trusted in God to become resigned to any fate, Esther wrote to her father November 2, 1757:

> *Honored Sir, I was something dampened by hearing that I should not see you until spring. But it is my comfort in this disappointment, as well as under all my afflictions, that God knows what is best for me, and for his own glory. Perhaps I doted too much on the company and conversation of such a near and dear affectionate father and guide. I cannot doubt but all is for the best, and I am satisfied that God should order the affair of your removal as shall be for his glory, whatever comes to me.*
>
> *Since I wrote my mother's letter, God has carried me through new trials and has given me new supports.*

My little son has been sick with a slow fever and has been brought to the brink of the grave, but I hope in mercy God is bringing him up again. I was enabled to resign the child (after a severe struggle with nature) with the greatest freedom. God showed me that the child was not my own, but his, and that he had a right to recall whatever he had lent whenever he thought fit; and that I had no reason to complain, or to say God was hard on me. This silenced me. In this time of trial I was enabled to enter into a renewed and explicit covenant with God. A few days after this, in talking of the glorious state my departed husband must be in, my soul was carried out in such longing desires after this glorious state that I was forced to retire from the family to conceal my joy . . . I think I had a foretaste of Heaven . . . God is certainly fitting me for himself; and when I think it will be soon that I shall be called hence the thought is transporting.

Esther's husband died in September 1757. Jonathan Edwards, after much persuasion, accepted the presidency of Princeton. Six months later he died from the inoculation for smallpox. Sixteen days later, April 7, 1758, Esther died of smallpox. She was twenty-seven. Within six months her mother, Sarah Edwards, passed to her reward—the fourth member of the family to die within a year. And so, in this brief space of time Sally and Aaron were robbed of life's richest boon—a mother's love and a father's protection.

The orphans went to live with their uncle, Timothy Edwards, at Elizabethtown, New Jersey. Sally was sent to school in Boston, from where she wrote that while she wanted very much to see her brother Aaron, she did not like the trip through the "Green Woods," for they were so dark and forbidding. The Puritanical severity of Timothy Edwards proved a poor substitute for their loving mother. Aaron's high spirits rebelled at discipline that was enforced with a rod, and on several occasions he ran away from home.

One of Aaron's early childish pranks to receive attention was the result of his throwing ripe cherries from the top of a cherry tree at an elderly lady, a guest of the home, who was primly clad in silk. Promptly the lad was reported to Uncle Timothy. Aaron was summoned to the study to receive treatment according to the Puritanical method of the household: First came a long lecture on the enormity of the offense, accompanied by a long prayer for the offender's reformation. From the beginning of these ceremonies the boy well knew how they would end, and he could correctly estimate the extent of the punishment by the length of the prayer and exhortation. A terrible castigation followed, or as Burr put it: "He licked me like a sack."

Those were days when the aged received homage from the young, or, failing in this, they were sure to be reminded of their lack of remission. The children of Jonathan Edwards, for example, arose at the entrance of their parents, and when they met in the street a clergyman or an old person, they stood aside, took off their hats, bowed, and waited until the honored one had passed. In the eyes of his uncle Timothy, the boy's affront to his elderly guest took on the proportions of a crime of magnitude.

At the age of ten, Aaron suffered an attack of wanderlust such as frequently affects an active boy. His impelling desire was for the sea. He went to New York, where he secured a post as cabin boy on a vessel that was loading. After a few days he espied a clerical-looking gentleman coming rapidly down the wharf whom he recognized as his uncle. Quickly he sprang up the rigging and climbed to the masthead. Here he was discovered and ordered down. Recognizing that his uncle could never reach him in this perilous position, he declined to descend, at least until he had negotiated terms of surrender. These were that nothing harmful should befall him because of his runaway. The agreed terms of his surrender and return were that he should resume his studies.

Aaron was diminutive in size, thin, delicate, and sensitive, but extremely fond of the outdoors—hunting, fishing, and rowing. Exercise in the sunshine added color to his cheeks and vigor to his stride. Eventually he became very rugged. His intimate friend and playmate was Matthias Ogden, brother-in-law of Timothy Edwards, with whom a close comradeship was established, and one that was to last through their lives.

He also formed a lifetime friendship with their tutor, Tapping Reeve, who later romanced and married Sally. Reeve took his bride to Litchfield, Connecticut, to live. Here he established the first law school in the United States and was elevated to the superior judgeship, then to chief justice of the supreme court of his state. An invalid much of her life, Sally Burr Reeve died in 1797.

That mind is truly great which can bear with equanimity the trifling and unavoidable vexations of life, and be affected only by those events which determine our substantial bliss.

– Aaron Burr
Private Letters

2
Aaron and Princeton

Aaron Burr and Princeton enjoyed a common fatherhood. Their births were not widely separated. Their germination was in the midst of a religious awakening and a political revolution that led to the American Independence. If Jonathan Edwards was father of the awakening that led a modern reformation among the colonies, the Reverend Aaron Burr was one of its greatest evangelists.

If ever a child was born of Puritan parentage and of an educated ancestry amid religious environment, it was the second Aaron Burr. When he was only seven, his uncle Pierrepont Edwards wrote, "Aaron is here, is hearty, goes to school and learns bravely."

At eleven, Aaron's energy and application to his books had marked him for distinction. He applied to the College of New

Jersey, which later became Princeton University, but was denied admission, not because he lacked the mental equipment but because of his diminutive size.

Deeply mortified, little Burr continued his studies alone. At thirteen he applied for admission to the junior class. He was denied this classification but was enrolled as a sophomore. Nettled at this slight to his student standing, as he saw it, he was determined to prove his worth, and he did. He led all his classmates, finishing his first year far out in front. Discovering that his mental activities were less responsive in the afternoon than in the morning, he assigned this to overeating, became very abstemious, and soon thereafter found that he could study sixteen and even eighteen hours a day.

In his junior year Aaron was awarded first place for "reading the English language with propriety, answering questions on orthography and reading the Latin and Greek languages." When Aaron graduated in 1772 at the age of sixteen, his good friend William Paterson, a Princeton alumnus of the class of 1763, wrote of the ceremony, "Speakers tolerable—none very bad or very good. . . . Burr made a graceful appearance."

As a senior Aaron read extensively but, according to his report, spent considerable time in the pursuit of pleasure. By borrowing from the university treasurer he spent his allowance before he actually received it, thus contracting a habit of running into debt that proved a millstone about his neck throughout his life.

It was in the month that Aaron graduated from Princeton that Alexander Hamilton was sitting among the ruins of St. Croix, contemplating the havoc wrought by a tropical storm and erecting his youthful "castles in the air," the architect of which was probably his tutor, the Reverend Hugh Knox.

Apparently Burr and Hamilton did not encounter each other as youths—unless they unknowingly passed on the streets of Elizabethtown in the summer of 1773; Hamilton was there preparing for college, while Burr often visited Matthias Ogden and many of his father's old friends in the old town during that season.

The essays of Aaron's college days were written under the eye of William Paterson. Two of the subjects were "The Passions" and "Style." "The passions," wrote Aaron, "if properly regulated, are the gentle gales which keep life from stagnating, but if let loose, the tempests which tear everything before them."

Then Aaron inquires, "Do not the provinces plundered and laid waste by fire and the sword; do not nations massacred and slaughtered by the bloody hand of war; do not all these dreadful and astonishing revelations recorded in the pages of history show the fatal effects of lawless passion?"

Of this Aaron was quite sure; also, that it is a "part of reason to soothe the passions and keep the soul in pleasant serenity and calm; if reason rules, all is quiet, composed and benign; if reason rules, all the passions, like a musical concert, are in unison."

Aaron's definition of "Style" was "an elegant simplicity of language. . . . A simple style, like a simple food, preserves the appetite. But a profusion of ornament, like a profusion of sweets, palls the appetite and becomes disgusting."

Aaron joined the American Whig Society, but withdrew to join the Cliosophic Society, its reorganization having taken place in 1770. Since the parent organization was patronized by William Paterson, Oliver Ellsworth, Robert Ogden, Tapping Reeve, Luther Martin, Samuel Spring, and Aaron's uncle Jonathan Edwards, it is quite likely that these friends were instrumental in the change.

Burr has accused himself of dissipation; however, since he neither ate nor drank to excess at any time in his life, apparently his dissipation consisted of reading the products of the best minds, some of which were tabooed by his puritanical forefathers, as well as by his student associates. Independent thought and action early led Burr into forbidden paths. He was eager for the truth and dared to follow such provocative pens as Paine and Voltaire.

Frederick the Great, the Seven Years War, and the rumblings of the French Revolution caught Burr's ear and quickened his pulse. A new era was in the offing, and his sensitive soul was awake to its coming. He was a prodigious reader of the lives of great men, especially those whose strategic prowess had paved the way to military glory.

For several generations after Burr's time there, students of the Princeton campus were taken to a spot to be told a story of Catherine Bullock—which the traducers of the youthful Burr contrived to keep alive—to the effect that Burr had seduced her as the result of a wager. A Princeton reference librarian of the name of Collins, however, has furnished evidence that Miss Bullock did not die of a broken heart; on the contrary, that she died in the home of her aunt at Prospect, that the cause of her death was consumption, and that she died with the love and esteem of her family—a thing that would have been improbable in her day had she strayed from the paths of virtue.

In Burr's schooldays, Princeton was a tiny village situated in a great forest. The inhabitants were chiefly Quakers and Dutch. It was miles from a large town, being situated on the main highway about halfway between New York and Philadelphia. Travelers going in either direction usually stopped for the night. A coachload of people and a number of other travelers were at the college tavern almost every night.

At a billiard table kept chiefly for the entertainment of the guests, one night Burr played for stakes and won. He was so degraded by the circumstance that he resolved that never again would he play any game for money, a resolution that he faithfully kept throughout his life.

During Aaron's senior year a great religious revival swept through the school. Many students were interested and joined the church. Aaron was urged to accept the faith of his father and mother, failing which he was threatened with the penalties of the hellfire doctrine of his grandfather Edwards. Conscience-stricken, Aaron sought the counsel of Doctor Witherspoon, since he respected the religion of his parents and the influence of four generations was in his blood.

John Witherspoon had been president for three years. He was a Scot Presbyterian in whose veins flowed the blood of John Knox and the Covenanters, who believed the prevailing excitement was not truly religious but rather fanatical. Thus the spiritual ardor of the youth was allowed to cool upon the altar of Scot conservatism.

Aaron spent the spring and summer of 1773 in the vicinity of Elizabethtown, reading, swimming, boating, and fishing. Military tactics caught his eye and absorbed his inquiring mind, as did the maneuvers of the British on Staten Island, for the world was topsy-turvy with the preparations for war and its clarion call to youth.

When one learns that Aaron was small of stature and possessed a big mouth and small ears, it appears a bit paradoxical that he should have been considered handsome. The chief attraction of his large head were his deep, round hazel eyes, which flashed so irresistibly that no one who looked into them ever forgot their charm—smiling and captivating, but at times so penetrating as to strike terror in those minds he sought to fathom.

Aaron was dominating. He possessed such natural leadership even as a boy that his associates dubbed him "Chief." His personality was presided over by a preternaturally keen mind. In youth he guarded his emotions and persistently schooled his mental processes that he might be prepared for every emergency and master of every situation.

Having decided that vanity dominated the fair sex, Aaron indulged flatteries while in their presence, although he preferred their society to the male, over whose minds he subtly exercised an almost irresistible power. Even in youth he was captivating and perturbing, a strange personality who was to become a powerful factor in the legal, military, and political development of America.

After persistent persuasion by friends and relatives, Aaron began preparation for the ministry; over and over he had been told "remember, it was the prayer of your father and mother" that he should become an apostle of Paul. The study of theology was begun at Bethlehem, Connecticut, under instruction by an old friend of his father, the Reverend Joseph Bellamy.

A few months demonstrated that Aaron Burr possessed an inquiring mind that carefully investigated every question with an

honest endeavor to learn the truth. Doctor Bellamy prided himself on his skill in presenting the Socratic questioning method in
which Benjamin Franklin had indulged. The object was to prevent
the pupil from accepting any dogma. This proved a dangerous
method for the learned teacher of theology to use when young
Burr was allowed to ask questions, for soon we find him writing
his friend Ogden, at Elizabethtown, that he had the good old doctor completely "under his thumb!"

When Aaron took leave of the Reverend Doctor Bellamy in
the summer of 1774, he recorded that in his opinion "the road to
heaven was open to all alike." Immediately he turned his attention
to the law, and placed himself under the instruction of his dear
friend, Tapping Reeve, his brother-in-law, with whom he could be
near his sister Sally.

At Litchfield, Connecticut, Aaron found an air of intellectual and religious toleration. Blue laws were relaxed. No longer
were penal statutes against the Quakers enforced, and legally
prescribed prayer books and legislative observance of Christmas
were dead letters. Here, too, he had a violent flirtation with pretty Miss Dorothy Quincy, who was summering at Fairfield forty
miles away. She protested that she was not permitted to spend
one moment alone with Mr. Burr, whom she found "a handsome
young man with a pretty fortune." At this time Miss Quincy was
engaged to marry John Hancock.

Other girls fell in love with Aaron; one "actually professed
love to me," Aaron was afterward to admit to Matthias Ogden.
"I felt foolish enough, and actually gave as cautious a turn as I
could, for I am destined to suffer her future hostility."

Aaron was at the impressionable age where beauty quickens
the pulse. He came near wedding, but because of a delayed fer-
ry the elopement was stopped. The prospective bridegroom was
ducked in the river by the irate parent and brother of the bride-
to-be, who was hastily snatched away, and time and destiny gave
example to Burns's observation that "The best laid schemes o'
mice an' men, Gang aft a-gley."

That combination of qualities . . . which fits a man to be a successful military commander, he possessed in a more remarkable degree, perhaps, than any other American who has won distinction in war. If [Burr] had been as much in the eye of Napoleon as he was in Washington's, the emperor would have made a marshal of him, and he would have shared with Napoleon his splendid immortality.

– James Parton
The Life and Times of Aaron Burr

3
At the Cannon's Mouth

The eagerness displayed for his studies did not compare with the enthusiasm with which the young Burr discarded his books to grasp a sword. Burr was sure he was born to command. His stripling appearance notwithstanding, did he not tower three inches above Napoleon, who was soon to conquer the world?

Burr's courage was perfect. His senses could not be startled; disaster and horror only steeled his nerves. He was a good horseman, a trained helmsman, a fair fencer, and a crack shot. He had studied every available authority of some of the best critics of the Revolution. That he was born to command was demonstrated at Quebec.

It was on the battlefield and at the "cannon's mouth" that Aaron Burr's sterling qualities of character were revealed. In old age, as Burr contemplated life's accomplishments, it was his judgment that his legal honors and political prowess were commonplace when compared with his military achievements.

Even the study of Blackstone could not prevent Burr's blood being stirred by the news of the Stamp Act of Massachusetts, the Riot Act in New York, the Boston Massacre, the Tea Party, the Port Bill, and the Continental Congress. It was in the midst of these that he wrote to Matthias Ogden concerning the Barrington mob that had destroyed the home of a Tory who was "suspected of being unfriendly to the liberties of the people."

Burr saw fifty men enter the town on horseback, each armed with a white club, heard the bells ringing and drums beating, and beheld soldiers marching. Would Ogden join him? He would, and immediately the two were off for Cambridge, Massachusetts, with a letter from John Hancock to General Washington recommending "Mr. Ogden and Mr. Burr, of the Jerseys."

But Washington's ragged, untrained recruits put a damper on the spirits of the eager pair. Learning that Colonel Benedict Arnold was enlisting men for an expedition against Quebec, with prospects for immediate action, the Jersey boys quickly enlisted, as did Captain Samuel Spring.

After the capture of Fort Ticonderoga in May, two expeditions against Quebec were planned: one under General Philip Schuyler by way of Lake Champlain into the St. Lawrence, the other under Benedict Arnold straight to Quebec through the wilds of Maine.

If the latter was less tactically conceived, it offered greater adventure; besides, the Kennebec and Chaudier rivers flowed into the St. Lawrence opposite Quebec, affording opportunity to take the city by surprise. When General Schuyler was temporarily retired on account of illness, his command was transferred to General Richard Montgomery, who had seen service under the distinguished General Wolfe.

Assembling at Newburyport, Massachusetts, were three companies of riflemen and two battalions of volunteers; it was to join these that Burr and his companions walked sixty miles to Cambridge. A number of family letters greeted him protesting against his participation in the dangerous undertaking; one, from the family physician, Dr. James Cogswell, implored, "You are not strong enough, it is impossible for you to endure the fatigue, you will die, I know you will die."

A message from his guardian, Timothy Edwards, ordered Burr to come home; to the bearer he indignantly inquired, "How do you expect to take me back, if I should refuse to go? If you were to make any forcible attempt on me, I'd have you hung up in ten minutes." After a more persuasive message failed to return Burr to his anxious relatives, a bag of gold from Edwards was delivered, and the messenger returned alone to Stockbridge.

The eleven hundred youthful warriors were divided into four divisions that set out on consecutive days, Colonel Arnold on September 25, and the second division under General Greene, with whom were Aaron and Matthias, on the following day. Sleet and snow froze their clothes; soon their boots were worn out, and their bare feet trod the frozen ground.

The green, poorly constructed boats were dashed to pieces against the rocks. Their food spoiled; then it was exhausted. For eight days they were without meat. Some of the men feasted on the quarters of a dog that had been left hanging in a tree by the preceding divisions, but others had not even dog meat.

Disheartening messages concerning the other divisions reduced morale. Less than half of their number survived to reach Quebec. The expedition proved one of the most heartbreaking adventures of the Revolution.

It was November 30 that Colonel Arnold wrote General Montgomery, "This will be handed to you by Mr. Burr . . . son to the former President of New Jersey College [who] has acted with great spirit and resolution on our fatiguing march. His conduct . . . will be sufficient recommendation to your favor."

While a thousand soldiers dallied before Quebec, Burr organized fifty personally selected men whom he trained in scaling the walls of the city on almost perpendicular ladders; the plan of assault was to send three simultaneous attacks against the Upper Town to distract attention from a fourth upon the bastion.

Burr's plan was rejected. The charge was made against Lower Town at five o'clock on the morning of December 31, 1775, during a heavy snowstorm. As the four divisions advanced, Captain Burr marched by the side of General Montgomery. Having passed the palisades, they were about to take the blockhouse, from which the garrison had fled, when suddenly one of its number returned and fired the blockhouse gun.

Of the head of the column, only Burr and the French guide escaped. Montgomery died in the arms of his staff officer, Captain Burr, who rallied the column and endeavored to push forward; however, Colonel Campbell, now in charge, ordered a retreat, and amidst "a shower of musketry" Burr attempted to carry the body of Montgomery from the field, but the snow made the task too difficult for him.

The attack on Quebec failed, but it has left imperishable fame and glory for Aaron Burr, whose intrepid conduct had thrilled his comrades and resulted in his promotion to brigade major. In February he wrote to his sister Sally that "Dirty, ragged, money-less and friendless" he had been returned to Montreal, to Camp Sorrel, to Fort Shamble, and finally to the States on "Public Business."

It was fortunate that the news of the attack on Quebec had not revealed that Burr was on Montgomery's staff, Tapping Reeve told him in January, for:

> *I concealed it from your sister until the eighteenth when she found it out; but in less than half an hour, I received letters from Albany, acquainting me that you were in safety and had gained great honour by your intrepid conduct. . . . It was happy for us that we did not know that you were an aide-de- camp, until we heard of your welfare; for we had heard that Montgomery and his aide-de-camps were killed without knowing who his aide-de-camps were.*

When Burr's fame reached Washington, he invited him to become a member of his staff, which was housed in Richmond Hill in New York. Alexander Hamilton did not join the staff until March 1, 1777.

Burr soon perceived that General Washington possessed a limited education, and that he lacked technical military knowledge that Burr expected in a commander-in-chief. Although the headquarters throbbed with military spirit, it denied Burr the opportunity for the action he had experienced on the battlefield, and under this new restrictions he chafed.

In his *Life and Times of Aaron Burr*, James Parton wrote, "General Washington was as fond of adulation as he was known to be sensitive to censure, and no officer could stand well with him who did not play the part of his worshiper. He could not bear near his person, said Burr, a man of independent habit of mind."

Washington was not chosen commander-in-chief because those responsible for his elevation thought him a military genius, but rather because they had confidence in his integrity, honor, and business ability—especially his ability to gather the sinews of war. They wanted the support of Virginia and other Southern colonies. Massachusetts and New York bore the original brunt of war, and only George Washington could bring to their aid the South.

Marvelous deeds did not crown the youth of Washington. Like Franklin and Jefferson, he was considered a dull boy in school, yet he was endowed with energy and frugality. He was not born rich. He accumulated seventy thousand acres of good land and married a rich widow who brought to his estate two hundred thousand dollars in cash, sixty-five thousand of which went into the Revolutionary War.

Washington's figure inspired respect. His tall stature, large hands, and number-thirteen boots gave him an imposing appearance that approached the majestic. With all this he was inclined to be a bit haughty; still, he was commanding, dignified, and even handsome.

Captain Burr was ill at ease at Richmond Hill, and on the recommendation of John Hancock he was transferred as aide to

General Israel Putnam. This fiery old Connecticut Yankee had suffered alike with General Washington from a lack of youthful educational advantages; both failed in a facility of expression in polite English. However, neither hesitated to substitute "cuss-words" for sake of emphasis while commanding an army.

It appears a bit paradoxical that Burr should have been critical of Washington's lack of military tactics, inasmuch as he was immediately to become appreciative and even sympathetic toward General Putnam. In fact the blunt-spoken, hard-riding old Indian fighter so completely won the youthful Burr that soon he was referring to him as the "good old general."

Under General Putnam's protection Major Burr found the beautiful Miss Margaret Moncrieffe, a cousin of the late General Montgomery, and a daughter of the British general stationed on Staten Island, at whose instigation she had come to New York to be placed under General Putnam. Fascinated by the clever miss, who apparently was not more than fourteen, Burr wondered why one so young should be placed in a position within reach of military secrets that were not trusted to seasoned American soldiers. He resolved to solve the mystery. To do so he paid her court. To his surprise she took the initiative, inviting long strolls in the moonlight and even along the battery, giving rise to rumors of more mutual interests. But the more cautious Burr soon demonstrated that he was the better spy. The general's charge was arrested and sent to Kingsbridge. If General Putnam was amazed at the revelation, he was doubly appreciative of the promptness with which Burr had the girl sent to a place of safekeeping.

In August of 1776, Major Burr, at the direction of General Putnam, was assigned to General Alexander McDougall to inspect the men and fortifications that General Washington had so hurriedly thrown together in preparation for the Battle of Brooklyn. His report was caustic. Burr recommended that the fortifications be abandoned, and at the same time he originated the suggestion that New York City also be abandoned and burned. When this came to the attention of the commander-in-chief, Burr's report was ignored, save that he was characterized as "the little upstart." But soon the fleeing battalions that Burr desired removed in military order were conveyed across the East River in disgrace and disaster, and Burr's recommendations were to be approved after the retreat by General Nathanael Greene and John Jay. But Washington never forgave Burr for his "recommendations."

Though Burr's report concerning the abandonment of Brooklyn Heights, and his suggestion that New York also be burned and allowed to fall into the hands of the British, was later approved by some of the best counselors of Washington, it aroused in the commander-in-chief a lasting antipathy for Burr, whose talents were so often the envy of many associates and contemporaries.

In the abandonment of New York, General Gold Selleck Silliman's brigade was overlooked, and left occupying the small fort. Lieutenant Isaac Jennings and Private Andrew Wakeman afterward reported:

> *We had but just got into the fort when Aaron Burr rode up and inquired who commanded there; Colonel Henry Knox presented himself, and Burr asked the Colonel what he did there, and why he did not retreat with the army. The Colonel replied that it was impossible to retreat, as the enemy were across the island, and that he meant to defend that fort; Major Burr ridiculed the idea of defending the place, being, as he said, without provisions or water or bomb proof . . . and again urged Colonel Knox to retreat to Harlem Heights; but Colonel Knox said it would be madness to attempt it.*
>
> *A smart debate ensued, the Colonel adhering to his opinion. [But] Burr addressed himself to the men, and told them if they remained there, they would before night be all prisoners and crammed into a dungeon, or hung like dogs. He engaged to lead them off, and observed that it would be better that one half*

should be killed fighting, than all be sacrificed in that cowardly manner. The men agreed to follow him, and he led them out. . . .

About four miles from town we were fired upon by a party of the enemy. Burr galloped directly to the spot the firing came from, hollering to the men to follow him. It proved to be only . . . a company of the enemy, who immediately fled. Burr and his horsemen pursued and killed several of them; while he was thus engaged the head of the column had taken the wrong road. . . . Burr came up and hurried us to the left, into a wood, and rode along the column from front to rear, encouraging the men, and led us out to the main army with very small loss.

The coolness, deliberation and valor displayed by Major Burr, in effecting a safe retreat without material loss, and his meritorious services to the army on that day, rendered him the object of peculiar respect from the troops, and the particular notice of the officers.

Captain Alexander Hamilton's company of New York artillery, a member of the brigade under Knox, on that historic afternoon managed to escape capture or possible annihilation by the British. In his biography of Hamilton, under the title *Portrait of a Prodigy*, David Roth wrote, "Oddly enough he was saved by the most improbable emissary Hamilton's guardian angel ever employed."

After noting that "It was the first time that Hamilton ever saw Burr; that he was a singularly handsome youth, even smaller than himself," Roth observes, "Burr was bearing lightly the burden of a great name, the reputation for precocious brilliance and the laurels of remarkably distinguished conduct at the siege of Quebec."

Of this meeting between two of the most brilliant men of the Revolution, Roth writes:

Impatiently, the natty young officer demanded to know what they were waiting for. Brushing aside the sweating Knox's melodramatic explanation, he offered to guide them along a road that was still open. Knox refused to take the chance, his massive frame towering over the dapper little Major as he thunderously proclaimed his intention to fight and die on the spot. There was no time for argument, and Burr never had much use for heroics. With the authority of an aide to Knox's superior [General Putman] he turned from the giant to ask the men if they really wanted to rot in the pestilential British hulks. The Colonel lacking the Major's dash, they did not hesitate and in a few minutes the column was in motion behind the Major's debonair figure. Night found them breathless but safe with the rest of the army on Harlem Heights.

As ungrateful and unjust as it may appear, official headquarters took no notice of Major Burr's skill and bravery as displayed on this occasion. This evidently provoked the youthful officer, for he wrote to General Washington, "I would beg to know whether it was any misconduct in me, or any extraordinary merit or services in them, which entitled the gentlemen lately put over me to that preference?"

Major Burr remained on General Putnam's staff for nine months after the evacuation of New York. His brilliant feat in saving Knox, Hamilton, and their men became the talk of the army and was to be accentuated by a similar situation after the surrender of Fort Washington, where another brigade was left behind and, for the want of a Burr, was captured by the enemy.

While at Peekskill with General Putnam in July 1777, Burr was promoted by General Washington to lieutenant colonel on Colonel William Malcolm's staff. Malcolm, whose regiment had been raised as a hobby of the wealthy merchant of New York, laid no claims to military talent. Consequently he conveyed control so completely to

Burr that it was thereafter known as Colonel Burr's regiment.

Judge Gardner of Newburgh wrote, "I served with this regiment all the time it was under the command of Colonel Burr, being about two years, and he never permitted corporal punishment to be inflicted in a single instance; yet no regiment in the army was under better discipline."

One of the conspicuously successful exploits of 1777 was the repulse of the marauding expedition of more than two thousand Tories under ex-governor Tryon, who had plundered their way from Connecticut through Orange County New York. Malcolm's regiment was at the Clove (now the village of Suffern), when Colonel Burr marched to Hackensack, having heard that enemy forces were there in considerable numbers. While they were en route, Major General Putnam sent a messenger suggesting that Colonel Burr retire with the public stores to the mountains, to which Burr replied that he could not run away from an enemy that he had not seen, and that he would be responsible for both public stores and his men.

At Paramus Colonel Burr found considerable bodies of militia, in great disorder, and doing much mischief to the neighboring farms. After putting the militia to repairing the fences that the enemy had destroyed and placing his guards, Colonel Burr set out with thirty men to reconnoiter. About ten o'clock at night it was learned that they were within a mile of the enemy pickets. Gardner says:

> *Colonel Burr then went alone to discover the position of the enemy. He spent the night in locating the enemy and then aroused us, forbade any man to speak or fire on the pain of death. He led us between the sentinels in such a way that we were within a few yards of the picket guard before they suspected our approach. He then gave the word, and we rushed upon them before they had time to take their arms, and the greater part were killed.*

Colonel Burr immediately sent [a messenger] to Paramus to order all troops to move and to rally the country. Our little success had so encouraged the inhabitants that they turned out with great alacrity and put themselves under the command of Colonel Burr. But the enemy, probably alarmed by these threatening appearances, retreated the next day, leaving behind the greater part of the cattle and plunder which they had taken.

Orders to join the main army in Pennsylvania made it impossible to pursue Tryon's band. Colonel Burr's regiment was immediately on the march to Valley Forge, where it spent the winter of 1777 and '78. By a curious fate he was again associated with Benedict Arnold, with whom he had gone to Canada. Burr never regarded the Irish adventurer as worthy of confidence, and watched with suspicion Arnold's intrigues to remove Washington from command.

Valley Forge is associated in Revolutionary memory with hardship, where hunger and privation stalked, where men strove mightily to withstand cold and sickness, where Washington is pictured as wrestling with God for succor. It was out of these sufferings and misery that men like General Horatio Gates wrote, "Heaven is determined to save your country, or a weak general and bad counselors would have ruined it." Even John Adams was sputtering about the idolatrous worship of George Washington! As early as 1776 General Charles Lee had added to the criticism that Washington at the most was damnably deficient, and it was out of this hour of peril that the traitor Arnold was able to fan a flame of distrust.

In July 1778 General Washington, through Lord Stirling, ordered Colonel Burr to Elizabethtown to spy out the activities of Upper New York Bay from Bergen Heights, "Weehawk or Hoebuck." This assignment Burr accomplished with such distinguished success that he must be credited with having supplemented voluntary espionage with military intelligence, as the work is now designated. This recognition, however, has been denied to Burr because of the political conspiracy that politics has so long succeeded in laying at his door—or, possibly, because to recognize that Burr laid the foundation for the military intelligence division of the army would discredit his accusers. Washington recognized and credited Burr with creating an entirely new concept concerning the movements of the enemy; why deny him proper credit for this distinguished arm of service any longer?

Earlier, out of the blistering June heat during the Battle of Monmouth, where General Washington sought to cut off the movement of the British from Philadelphia to New York, Colonel Burr had suffered sunstroke. This combined with exposure and fatigue impaired his health. In October he took a furlough, but this was not sufficient to restore his strength, and he wrote General Washington for permission for a more prolonged absence:

> *Sir, the excessive heat and occasional fatigues of the preceding campaign have so impaired my health and constitution as to render me incapable of immediate service. I have, for the three past months, taken every advisable step for my recovery, but have the mortification to find, upon my return to duty, a return of sickness, and that every relapse is more dangerous than the former. I have consulted several physicians; all assure me that a few months' retirement and attention to my health are the only probable means to restore it.*
>
> *A conviction of this truth, and of my present inability to discharge the duties of my office, induce me to beg your Excellency's permission to retire from pay and duty until my health will permit, and the nature of the service shall more particularly require my attention, provided such permission can be given without subjecting me to any disadvantage in point of my present rank and command, or any I might acquire during the interval of my absence.*

I shall still feel and hold myself liable to be called into service at your Excellency's pleasure, precisely as if in full pay, and barely on furlough; reserving to myself only the privilege of judging the sufficiency of my health during the present appearance of inactivity.

General Washington's reply ran:

You, in my opinion, carry your ideas of delicacy too far when you propose to drop your pay while the recovery of your health necessarily requires your absence from the service. It is not customary and it would be unjust. You therefore have leave to retire until your health is so far reestablished as to enable you to do your duty. Be pleased to give the Colonel notice of this, that he may know where to call you should any unforeseen exigency require it.

Since his suggestion concerning his pay was not accepted, Colonel Burr returned to West Point, where he rejoined his regiment.

Two months later Colonel Burr took final leave of Malcolm to join General McDougall's Westchester operations, where he commanded the lines from the Hudson River to Long Island Sound. It was at the request of his old Brooklyn commander, General McDougall, that Burr was assigned to this hazardous task, because, as McDougall said, he was determined to restore discipline and order and provide reliable protection for the inhabitants.

Infested with mixed Tory and Whig loyalties, the civilian population had long endured marauding bands from both armies. Burr shortened his lines and established headquarters at White Plains, only to discover that his predecessor, Colonel Littlefield, was starting on a "scouting" expedition. Burr directed that he proceed as far as Throgs Neck and that no private property be molested. When the scouts returned with one prisoner and a large quantity of plunder, Colonel Burr wrote the general that he "could gibbet a half dozen good Whigs with all the venom of the inveterate Tory." General McDougall replied, "I authorize you to be sole judge. In the exercise of this trust, it is my wish that you should lean to the honour of our arms."

Maps showing every path and stream were prepared, and McDougall's voluntary horsemen patrolled the roads, in what was, perhaps, the first of America's mounted constabulary. Burr classified the inhabitants according to their occupations and political leanings; he forbade the passage of his lines to anyone living elsewhere. Sanitary measures were inaugurated in camp, disreputable characters of either sex were banished, a respect for property was promoted, and punishment for all infringements was inflicted with impartiality.

Immediately the "itch for scouting" disappeared with the opportunity for stealing. Colonel Burr slept in his clothes; he would appear unceremoniously in the midst of a storm and just where he was least expected; he led nocturnal attacks against enemy blockhouses. His thoughtful care of his men soon earned their respect and cooperation.

As a soldier, officer, and commander, Colonel Burr was informed as to every situation; he was cautious that his men were not unduly exposed to danger; he carefully guarded their health and soon became the inspiring leader, whose every wish was respected and whose commands were eagerly obeyed—this veteran of four campaigns who was but twenty-three years old.

With firsthand information from many men who were associated with Colonel Burr, James Parton wrote:

> *He revealed a combination of qualities more remarkable, perhaps, than any other American who won distinction in the Revolutionary War. If Burr had been as much in the eye of Napoleon as he was in Washington's, the Emperor would have made a marshal of him, and he would have shared with Napoleon his splendid immortality.*

It was a love marriage, that of Aaron Burr and Theodosia Prevost; and when Theodosia, the daughter, came, Burr's star was fixed. The love of Burr for his Theodosia raises him high above the ranks of ordinary mortals, who too often bring children into the world to loose them to return to the infinite, perhaps the poorer for their earthly pilgrimage.

– Walter F. McCaleb
The Aaron Burr Conspiracy

4
Theodosia of Paramus

The romance between Theodosia Barstow Prevost and Aaron Burr was a product of the Revolution. Just when it began is not clearly established, but Colonel Burr was a frequent visitor at her Paramus, New Jersey, home, the Hermitage, in 1780. For some time he had been in the habit of having himself and his horse ferried across the Hudson to elude the British and to spend a few hours with the lady who had lost her husband, a British officer, in the service of the Crown in the West Indies. That their interests at the outbreak of the Revolution were opposed appears later to have led their friends to conjecture.

The records reveal that in August 1778 New York Governor George Clinton authorized a sloop with a "flagg of truce with three drums and fifes" for the purpose of conducting within the

British lines the families of certain Tories who had preferred to affect "allegiance to the King of Great Britain." That this courtesy was rendered by Colonel Burr is established by his endorsement on the certificate "Mrs. Prevost and Miss De Visme with one man servant in consequence of Lord Stirling's leave to pass to New York and return, are admitted on board this flagg."

While a guest of Mrs. Prevost at the Paramus Hermitage, Colonel Burr witnessed one of the tragedies of war when a cavalry escort permitted its charge, a veiled and distraught lady, to seek a moment's rest during her perilous flight to New York. This distracted lady proved to be Mrs. Benedict Arnold, who was fleeing from the disgrace of her husband in his attempt to surrender his West Point command to the British. Not only was Mrs. Arnold a friend of the Prevost family, but she and Colonel Burr had been friends from childhood.

Apparently it was wagging tongues that induced Colonel Burr's boyhood friend Colonel Robert Troup to write:

> *I feel irresistibly impelled to recommend to your kindest attention one of my female friends in distress. I mean Mrs. Prevost, who has been justly esteemed for her honor, virtue and accomplishments. . . . During the whole course of this war she has conducted herself in such manner as proves her to possess an excellent understanding as well as a strong attachment to our righteous cause. . . . Without the least deviation from truth I can affirm that Mrs. Prevost is a sincere and cordial well wisher to the success of our army, which will be an additional reason with you for showing her all the civilities in your power.*

Mrs. Prevost was fortunate in descending from two of the best families in the Colonies. Her father, Theodosius Barstow, was a lawyer at Shrewsbury, New Jersey, being the son of the Reverend John Barstow, who founded St. Peter's Episcopal

Church in Westchester. Her mother's great-great-grandfather, Nicholas Stillwell, came from Surrey to be one of the early tobacco planters of Yorktown, Virginia. He was a famous Indian scout, who earned the title of "Valiant" Stillwell. In 1639, when there was need to curb excessive cultivation of tobacco, and when it was decreed that crops should be "viewed," and half of the crop burned, Stillwell was chosen as a "viewer" possessed of experience and dignity.

It was after Theodosia's mother had married Philip De Visme and was living at Paramus, New Jersey, that Theodosia in 1763 married Jacques Marc Prevost, who was killed while on duty with the British forces in the West Indies. Colonel Prevost was a brother of General Augustine Prevost, commander of the British forces in South Carolina. Since Theodosia Prevost was a descendent from officials of the Crown, stepdaughter and niece by marriage of five British officers and related directly to many prominent Whigs, what was more natural than that she should suffer criticism for her association with, and friendship for, the distinguished young American officer Colonel Aaron Burr. Concerning this, in May 1781 she wrote:

> *Our being the subject of so much inquiry, conjecture and calumny, is no more than we ought to expect. My attention to you was ever pointed enough to attract the observation of those who visited the house. Your esteem more than compensated for the worst that they could say. When I am sensible I can make you and I happy, I will readily join you to suppress their malice. But, till I am confident of this, I cannot think of our union. Till then I shall take shelter under the roof of my dear mother, where, by joining stock we shall have sufficient to stem the torrent of adversity.*

In the fall of 1780 Aaron Burr and Robert Troup resumed the study of law with William Paterson as instructor, but they were opposed to his insistence of a thorough preliminary grounding in legal principles and soon turned to Thomas Smith, who lived at Haverstraw and appeared to afford a shorter cut to active practice.

Mr. Smith had a good library and plenty of leisure time. With him Burr in the spring of 1781 made a peculiar and characteristic arrangement. For a certain sum the lawyer agreed to devote a specified time to his pupil every day and to answer any questions he might propose. Burr now read law, literally day and night, sometimes spending twenty hours in twenty-four studying, taking notes, and reserving doubtful points to be elucidated by his instructor.

By October 1781 he was ready for his examinations. With a letter from General McDougall to General Philip Schuyler he departed for Albany to solicit a license to practice law. The letter stated that since Colonel Burr was a stranger in that part of the country, General McDougall had taken this method of introduction, commending him as:

> *A soldier, an officer, and a worthy citizen, and commanded the advance corps of the army in the Southernmost part of this state in the winter of 1779, during which time he discharged his duty with uncommon vigilance. I am persuaded by my knowledge of him that he will merit every attention you may think proper to show him.*

Burr was confronted at Albany with a rule that candidates for examination must have spent at least three years in the study of law. The time he had devoted to the subject before the war together with his recent devoted studies totaled less than one third of this period. After conferring with Judge Yates, he wrote the chief justice:

> *Before the Revolution, and long before the existence of the present rule, I had served some time with an attorney of another state. At that period I could*

have availed myself of this service; and, surely, no rule could be intended to have such retrospect as to injure one whose only misfortune is having sacrificed his time, his constitution and his fortune to his country.

It would give me sensible regret were my admission to establish a precedent which might give umbrage to the bar; but should your opinion accord with my wishes with respect to the indulgence due to my particular case, the expression of it to any gentleman of the profession, would doubtless remove the possibility of discontent.

Perhaps I assume a freedom which personal acquaintance only would warrant. I beg, sir, you will ascribe it to the reliance I am taught to place in your goodness and the confidence with which your character inspires even those who have no other title to your notice.

While the youthful aspirant awaited with some impatience the decision of the bar, he wrote to Theodosia:

I always keep a memorandum for you. . . . when I think of anything at any time of day I wish to write, I make a short note in a manner which no other person would understand . . . I would recommend the same to you, unless you choose to write at the moment when you think of anything. . . . I really fear Judge Yates is playing the fool with me. Still evasive, though plausibly so. . . . My mind is so engrossed by new views and expectations, that I cannot disengage it. I have not, these five days past, slept more than two hours a night, and yet feel refreshed and well.

Eventually the examining counsel suspended the rule, apparently with a reservation that an examination would dispose of the aspirant, but Burr passed a brilliant examination. He was admitted to the bar January 19, 1871. On April 17 he was admitted as counselor. He was then twenty-six years of age.

Colonel Burr opened his law office in Albany. Immediately there were clients, so Burr decided it was time to wed. He and Theodosia were married July 2, 1782. For many years Paramus and Albany each claimed to be the scene of the nuptials. A letter now in the possession of the New Jersey Historical Society favors the Paramus Hermitage, or the home of Doctor Joseph Brown, whose wife was a sister of Mrs. Burr.

After reaching Albany, Theodosia wrote:

It was neither what you had a right to expect or what I wished. Caty's journey was not determined on till we were aboard the sloop. Many of our friends had accompanied us and were waiting to see us under sail. It was with difficulty that I stole a moment to give my sister a superficial account. Caty promised to be more particular, but I fear she was not punctual.

You asked Carlos the particulars of our wedding. They may be related in a few words. It was attended by two singular circumstances. The first is that it cost us nothing. Brown and Caty provided abundantly and we improved the opportunity. The fates led Burr on in his old coat. It was proper my gown should be of suitable gauze. Ribbons, gloves, etc. were favors from Caty.

The second circumstance was that the parson's fee took the only half Joe Burr was master of. We partook of the good things as long as they lasted and set out for Albany where the want of money is our only grievance. You know how far this affects me.

We are impatient to have you with us. We count the weeks. You must not, you will not, disappoint us. The air of Albany is healthy. But why enumerate inducements? My friends know the pleasure they will give us—that their presence will crown the felicity of a brother and sister who love them with tenderness and affection. Your tender concern for us is a testimony of your regard, and summons a tear of gratitude and love. Yes, my sister, I realize my joy fully.

Aaron and Theodosia received a gracious welcome in Albany. Their friends were legion. Numerous congratulations came from the prominent men of the state, including Governor Clinton and Judge Hobart. William Livingston wrote, "I have but a Moments Time to Congratulate you on the late happy Circumstance of your marriage with the Amiable Mrs. Prevost. Confident that the Object of your Choice will ever meet Universal Esteem."

Among the families with whom, during the Revolution, Burr had been on intimate terms—the Clintons, the Livingstons, the Schuylers, the Van Rensselaers—there was surprise that Colonel Burr, the most prominent young man in the state, handsome, fascinating, well-born, educated, and brilliant, whose addresses no young lady would have chosen to repulse, should have picked a widow ten years older than himself with precarious health, small estate, and without beauty. It aroused speculation then; it has puzzled his biographers since.

Theodosia Barstow Burr was to furnish the answer. She was one of the cultured ladies of her day, a student of French and English literature as well as philosophy, a woman of exquisite manners that graced a charming personality—a creature that Aaron Burr adored. In his own language she was a woman whom he loved because she had the truest heart, the ripest intellect, and the most winning and graceful manners of any woman he ever met.

Later, when Burr was regarded as the intellectual peer of the Senate, he declared that he owed whatever success he had attained largely to his wife, and that if a measure of perfection were his, the touch of her artistry and the inspiration of her mind should be given credit.

The mental and spiritual union of Aaron Burr and Theodosia Prevost persisted throughout their wedded lives. It ripened and sweetened with the years, and it found its complete fruition in Theodosia, their daughter, who was born in Albany on June 21, 1783. A second child, Sally, was born in New York in 1787. The latter died when but two years of age with but the single record: "We lost our youngest child, Sally, a beautiful lovely baby."

Love letters of courtship seem commonplace in comparison with the record of connubial bliss that Theodosia and Aaron have left, letters that were written long years after they were wed, when devotion to the law kept Burr away from home much of the time and when Theodosia pours out her heart:

> *My Aaron had scarce quitted the door when I regretted my passiveness. Why did I consent to his departure? . . . My Aaron, dark is the hour that separates my soul from itself. . . . Heaven protect my Aaron; preserve him, restore him to his adoring mistress. . . . Love in all its delirium hovers about me; like opium, it lulls me to soft repose! Sweet serenity speaks, 'tis my Aaron's spirit presides. Surrounding objects check my visionary charm. I fly to my room and give the day to thee.*

Theo was now forty-three and for a decade love epistles had flitted constantly between this rare couple. There are scores of letters. One missive of their wedded bliss reads:

> *I pursued thee yesterday, through wind and rain, till eve, when, fatigued, exhausted, shivering, thou didst reach thy haven, surrounded with inattention, thy Theo from thee. Thus agitated, I laid my head upon a restless pillow, turning from side to side when thy kindred spirit found its mate, I beheld my much-loved Aaron, his tender eyes fixed kindly on me; they spake a body wearied, wishing repose, but not sick. This soothed my troubled spirit; I slept tolerably; but dare not trust too confidently. . . . naught but thy voice*

can tranquilize my mind. Thou art the constant object of love, hope, and fear.

Theo shared her pleasure with the children by putting the letters on the mantelpiece for them to find:

> *The surprise, the joy, the exclamations exceed description. The greatest stoic would have forgotten himself. A silent tear betrayed me no philosopher. . . . We talked of our happiness, of our first blessing, our best of papas. I enjoyed, my Aaron, the only happiness that could accrue from your absence. . . . Your letters always afford me a singular satisfaction—a sensation entirely my own. . . . My Aaron, it was replete with tenderness, with the most lively affection. I read and reread, till afraid I should get it by rote, and mingle it with common ideas; profane the sacred pledge. No, it shall not be. I will economize the boon. I will limit the recreation of those moments of retirement devoted to thee.*

Burr's letters to his wife, while less demonstrative, are no less devoted. Regarding their separation, he writes:

> *You may judge with what reluctance I engaged in a business that will detain me so long from all that is dear and lovely. I dare not think of the period I have yet to be absent. What sacrifices of time and pleasure do I make to this paltry object—contemptible indeed in itself, but truly important and attractive as the means of gratifying those I love.*
> *No other consideration would induce me to spend another day of my life in objects of themselves uninteresting. . . . Oh, Theo! There is a most delightful grove— so darkened with weeping willows that at noonday a susceptible fancy like yours would mistake it for a be-*

witching moonlight evening . . . no rude noise interrupts the softest whisper . . . than the wild cooings of the gentle dove, the gay thresher's animated warbles, and soft murmurings of the passing brook. Really, Theo, it is charming . . . We will plant it with Jessamine and woodbine, and call it Cyprus. It seems formed for the residence of the loves and graces, and is therefore yours by the best of titles. It is indeed most charming.

As if to compensate Burr for its brevity, the years of his domestic life were serene and contented; his wife was devoted to his pleasure and comfort; she found her greatest pleasure in her husband and her children. Their inquiring minds and mutual desires for intellectual advancement, their beautiful home and their precocious child filled their lives to overflowing. The mental fitness of each and the spiritual union of both brought together contentment and an unusual degree of wisdom.

Poor Theo's last days of life were spent as an invalid. Burr proposed to resign from the U.S. Senate that he might be with her, but she instructed her daughter to write: "Ma begs you to omit the thoughts of leaving Congress."

Like many another who has suffered from cancer, Theo's mind was affected, concerning which she wrote to Tapping Reeve, "I pass many succeeding lingering hours—hours that can never be described . . . In the morning I wake with regret—at night I lie down with the hope of never waking to the disappointments of another day."

Death came after a prolonged illness. Theodosia died May 28, 1794. It was in Philadelphia that the colonel was to receive the "afflicting news that my once amiable and accomplished wife had died on the Sunday preceding." To Timothy Edwards he wrote:

Though her situation had long been considered as helpless, yet no apprehension was entertained of any immediate danger until a few hours before her death; she sank calmly and without pain into her last sleep. My little daughter, though much afflicted and distressed, bears the stroke with more reason and firmness than could have been expected from her years.

Aaron's Burr's love for his wife is inspiring, but not more profound and steadying than was her wisdom and fidelity. What a consoling refuge she would have proven in the tragic days that followed had she been permitted to dwell with him!

Aaron Burr's pocket watch. Historians and art critics have mislabeled the profile on the left as Theodosia his wife, and on the right as Theodosia his daughter. But the watch was ca. 1792, at which time Theodosia his daughter would have only been nine years old, hardly the age of the profile on the right. And, on closer inspection, the figure on the left is that of a man, probably Burr himself, and the figure on the right most likely his wife.

Henry H. Anderson, Jr.

From 1791 dates Hamilton's repugnance to Burr, and soon after his letters begin to teem with passages expressive of that repugnance . . . and from this time, in whatever direction Burr sought advancement, or advancement sought him, his secret, inveterate opponent was Alexander Hamilton; until at length the politics of the United States was resolved into a contest between these two individuals.

– James Parton
The Life and Times of Aaron Burr

5
Eminence at the Bar

The spectacular rise of Aaron Burr at the bar in New York is without parallel. When he moved from Albany to a stately home in Maiden Lane in 1783, he chose a fertile field for his labors. Following the evacuation by the British after seven years of military occupation, the city of twenty-five thousand took on new life. Many new houses were built, more repaired and others rebuilt. Titles were jumbled by the confiscation of property. War services and damages resulted in interminable claims. Trade revived with astonishing vigor.

By debarring the Tories, the legislature had eliminated most of the older lawyers, many of whom had enjoyed lucrative clienteles. Burr embraced this opportunity and his business prospered phenomenally. Working long hours, he gave no respite to his adversaries, much less to his associates, who were frequently sent with a note at midnight to rout from bed a collaborating counsel from whom he demanded an immediate reply.

Burr received large fees for that day. He reports, "I have never undertaken the management of a cause of any moment in error under forty pounds." Annual receipts of the firm of Burr & Broome were more than twenty thousand dollars. Burr is known to have received ten thousand dollars for a single case.

The Prevost boys, sons of Mrs. Burr, received their law training as well as their preparation for business in the office with Colonel Burr. Apparently his excessive energy and enthusiasm inspired them to intensive study, for it resulted in a distinguished record of service, concerning which John Quincy Adams wrote in his diary:

> *Mr. Jefferson mentioned the extreme difficulty he had in finding fit characters for appointments in Louisiana, and said he would give the creation for a young lawyer of abilities, and one who could speak the French language, to go to New Orleans as one of the Judges of the Superior Court of the Territory.*
>
> *The salary was about two thousand dollars. He has been lucky in obtaining one such Judge in Mr. Prevost of New York, who had accepted the appointment and was perfectly well qualified, but he was in extreme want for another.*

Additional evidence of Burr's exacting standards of legal preparation and its influence at the bar is related by a noted traveler, John Davis, who wrote:

> *There is so decided a leaning in his favor, and such marked deference to his opinions, that exclamations of despair were frequently heard escape the lips of counsel whose fortune it was to be opposed by the*

eloquence of Burr. I am aware that this language wears the colour of panegyric, but the recollections which the facts excite in the breasts of his candid rivals will corroborate its accuracy.

Aaron Burr was a clever trial lawyer who was exceedingly adroit in the presentation of evidence. Some of his adversaries declared he was a magician because of the pitfalls he invented and into which he led them so ingeniously. Only five feet six, still, he walked with such military bearing and his manners were so courtly and graceful that he excited respect and admiration. Whenever Burr faced a jury, all eyes followed his movements; his distinctly enunciated words reached every ear. His style was conversational, never oratorical, yet his power over a jury was such that some of his rivals declared that he unduly influenced them. Only Hamilton has ever been compared with him at the bar.

If the fires of jealousy burned the breast of Hamilton during their professional and social intercourse, there is nothing in their personal or family lives to indicate it. The two families were surprisingly intimate. Hamilton was fond of Burr and often dined with him. No one who is acquainted with the lives of these two distinguished Americans can escape the conviction that, until politics and business divided them, they dwelt in peace and with mutual admiration.

After revealing his association with Burr in Congress, General Erastus Root records that in the height of his celebrity as a lawyer and scholar, Burr's reasoning powers were at least equal with Hamilton's. Their modes of argument were very different:

Hamilton was very diffuse and wordy. His words were so well chosen and his sentences so finely formed into a swelling current that the hearer would be captivated. The listener would admire, if he was not convinced. Burr's arguments were generally methodized and compact. I used to say of them, when they were rivals at the bar, that Burr could say as much in half an hour as Hamilton in two hours. Burr was terse and convincing, while Hamilton flowing and rapturous. They were much the greatest men in this state, and perhaps the greatest men in the United States.

After spending that span of life which has been allotted in Holy Writ in research and mental association with these two illustrious characters, Parton finds it evident that Burr was more discriminating, possessed a steadier nerve, and was master of every momentous struggle—even at Weehawken!

What happy years were those which Colonel Burr passed in the practice of law in New York before he was drawn into the political vortex! His wife was full of affection and helpfulness, making him the happiest while he was at home and superintending, with wise vigilance, his office and his household when he was abroad. Her two sons were students in Colonel Burr's office, and aided him most efficiently in the prosecution of his business. One of them frequently accompanied him on his journeys as an amanuensis and clerk, while the other represented him in the office in New York.

On at least three different occasions Burr and Hamilton jointly defended an accused. One of these was Levi Weeks, a young carpenter, who was known to share the commonly bestowed affections of Gulielma Sands, who was murdered and her body deposited in a well in 1799.

After the grand jury had indicted Weeks he became the object of a mass hysteria that would sacrifice him to appease its misguided rage. An alibi accounted for the manner in which he had spent the evening "except for a few minutes," whereupon the court declared that there was not sufficient proof to warrant a decision against the accused.

A remark to which time has given peculiar gravity was hurled at Hamilton the day following the trial, when one of the relatives of the deceased exclaimed, "If thee dies a natural death, I shall think there is no justice in heaven." Following this curse, the trial judge, Justice John Lansing, permanently disappeared, and this only a short time after the tragic death of Hamilton.

Colonel Burr located in New York with the intention of devoting himself exclusively to the law. He had contributed four of his best years to the Revolution. These had cost him his fortune and his health. To rear and educate his family, to possess the finest library obtainable and live in the best home in New York: these, in addition to his profession, appear to have been his chief ambitions. Against his protest he was chosen a member of the Assembly in April 1784.

To his first session in the Assembly he gave slight consideration and attended few of the deliberative meetings. In the second session he espoused a movement for the abolition of slavery in New York. This resulted in his becoming chairman of the committee that revised the laws in 1800. He served for seven years as a member of the Board of Governors of New York Hospital. Colonel Burr was a member of the commission that disposed of the wild lands of the state in 1791 and was the only man whose record escaped the calamitous scandal that resulted in their sale.

In the gubernatorial election of 1789 Burr supported Judge Robert Yates for governor, but George Clinton was re-elected and revealed some of the political tactics of a Napoleon by appointing Yates as chief justice of the Supreme Court and Aaron Burr as attorney general.

Such recognition of Burr's legal ability when he had practiced law but seven years marked him in the public esteem. Two years as attorney general added enough to his reputation as a lawyer and diplomat that the legislature elected him to succeed General Philip Schuyler, Alexander Hamilton's father-in-law, in the United States Senate.

Senator Schuyler had served for the "short term" of two years, having been a member of the first Congress. Schuyler's de-

Aaron Burr in 1794 copy of a Gilbert Stuart portrait, by John Vanderlyn

feat caused a sensation. It infuriated Hamilton, whose vanity was to suffer often thereafter at the hands of Burr. From the day of General Schuyler's defeat Hamilton never lost an opportunity to vilify the man he had previously acknowledged as friend, neighbor, and legal associate as well as a competitor worthy of his steel. Now he wrote, "I fear [that Burr] is unprincipled . . . he is for or against nothing, but as it suits his interest or ambition. . . . I feel it a religious duty to oppose his career."

When these two ambitious politicians came to the parting of the way, the political destinies of the state of New York were controlled by three great families—the Clintons, the Schuylers,

Alexander Hamilton in 1806 portrait by John Trumbull

and the Livingstons. George Clinton was undisputed leader of the anti-Federalists, who gradually merged as Republicans. Clinton was able, honest, tough, wary, and democratic. For eighteen years this rugged son of Northern Ireland had been re-elected every second year as governor.

The Schuyler clan was rich and aristocratic. Their chief, General Philip Schuyler, was proud and haughty. He was the guardian of the clan. Clinton had defeated him for governor in 1777 and the sting of that defeat had never been removed.

Perhaps the Livingston clan was larger than both of the others. In addition to being rich, its members, most of them wealthy, were politicians, clergymen, judges, and lawyers. Many were resentful that one of their clan had not been chosen with Schuyler as an original U.S. senator instead of Rufus King. They were sure Robert Livingston should have been the first chief justice of the United States in the place of John Jay.

These are some of the political factors that caused the schism among the Federalists—a breach that contributed to the defeat of Schuyler and the election of Burr to the United States Senate. Burr was only thirty-four, and his political alliances were independent. His ancestry, scholarship, distinguished military service, and record as a lawyer and as New York attorney general were outstanding, yet these alone could scarcely have accomplished his election. Disaffected Federalists were a large factor in the choice of Burr.

With a substantial majority in the legislature, had the Federalists really desired his return to the Senate, General Schuyler would have been chosen, as Hamilton so confidently expected. Twelve members of the state senate voted for Burr; four voted for Schuyler. Burr's majority in the Assembly was five.

Schuyler was personally rejected because he was a haughty old soldier who held himself aloof from the masses. He insisted that the vulgar public be excluded from the United States Senate, which to him was an American House of Lords. Washington, Adams, and Hamilton shared Schuyler's English precept. To all of these, to be member of the Senate was a badge of aristocracy. Hamilton's scintillating pen, social standing, and wealthy association led to his elevation as secretary of the treasury, which was then the most powerful position in the cabinet.

Hamilton was father of the Federalist party, and while his appointment may be regarded as a reward for his brilliant services to General Washington, as secretary of the treasury he became confidential adviser, where his services extended to such encyclopedic proportions that he was the most powerful factor in the administration. Hamilton's ego gradually led him to assume a position equivalent to prime minister, often to the embarrassment of Washington and to the disgust of Adams and Jefferson. Hamilton's influence over the Federalist Party during the administrations of Washington and Adams probably has never been equaled during the first one hundred fifty years of the United States. James Parton wrote of Burr's victory:

> *Schuyler felt his defeat acutely, and Hamilton was painfully disappointed. It was of the utmost possible importance to the Secretary of the Treasury to have a reliable majority in Congress; and the presence of a devoted father-in-law, in a Senate of twenty-eight members sitting with closed doors, was convenient.*
>
> *From 1791 dates Hamilton's repugnance to Burr, and soon after his letters begin to teem with passages expressive of that repugnance. . . . from this time, in whatever direction Burr sought advancement, or advancement sought him, his secret, inveterate opponent was Alexander Hamilton; until at length the politics of the United States was resolved into a contest between these two individuals.*

About this time a thousand people died in New York from yellow fever. This calamity was traced to impure drinking water due largely to the lack of a water system. Aaron Burr promoted a bill through the legislature that provided for the construction of such a system, and that the surplus capital might be employed in any way not inconsistent with the laws and the Constitution of the United States and the state of New York.

This legislation permitted the organization, using surplus earnings, of a third bank in New York City, a thing Hamilton and his associates, who controlled the branch Bank of the United States and the Bank of New York, had been able to prevent. Immediately the Bank of Manhattan was organized. It was a friendly institution where anti-Federalists could do business. But the friends of Hamilton were outraged and bitterly criticized him for allowing Burr to outwit him. As press agent for the Federalist group, Robert Troup wrote, "Burr is unprincipled, without virtue, ambitious, immoral and unscrupulous."

At the Constitutional convention Hamilton opposed attempts to require a residency period before immigrants could become members of Congress. However, he was overruled, as the delegates established prior residency requirements for both houses. Hamilton's greatest ambition was never realized. The facts are simply that the voters never elevated him to a position of trust. He was always appointed to office as a political reward—never elected under the Constitution which he helped frame.

Two of the most painstaking students of Burr and Hamilton, Samuel Wandell and Meade Minnigerode, after many years' research, wrote:

> *Hamilton and Burr had been friends; they had much in common. . . . shared the same outstanding qualities of mind. . . . as lawyers and men of culture. . . . they were possessed of the same charm of wit and eloquence; exhibited the same generous, spendthrift habits. . . . they exerted the same. . . . disregard of the accepted requirements of private morals. . . . however, they differed fundamentally; Burr's ancestry was impeccable, the West Indian from Nevis could not deny John Adams's remark that he was "the bastard brat of a Scotch peddler."*

Pointing out that Hamilton's secret hatred, his underhanded obstruction, his stealthy defamation of Colonel Burr began with the defeat of General Schuyler, the historians report that Burr had gained an implacable enemy, taken upon himself the perils of a ruthless feud, subjected himself to the constant provocations of a jealous calumny. At every turn, now, the colonel was to feel the invisible hand, to hear the disguised voice of the West Indian.

No other man in history has been both pen and voice of a political organization as was Hamilton in the creation of the

Federalist party. No other man has sat at, or near, the elbow of two presidents to guide their political destinies as did Hamilton with Washington and Adams. No other man in history has staked all and lost, as did Hamilton when he attempted to destroy Aaron Burr. Alexander Hamilton influenced, even largely controlled, every organization and every individual with whom he came in contact except Aaron Burr. Burr was master in every contest with Hamilton save Hamilton's pen—which became the agent of destruction for both!

I really believe ... few parents can boast of children whose minds are so prone to virtue.

– Mrs. Aaron Burr
Private Letters

6
The Filial Daughter

For generations the Burr family had been teachers, preachers, lawyers, and militiamen. They had occupied public office as members of court, auditor of colony, speaker of the house, and magistrate. The Reverend Aaron Burr was a distinguished teacher and preacher, and, like his son, he was obsessed by a desire to teach. Theodosia's father was determined that she should demonstrate to the world that the feminine mind was capable of receiving serious training and, if given opportunity, would prove a worthy competitor for the male mind. Theodosia's mother was well read and possessed a personality that had motivated her husband to write:

It was a knowledge of your mind which first inspired me with respect for that of your sex, and with some regret, I confess, that the ideas which you have often heard me express in favor of female intellectual powers are founded on what I have imagined more than what I have seen, except in you. I have endeavored to trace the causes of this rare display of genius in women and I find them in the errors of education, of prejudice and of habit.

Boys and girls are generally educated much in the same way till they are eight or nine years of age, and it is admitted that girls make at least equal progress with the boys; generally, indeed, they make better. Why, then, has it never been thought worth the attempt to discover, by fair experiment, the particular age at which the male superiority becomes so evident?

Today, when after a century and a half the female mind has enjoyed opportunity for education and comparison with its male competitor, few people realize that in Burr's day a girl was scarcely considered worth educating. There was no public school and only the boys were sent to college.

It is interesting to observe that Theodosia Burr and Washington Irving were not only born in the same year, but that they were school friends, both of whom desired an education. Irving had his choice of Harvard, Yale, or the College of New Jersey, but Theodosia, because she was a girl, was barred from attending college in America. Of all public men, only Benjamin Franklin spoke of the "propriety of educating the female sex in learning."

Theodosia's mother was descended from the tobacco-growing colonists of Virginia who had traded their product for European brides. This rare product of barter proved a great moral and intellectual influence in the civilization of the New World.

Burr concedes that his first obsession for the education of his daughter was aroused by what he saw in her mother. May not the daughter as well as the mother have received from ancestral forbears the spirit as well as the blood of these "young, handsome, honestly educated maids" whose passage to America was paid for in tobacco?

In an attempt to carefully educate Theodosia, she was served a bread-and-meal diet for breakfast after a night alone in a remote room of the home without fear or nerves. Puritanical? It was the Burr method!

Theodosia must be more than just his flesh and blood, the product of his mind, the creation of his spirit, the apotheosis of his intellect, and the fruition of his hopes. She must mirror and multiply his virtues, especially those he had discovered in her mother.

With all his dreams of womanly grace and mental achievement, fear for female frailties crept into Burr's mind. This he reveals in a letter to his wife:

> *If I could foresee that Theo would become a mere fashionable woman with all the attendant frivolity and vacuity of mind, adorned with whatever grace or allurement, I would earnestly pray God to take her forthwith hence. I hope . . . by her to convince the world what neither sex appear to believe, that women have souls.*

Theodosia's mother was little less intellectual than her father. When the daughter was two years old, the mother wrote:

> *Your dear little Theodosia seeks you twenty times a day; calls you to your meals, and will not suffer your chair to be filled by any member of the family. She cannot hear you spoken of without apparent melancholy; insomuch that her nurse is obliged to exert her invention to divert her and myself to avoid mention of you in her presence. She was one whole day indifferent to everything but your name. Her attachment is not of the common nature.*

Burr's legal duties kept him away from home much of the time. During his absence the chief topic of his letters was the children—for there were two, Theodosia and Natalie, the latter a French child that he had adopted, who was reared and educated with equal care in his home. Of the children he wrote:

> *The letters of our dear children are a feast. . . . To hear that they are employed, that no time is absolutely wasted . . . insures their affection, or is the best evidence of it. It insures, in its consequences, everything I am ambitious of in them. Endeavor to preserve regularity of hours; it conduces exceedingly to industry.*

In reply Mrs. Burr wrote:

> *I really believe, my dear, that few parents can boast of children whose minds are so prone to virtue. I see the reward of our assiduity with inexpressible delight, with gratitude few experience. My dear Aaron, they have grateful hearts.*

In her tenth year Theodosia was reading French with such facility that it was difficult for her father to keep her supplied with texts that merited his approval. He was always correcting her letters; yet he found much in them to approve—to encourage her to become a real student.

Theodosia grew up to be one of the happiest of children, an eager reader, a facile writer, an accomplished musician, a graceful dancer, a spirited equestrian, thoroughly in love with her home, where she presided with a grace that captured the hearts of her father's guests and won their approval. Such was the realization of his plans for her education. If she worshipped her father, she basked in the sunshine of her mother's grace and wisdom. Here is an example where love and attention to a "youngster" was wisely bestowed, and was to bless rather than spoil, as it usually does.

What a terrifying schoolmaster Burr would prove today with all his phenomenal powers for study, his passion for instruction and criticism, his mania for regulations and correction, even encouraging his brilliant wife to pursue new courses: "You have often wished for opportunities to read; you now have, and, I hope, improve them. I should be glad to know how your attention is directed. Of the success I have no doubt."

Never satisfied with present efforts and achievements, he must push on, and he outlines a course of reading: in Gibbon she must not pass a word she did not understand; Plutarch's *Lives* should give pleasure; in Paley's *Philosophy of Natural History*, "be sure to make yourself mistress of all the terms. But, if you continue your Gibbon, it will find you in employment for some days. When you are weary of soaring with him, and wish to descend into common life, read the *Comedies* of Plautus."

Apparently Theodosia the daughter shared her father's obsession for the ability to think clearly and to reason wisely. Colonel Stone in his *Life of Joseph Brant* tells how in her fourteenth year Theodosia Burr, then regarded as a young lady, entertained in the absence of her father. Burr was in Philadelphia as senator. After entertaining the distinguished chief there, Burr gave him a letter to his daughter requesting that the Native American be shown every possible courtesy. Stone writes:

> *The Forest Chief was received with all the courtesy and hospitality suggested. Miss Theodosia performed the honors of her father's house in a manner gratifying to her parent and creditable to herself. Twelve plates were served and among the eminent guests were Bishop Moore and doctors Hosack and Bard.*

Theodosia wrote her father that she had been somewhat at a loss to select the dishes as would suit the palate of her principal guest, given the many tales she had heard of "the Cannibals that each other eat, / The Anthropophagi, and men whose heads / Do

Theodosia Burr in 1802 portrait by John Vanderlyn

grow beneath their shoulders." She added playfully that she'd had
a mind to request the hospital to contribute a human head to be
served like a boar's head in ancient hall barbaric. But, after all, she
found him a most Christian and civilized guest in manners.

In the days that Theodosia blossomed into young woman-
hood her father's success was second to no man's in New York.

His ancestry was pre-eminent in the young republic. His military services during the Revolution were conspicuous. As United States senator he and his daughter were much in the public eye. As Theodosia rode about Manhattan Island on her pony, followed at a respectful distance, as was the custom, by one of her father's slaves mounted on a coach-horse, she was probably the happiest young woman in the city and the most envied.

At this time Burr maintained a town house and another a mile and a half out in the country on the banks of the Hudson. This was the historic Richmond Hill mansion, made famous during the Revolution as the headquarters of Washington. It was a massive, imposing wooden structure with lofty portico of Ionic columns that faced the river. The home was located in the midst of a great lawn of ancient native trees and trained shrubbery. The grounds extended to the banks of the Hudson and comprised about a hundred and sixty acres. It was the finest country estate on the island. Theodosia's letters reveal that she gloried in roaming over these grounds and that she was acquainted with the flowers, birds, plants, and trees. Like her father, she was a student of nature.

Naturally Theodosia had many admirers including Washington Irving. Joseph Alston apparently realized that brains and beauty were rare companions. He pressed for her hand with all the chivalry of the old South. Theo protested that they were both too young to wed, quoting Aristotle's opinion that a man should not marry before thirty-six. Alston's pleading was supplemented by a million-dollar fortune. Joseph was twenty-two, Theodosia seventeen.

Because Colonel Burr was a member of the legislature and was living at Albany in early 1801, the wedding took place at the state capital, where a week of the honeymoon was spent. The newlyweds spent another week at Richmond Hill, then journeyed to Baltimore to be joined by Theo's father, in whose carriage the trio traveled to Washington. Here Joseph Alston and his bride witnessed the inauguration of Aaron Burr as vice president and Thomas Jefferson as president.

In 1801 the capital of the United States was little more than a series of mud holes along a new road leading from the president's mansion to the capitol, and possessed little to attract and detain Theodosia and Joseph. Soon they floated down the Potomac and along the Atlantic to Charleston to receive as enthusiastic and cordial a reception as that warm-hearted city ever showered upon anyone.

For three years Theodosia was the beneficiary of health and wealth and a full measure of the love of her husband. She possessed a luxurious home in Charleston, spent her summers in the mountains and in Richmond Hill, and was everywhere honored because of her charming personality and ready wit, and as one of the most widely cultured women of her day. The national fame of her father and the standing of her husband in South Carolina were focused upon her. A full measure of life's happiness came after two years with the birth of her son, Aaron Burr Alston, who became the pride of his parents and grandfather, whose ambition was that he be trained and educated; "Little Gampy," as he called him, must be worthy of his ancestry.

When her father was charged with being a traitor, Theodosia joined him at the trial, where she faced his accusers with a faith that was absolute and revealed that for him she would cheerfully have faced the scorn of his enemies and the derision of the world, and shared any fate to which his misfortune could have led him.

No father ever loved his child more, nor more laboriously proved that love than Aaron Burr; no child ever repaid a father's devotion and tenderness with a love more constant than Theodosia.

That such a woman's faith and devotion were never to waver awakened this author to suspect that the true Aaron Burr was an entirely different person from that pictured by Hamilton, Jefferson, Wilkinson, and Eaton. Certainly he was not all good, but the evidence removes him far from being the devil painted by his accusers!

For Theodosia to have shared the calumny of her father and out of such misfortune to have recorded, "I would rather not live, than not to be the daughter of such a man," places both in an exalted position, which, when supported by the evidence, should give to both immortality!

How shall I describe . . . my sensations and reflections at that moment. [Washington] had compelled me to promote over the heads of Lincoln, Clinton, Gates, Knox, and others . . . the most restless, impatient, artful, indefatigable, and unprincipled intriguer in the United States, if not in the world. . . . But I was not permitted to nominate Burr.

– President John Adams,
Private Letters

7
The Gentlemen
from New York

Aaron Burr took the office of senator in Philadelphia on October 24, 1791. The following day President Washington delivered his first message to Congress, when a most unusual thing occurred: Aaron Burr, who had served as senator only one day, was chosen to draft a reply to the president. After accepting the product of Burr's pen without change, the Senate convened in the home of George Washington, where it was read by vice president John Adams.

In a letter to his wife in New York, Burr wrote:

I am at length settled in winter quarters. The house . . . is inhabited by two widows. The mother about seventy, the daughter about fifty. . . . The old lady is deaf. .

. . I receive many attentions and civilities, many invita-
tions to dine, all of which I have declined and have not
eaten a meal except at my own quarters. . . . Send me a
waistcoat, white and brown such as you designed. You
know I am never pleased except with your taste.

One of Burr's first proposals was that the Senate's deliberations be open to the public, but it took patience and perseverance
to accomplish this democratic procedure.

In inviting Burr, a new member, to reply to the president's
message, the Senate had shown him an unusual courtesy. Before
that session was over, however, the president rudely rebuked him.
Burr was always a student, and with a view of writing a history of
the Revolutionary War began his research among the files of the
secretary of state. After arranging that a messenger build a fire for
him, Burr would go to the department at five o'clock in the morning. To facilitate his work he had his breakfast brought to him. A
clerk assisted in copying as well as doing the research, until one
day President Washington learned of the practice and issued a
peremptory order forbidding such research by Aaron Burr; Burr's
history of the Revolution was never written.

Desiring information concerning the late surrender of western posts, Burr addressed a note to Jefferson requesting permission to make this particular investigation. The secretary of the
state replied that it had been concluded improper to communicate
the correspondence of existing ministers.

In view of the persistent Native American troubles, in his
message to Congress the president had urged larger military es-
tablishments. As chairman of the committee to consider the president's recommendations, Burr gave these recommendations hearty
support, his military experience having impressed upon him the
necessity for such protection.

After George Clinton had been re-nominated as candidate for
governor in 1792, the Federalists endeavored to induce Aaron Burr
to become the opposition candidate, and the field was thoroughly

canvassed with a view of drafting Burr. The rank and file of the Federalist party argued that since Burr belonged to no party, and would be supported by men of moderate means of all parties, it would be wise to secure the advantage of his name and talents.

The Federalists could win with Burr at the head of the state ticket, was the opinion of James Watson, who wrote: "besides, if we do, will it not attach him to the Federalists?" Hamilton, however, who was, as James Parton wrote, "The unquestioned leader of the Federalists in the state," vetoed the movement. A word from him would, in all probability, have made Burr governor in 1792. But that word was not spoken.

Burr declined the proposed nomination, after which John Jay resigned as chief justice of the U.S. to accept it. At the election returns by the Federalist count were nearly four hundred in their favor; the Republicans, however, refused to concede Jay's election on the grounds that fraud had been committed.

The question was one of technical irregularity in three counties. Thus Senators Aaron Burr and Rufus King were asked to decide. They, too, disagreed, each finding for the party of his preference. Burr suggested that they decline to make a public statement, but King promptly filed his opinion. Burr responded with a counter-decision, which the canvassers supported with a vote of seven to four. Clinton was declared re-elected.

The contest was taken before the Legislature. Burr represented Governor Clinton's case, which was approved by a vote of thirty-five to twenty-two. Since the legal points at issue were still subjects of debate, Burr secured from some of the best judicial minds of the hour concurrent opinions, which he published.

Alexander Hamilton registered a protest against the decision of the Legislature as follows:

> *I have hitherto scrupulously refrained from interference in elections. In my opinion, the occasion is of sufficient importance to warrant a departure from that rule. It is incumbent upon every good man to resist the present*

Aaron Burr bust by Leith Adams, commissioned by the Aaron Burr Association and installed in the Morris-Jumel Mansion on Morningside Heights southeast of Riverside Church a.k.a Rockefeller Cathedral.

designs. Mr. Burr's integrity as an individual is not un-impeached. As a public man, he is one of the worst sort.

Burr aims at putting himself at the head of what he calls a "popular party" as affording the best tools for an ambitious man to work with. Secretly turning liberty into ridicule, he knows as well as most men how to make use of that name. In a word, if we have an embryo-Caesar in the United States 'tis BURR.

In the midst of Burr's senatorial activities Governor Clinton tendered him a place on the Supreme Court of New York. This he promptly declined.

The Republican party in caucus appointed James Madison and James Monroe as a committee to ask President Washington to appoint Burr as minister to France. With Jefferson and Hamilton sitting at his elbow as members of his cabinet, and with his long-known repugnance toward Burr, he declined.

The president gave as his reason for refusing to appoint Colonel Burr as minister to France that he was not assured of his integrity.

The Republican caucus returned Madison and Monroe, who insisted that Burr was so preeminent in the party in fitness and integrity that they had no other choice. This they did for the third time, when Washington in anger declared that he "would not appoint Aaron Burr!" Then, as if to mollify his offense to the committee and the party, said he would gladly appoint Mr. Monroe.

Thus was established the political stop-gate against Aaron Burr—Washington against Burr, Hamilton against Burr, and Jefferson against Burr. Each of these distinguished gentlemen assumed that it was his divine mission to stop Aaron Burr politically.

Hamilton had publicly declared it to be "his religious duty." Washington now made it his military prerogative, and Jefferson made it the supreme effort of his life.

Later, in recognition of Colonel Burr's military record, President Adams proposed to General Washington that Burr be appointed a brigadier general, but Washington demurred, saying, "By all that I have known and heard Colonel Burr is a brave and able officer; but the question is, whether he has not equal talents at intrigue."

In complete disgust President Adams wrote, "How shall I describe my sensations and reflections at that moment? He had compelled me to promote over the heads of Lincoln, Gates, Clinton, Knox and others, and even over Pinckney, one of his own triumvirates, the most restless, impatient, artful, indefatigable and unprincipled intriguer in the United States, if not in the world [Alexander Hamilton]; but I was not permitted to nominate Burr!"

George Washington in 1798 portrait by Gilbert Stuart

The Federalists were confident at first that they could de-bauch Colonel B.... His conduct has been honorable and decisive and greatly embarrasses them.

– Thomas Jefferson
Private Letters

8
Hamilton Elected Jefferson President

Profiting by its defeat caused by internal strife in 1792, six years later the Federalist party chose General Philip Schuyler as senator from New York. Aaron Burr resumed the practice of law, but found time to reorganize the Republican party.

The prospects of the "outs" were gloomy. It was the first time in any city in America that each ward was organized and a dependable record made of its political status. This "grass-roots" organization, as it was later called in the West, took place at Richmond Hill. Here Theodosia sat beside her father and listed the voters for the Tammany Society, which had been reorganized in 1789. "Tammany's democratic principles," recorded John Pintard, "will serve in a measure to correct the aristocracy of our city."

Hamilton selected the names that appeared on the Federalist ticket. Only persons who were responsive to his instructions were named. He planned to defeat John Adams for re-election by securing a larger number of votes for C. C. Pinckney and thus reversing the party's choice by electing Pinckney as president and Adams as vice president. Hamilton hated John Adams.

After the Federal ticket was published, Burr named as Republican electors: George Clinton, General Horatio Gates, Samuel Osgood, Henry Rutgers, Elias Neusen, Thomas Storm, George Warner, Philip J. Arcularius, James Hunt, Ezekiel Robbins, Brockholst Livingston, and John Swartwout. Each name gave peculiar strength to the ticket, but it required all of Burr's power of appeal to induce the nominees to stand for election. At the outset this appeared an impossibility; however, the personal challenge of Burr to each elector, even to old Governor George Clinton, brought to the voters such a combination of political strength that the city voted the Republican ticket by a majority of 490.

This was the third time that Aaron Burr had engineered and accomplished the defeat of Alexander Hamilton, in whom it aroused a spirit of political hatred that led to Weehawken.

As soon as the returns from all the states were received, it was apparent that Aaron Burr had received the same number of votes as vice president as Thomas Jefferson had received as president, and if some state did not adjust its electoral vote there would be a tie. This would automatically throw the election into the House of Representatives, where the Federalists were in control. If this political prerogative had been exercised by the Republicans, as it was by the Federalists in Rhode Island, the coalition of Hamilton and Jefferson against Burr would have been averted.

Jefferson wrote to Randolph, his son-in-law:

> It was intended that one vote be thrown away from Colonel Burr. It is believed that Georgia will withhold one or two from him. The vote will probably stand T. J. 73, Burr about 70. Pinckney probably

lower than that. It is unfortunate that some difference will be made between the two highest candidates, because it is said that the Federalists held a caucus and came to a resolution in event of their being equal that they would prevent an election, which they could have done by dividing the H of R.

In a letter to his daughter January 26, 1801, Jefferson wrote, "Hamilton is using his utmost influence to procure my election rather than Colonel Burr's." Three days later he wrote to his son-in-law, "The main body of Federalists are determined to elect Burr or prevent an election. I dare not trust more through the mail."

Realizing the Federalists would be defeated if Upstate New York selected Republican electors, Hamilton wrote to Governor Jay proposing that he call an extra session of the old legislature to choose presidential electors. Jay filed this letter with his personal rebuff: "Proposing a measure for party purposes, which I think it would not become me to adopt."

Hamilton's contempt for the electorate was deep-seated. Failing in this attempt to corrupt the governor and nullify the expressed will of the electorate, he wrote Charles Carroll of Carrollton:

There is too much probability that Jefferson or Burr will be President. The latter is intriguing with all his might in New Jersey and Vermont. If he does he certainly will reform the government a la Bonaparte. He is unprincipled and as dangerous a man as any country can hold.

Anticipating a tie-vote, the Republicans of Virginia and New York each promised to adjust its vote that Jefferson should be chosen president and Burr vice president. Neither kept its promise. When the Electoral College assembled in December, the Federalists cast one vote for Jay, sixty-four for Pinckney, and sixty-five for Adams. The Republican vote was seventy-three for Jefferson and Burr. This impasse automatically transferred the election to the House of Representatives, where the Federalists had a majority but possessed no candidate. The Constitution limited the candidates to the two highest.

This situation aroused unprecedented partisan intrigue. Hamilton and Jefferson formed an alliance to defeat and then to destroy the usefulness of Burr. Hamilton's caustic pen eventually led him to Weehawken. Jefferson's political policy of making charges that he knew were not true and that he could not prove led to trial. Burr was politically destroyed, but at what price to his traducers!

The electoral vote of Jefferson and Burr by states was the same, being: New York 12, Pennsylvania 8, Maryland 5, Virginia 21, North Carolina 8, South Carolina 8, Georgia 4, Kentucky 4, and Tennessee 3; total 73.

The electoral vote of the Federalists for Adams and Pinckney was: New Hampshire 6, Vermont 4, Massachusetts 16, Connecticut 9, New Jersey 7, Pennsylvania 7, Maryland 5, Delaware 3, North Carolina 4; Rhode Island voted Adams 4, Pinckney 3, and Jay 1. The total vote was Adams 65, Pinckney 64, and Jay 1.

Originally the Federalists planned to continue the balloting until March 4, when both offices would become vacant and probably another election would be held. A majority preferred Burr to Jefferson for president, and this would have been accomplished but for the opposition of Alexander Hamilton. The vote by states in the House of Representatives was as follows:

STATE	JEFFERSON	BURR
New Hampshire	0	6
Vermont	1	1
Maine	3	11
Rhode Island	0	2
Connecticut	0	7
New York	6	4
New Jersey	3	2

STATE	JEFFERSON	BURR
Pennsylvania	9	4
Delaware	0	1
Maryland	4	4
Virginia	14	5
North Carolina	6	4
South Carolina	1	4
Georgia	1	0
Kentucky	2	0
Tennessee	1	0
Total	**51**	**55**

In his *History of the Presidency*, Edward Stanwood wrote:

> *An active intrigue had been in progress among the Federalists, dating back almost to the day when they learned of their defeat, which had for its purpose the prevention of the election of Mr. Jefferson. . . . Hamilton's most powerful efforts to detach the Federalists from Burr were exerted on one member of the House of Representatives from Delaware, Mr. James A. Bayard. . . . the Federalists made strenuous efforts to obtain assurances from Burr that he would, if elected, administer the government as a Federalist.*

Samuel P. Orth, in his section on Aaron Burr, "Father of the Political Machine" in *Five American Politicians: Study in the Evolution of American Politics*, wrote, "The Federalists of New England preferred Burr to Jefferson; their letters, their pamphlets, all are frank in this avowal." He quotes the *Boston Sentinel*:

> *The Federal States in Congress will give Mr. Burr their suffrages. Mr. Burr has never yet been charged with writing libelous letters against the government of his country to foreigners, and his politics always have*

been open and undisguised. It is granted that he is ambitious, but he is no hypocrite and though he is like Bonaparte in some respects, he is possessed of none of the cold-hearted qualities of the Gallic Consul.

Continuing, Orth wrote:

> *Had the House of Representatives convened in December, 1800, to choose a president, the New England Federalists would have given their support to Burr. What influence overcame their predilections? There was only one power in the Federal party potent enough to avert the elevation of Burr over Jefferson. It was the power of Hamilton. The genius of that gifted man was now applied to the single object of keeping his hated rival out of the presidential chair. He first tried to steal the electoral vote of New York by having Governor Jay call an extra session of the legislature. . . .*
>
> *Hamilton then turned to his personal friends in the party. He wrote, expostulated, argued, pleaded. To all he pictured Burr as without principle, profligate, selfish; a Caesar, a Catiline, a Bonaparte whose election would disgrace the country if not hurl it to ruin. The perusal of Hamilton's letters reveals the skill with which he adapted his arts to the various individuals he desired to sway and leaves one wondering how much of the spirit of jealousy prompted his patriotism.*

Probably the best source of information as to what occurred during the two months following the failure of an election by the Electoral College and the assembling of the House is to be found in the forty volumes of the works of Washington, Adams, Jefferson, and Hamilton. To those who do not have access to his record, some letters during this interim will be illuminating.

To representative Samuel Smith of Maryland on December 16, Colonel Burr wrote:

> *It is highly improbable that I shall have an equal number of votes with Mr. Jefferson; but if such should be the result, every man who knows me ought to know that I should utterly disclaim all competition. Be assured that the Federal party can entertain no wish for such an exchange. As to my friends—they would dishonor my views and insult my feelings by harbouring a suspicion that I could submit to be instrumental in counteracting the wishes and expectations of the United States. And I now constitute you in my proxy to declare these sentiments if the occasion shall require.*

The political principles recorded by Aaron Burr in that letter are in great contrast to those recorded and practiced by Alexander Hamilton and Thomas Jefferson in their attempt to destroy Burr. No man of his day came nearer to living up to the golden rule than Aaron Burr, while the vicious attacks of his enemies are without parallel. Every eager student who would know the truth should take the pains to verify the information contained in the following letters, consult the bibliography of this volume, and continue the research until completely convinced that this information is trustworthy. Unfortunately the textbooks of our schools are vague, incomplete, and even misleading concerning the conspiracy against Aaron Burr. Only those students who are willing to do careful research will be sure of their facts. The subject will commend itself to all who would know their history.

On the very same date that Burr wrote the foregoing letter, Hamilton wrote to Oliver Wolcott, "Burr is bankrupt beyond redemption except by the plunder of his country . . . yet it may be well enough to throw out for a lure for him . . . to start for the plate and thus lay the foundation of disunion between the two chiefs."

The next day, December 17, Harrison Otis of Massachusetts

wrote to Hamilton, "It is palpable that to elect [Burr] would be to cover the opposition with chagrin and to sow among them seeds of a mortal division." Otis went on to ask, in effect, "Shall we open negotiations with Burr? If yes, How? Will he stand to his engagements? We in Massachusetts do not know the man. You do. Advise us."

Late in December, Hamilton wrote to Wolcott warning that:

If the Federal party succeeds in electing Burr late in December, it will have done nothing more nor less than place in that station a man who will possess the boldness and daring necessary to give success to the Jacobin system, instead of one who, for want of that quality, will be less fitted to promote it.

To accomplish this end Burr must lean on unprincipled men, and continue to adhere to the myrmidons who have hitherto surrounded him. To these he will, no doubt, add able rogues of all parties. These things are to be inferred to a moral certainty from the character of the man. Every step of his career proves that he has formed himself upon the model of Catiline, and that he is too cold-blooded and too determined a conspirator ever to change his plan.

On December 26, Hamilton wrote to Gouverneur Morris, "If there be a man in the world I ought to hate, it is Jefferson. With Burr I have always been personally well. But the public good must be paramount to every private consideration."

Then on the next day Hamilton wrote a long letter to Bayard of Delaware, the sole representative in the House from that state:

No engagement that can be made with [Burr] can be depended upon. While making it he will laugh in his sleeve at the credulity of those with whom he makes it; and the first moment it suits his views to break it, he will do so. Let me add that I could scarcely name a discreet man in either party in our state who does not think Mr. Burr the most unfit man in the United States for the office of President. Disgrace abroad, ruin at home, are the probable fruits of his elevation.

James A. Bayard was the key man to the great political conflict, but he held from the entreaties of Hamilton. He replied to Hamilton:

But there is another view of the subject which gives me some inclination in favor of Burr. I consider the state ambition of Virginia as the source of the present party. The faction who govern that state aim to govern the United States. Virginia will never be satisfied but when this state of things exist. If Burr should be President, they will not govern, and his acceptance of the office, which would disappoint their views, which depend upon Jefferson, would, I apprehend, immediately create a schism in the party, which would soon rise into open opposition.

I cannot deny, however, that there are strong considerations which give preference to Mr. Jefferson. The subject admits of many and very doubtful views, and before I resolve on the part I shall take, I shall wait the approach of the crisis, which may probably bring with it circumstances decisive of the event. The Federal party meets on Friday for the purpose of forming a resolution as to their line of conduct. I have not the least doubt as to their agreeing to support Burr. Their determination will not bind me, for though it might cost me a painful struggle to disappoint the views and wishes of many gentlemen with whom I have been accustomed to act, yet the magnitude of the subject forbids the sacrifice of a strong conviction.

General James Gunn of Georgia acknowledged a letter from Hamilton on the ninth of January. From Washington he wrote:

> *On the subject of choosing a President, some Revolutionary opinions are gaining ground, and the Jacobins are determined to resist the election of Burr at every hazard—most of the Jacobin members will be instructed not to vote for Colonel Burr.*
>
> *I have seen a letter from Mr. Madison to one of the Virginia representatives, in which he says that in event of the present House of Representatives not choosing Mr. Jefferson President, that the next House of Representatives will have a right to choose one of the two having the highest number of votes; and that the nature of the case, aided with the support of the great body of the people, will justify Jefferson and Burr Jointly to call together the members of the next House of Representatives, previous to the 3rd of next December, for the express purpose of choosing a President, and that he is confident they will make a proper choice.*

Governor John Rutledge of South Carolina acknowledged on January 10 receipt of a letter from Hamilton, and replied as follows:

> *My determination to support Mr. Burr has been shaken by your communication, and I shall make, among those who with you are anxious to preserve public order at this crisis, all the use of it that its reasonableness and value will enable me to do.*
>
> *Viewing Mr. Jefferson and Mr. Burr separately, each appears improper for the Presidency; but looking at them together, and comparatively, the Federalists think their preferring Burr will be the least mischief they can do. His promotion will be prodigiously af-*

flicting to the Virginia faction, and must disjoint the party. If Mr. B's presidency be productive of evils, it will be very easy for us to excite jealousy respecting his motives and to get rid of him.

While the Federalists were originally almost unanimously for Burr, Hamilton's letters were having a disturbing effect and causing a decided change of sentiment. True, Hamilton had lost much of his masterly control of the party, but he still wielded sufficient influence to elect Jefferson and defeat Burr, whom he would go to any length to remove from public esteem. It was January 16 that Hamilton resumed his letters to Bayard:

Your resolution to separate yourself . . . from the Federal party, if your conviction shall be strong of the unfitness of Burr, is certainly laudable. So much does it coincide with my ideas, that if the party shall, by supporting Burr as President, adopt him for their official chief, I shall be obliged to consider myself as an isolated man. . . . He is crafty and persevering in his objects; that he is not scrupulous about the means of success, nor very mindful of truth, and that he is a contemptible hypocrite.

Nor is it true that Jefferson is zealot enough to do anything in pursuance of his principles which will contravene his popularity or his interest. He is as likely as any man I know to temporize; to calculate what will be likely to promote his own reputation and advantage.

No other man of his day made such an exhaustive study of Hamilton, Jefferson, and Burr as James Parton. He wrote a biography of Jefferson and one of Burr, and out of this research Parton recorded "Hamilton's chronic dread of Burr's usurping the government . . . was . . . one of the symptoms of the Burriphobia which he labored."

Hamilton was of the opinion that the Constitution had been tried and found wanting. According to Parton, Hamilton, of the two, "was more likely to have made an attempt to subvert the government than Burr; for Hamilton was already convinced of the necessity of its subversion."

It was January 21 that Hamilton closed his case against Burr by writing to Theodore Sedgwick, "I never was so much mistaken as I shall be if our friends, in the event of their success, do not rue the preference they will give to that Catiline."

A majority of the 106 members of the House were Federalists. If a majority of the voters had sufficed, Burr would have been elected on the first ballet. Burr's vote was 55; Jefferson's total was 51; but the choice must be made by states. Delaware, as represented by Bayard, was just as strong in the final test of strength as Virginia with twenty-one representatives. And as it turned out, Bayard wrote his name on the pages of history more indelibly than his 105 colleagues—Bayard's vote elected Jefferson. Hamilton was the political brains and power that marshaled the Federalists onto the field of battle and whipped them into line—drove them from their preference for Burr to their choice of Jefferson. Hamilton was the power; Bayard became as putty in Hamilton's hands.

For thirty-five ballots New York, Pennsylvania, New Jersey, North Carolina, Virginia, Kentucky, Tennessee, and Georgia voted for Jefferson; New Hampshire, Massachusetts, Rhode Island, Connecticut, South Carolina, and Delaware voted for Burr. Eight states were for Jefferson and six for Burr. On the thirty-sixth ballot Bayard changed to Jefferson, and the agony was over. Nine states, a majority of whom were Federalists, had chosen a Republican for president.

The Republicans of the United States had voted for Jefferson for president, and for Burr as vice president. Burr's sense of political honor motivated him to decline the presidency at the hands of the Federalist.

Notwithstanding that he had voted persistently from February 11 until February 17 for Burr and opposed Jefferson, Bayard was so incensed at Burr's failure to cooperate in the struggle that he now wrote:

> *The means existed of electing Burr, but required his cooperation. By deceiving one man (a great blockhead), and tempting two (not incorruptible) he might have secured a majority of the states. He will never have another chance of being President of the United States; and the little use he has made of the one which has occurred, gives me but an humble opinion of the talents of an unprincipled man.*

After the balloting was over Bayard reported to Hamilton:

> *I was willing to take Burr, but I never considered it as a case likely to happen. . . . But I was enabled soon to discover that he was determined not to shackle himself with federal principles.*

Among the representatives was William Cooper, the father of James Fenimore Cooper, who wrote to Thomas Morris:

> *We have this day locked ourselves up by a rule of procedure to choose a President before we adjourn. We shall run Burr perseveringly. . . . A little good management would have secured our object on the first vote.*

Three days later, Cooper added:

> *Had Burr done anything for himself, he would long ere this have been President. If a majority would answer he would have had it on every vote.*

And this was the terrific contest whereby refusing to crook his finger in self-help Burr maddened the Federalists and aroused the jealousy of Jefferson until, like Hamilton, he could never thereafter see anything good in Burr. The coalition between Hamilton and Jefferson, which elected Jefferson, constitutes the outstanding debauchery of American politics.

While the contest was in progress, David A. Ogden, Hamilton's law partner, was sent to Albany to ascertain upon what terms Burr would accept the presidency from the Federalists. He reported that Burr refused to entertain any terms whatever.

Six years after this memorable contest, the necessity for correcting statements contained in Jefferson's diary resulted in the verification of Congressman's George Baer's record:

> *Much anxiety was shown by the friends of Mr. Jefferson, and much ingenuity used to discover the line of conduct which would be pursued by them. . . . There was no evidence of any effort on the part of [Colonel Burr] or his personal friends, to procure his election [while there were numerous assurances] of certain advantages in case Mr. Jefferson was elected.*

On this occasion James A. Bayard testified:

> *I never had any communication, directly or indirectly, with Mr. Burr in relation to his election to the presidency. . . . I repeatedly state that it was a vain thing to protract the election, as it had become manifest that Mr. Burr would not assist us, and as we could do nothing without his aid. . . . I never did discover that Mr. Burr used the least influence to promote the object we had in view. . . . I have no reason to believe, and never did think, that he interfered, even to the point of personal influence, to obstruct the election of Jefferson or to promote his*

own. I do not know, nor did I ever believe, from any information I received that Mr. Burr entered into any negotiation or agreement with any member of either party.

Under oath Samuel Smith corroborated Bayard's affidavit.

Hamilton was a persuasive politician. His letters to the Federalists in the House of Representatives elected Jefferson president. Yet Hamilton's record in that contest, like Jefferson's, is unworthy of a politician, much less of a statesman. Hamilton had bought a few acres near New York City to which he would soon retire. He wrote Gouverneur Morris:

Mine is an odd destiny. Perhaps no man in the United States has sacrificed or done more for the present Constitution than myself; and, contrary to all my anticipations of its fate, as you know from the very beginning, I am still laboring to prop the frail and worthless fabric. Yet I have the murmurs of its friends no less than the curses of its foes, for my rewards. What can I do better than withdraw from the scene? Every day proves to me, more and more, that this American world was not made for me.

"Burr's standing in the republic was absolutely as good as Jefferson's, and his elevation to that high office was less dreaded by the opposition than that of Jefferson," according to Thomas Edward Watson, author of *The Life and Times of Jefferson.* He adds:

Had Burr made the pledges which Jefferson's friends ... did make, there can be no doubt that he would have been President of the United States. It only needed that he should crook his finger in the way of active self-help. And had Aaron Burr become President who can say that he would not have made a good one? ...

By sheer force of will and intellect he wrested New York from the Hamilton-Schuyler faction. . . . He had never knifed a friend as Hamilton and Walcott stabbed John Adams.

Charles Carroll of Carrolton, a signer of the Declaration of Independence, who probably knew Jefferson and Burr as well as any contemporary, and who was regarded as one of the purest patriots and ablest statesmen of his day, wrote to Hamilton on August 27, 1800, that he preferred Burr to Jefferson for president because of "Burr's decision of character."

In February 1801, Carroll wrote to his son: "I hope Burr will be chosen by the House of Representatives. . . . Mr. Jefferson is unfit to govern this or any other country." Carroll concluded that "Burr is firm, energetic and decisive."

It was December 15, 1800, that Jefferson wrote to Burr he was sorry that he was to lose him from the original list as a member of this cabinet:

> *I feel most sensibly the loss we sustain of your aid in our new administration. It leaves a chasm in my arrangements, which cannot be adequately filled up. I had endeavored to compose an administration whose talents, integrity, names and dispositions should inspire unbounded confidence in the public mind. I [regret] to lose you from the list. . . .*

Hamilton must cease his lying attacks. And to silence Hamilton? It took a pistol shot, and the story of that encounter has been written all over our history. Possibly no single event has been so exaggerated, and certainly the dwarfed figure of Hamilton has been stretched until the canvas has cracked and torn. Presently we shall have a new portrait of him. I wonder whether we shall be able to recognize the man on the new frame.

— Walter F. McCaleb

9
The Vice President

During the historic struggle by the House of Representatives, Colonel Burr was in Albany as chairman of a committee charged with the revision of the laws of New York. Vice president Jefferson was in Washington receiving reports from his lieutenants and directing their activities. Burr declined to answer letters from the Federalists. He refused the presidency at their hands.

Mr. Jefferson conferred with the Federalists if not personally then through his political representatives. He accepted the presidency from the Federalists on terms identical to those on which previously it had been offered to Burr. Jefferson allowed certain Federalists to hold over; he appointed others to offices of trust and emoluments.

It was two months prior to the convening of the House that

the Electoral College had come to the impasse when Jefferson and Burr each had received seventy-three votes. The Constitution automatically certified the "two highest" as the only eligible candidates. One must be chosen president, the other vice president.

Originally the Federalists decided to ballot until John Adams's term expired, when they had hoped that he would succeed himself, or another election would take place. Their stand, however, became so untenable they were unable to hold out. Their meeting place became a madhouse. Nothing like it had been witnessed in the United States. The members were imbued with and succumbed to intrigue, political dishonor, and blind partisanship.

Out of the ravings of the House of Representatives was born Jefferson's animosity toward Burr. Here he was obsessed with the idea that Burr coveted the presidency and that he plotted to defeat him. Time and the records reveal the truth: Jefferson's envy and jealousy were aroused; he was motivated by political ambition. Burr's sin consisted in having been the first choice of the Federalists!

Only the student who has made vast research may have any conception of the ill will and political jaundice that motivated Jefferson during the four years that he was president and Burr was vice president. Their elevation to office resulted from the most malevolent political fight in history.

During the terms of Washington and Adams this government had been administered in complete sympathy with English ideals. For twelve years Alexander Hamilton was in a very large sense ruler of this country. The great measures of both administrations were the products of his brain. Strangely, Hamilton had no place in the hearts of the people; his anchorage to the public was that he was trusted by Washington. In addition to being the soul and intelligence of the Federalist party, Hamilton gave aspiring socialites respectability; he encouraged the court homage that Mrs. Washington and Mrs. Adams loved. Notwithstanding this, John Adams always mistrusted Alexander Hamilton.

Jefferson had escaped to France in 1785, thereby avoiding

the travail of the writing of the Constitution. He returned four years later to become secretary of state. He took office in March 1790. Hamilton was secretary of the treasury. Immediately Hamilton and Jefferson learned that they were radically opposed to each other in theories of government, all save one: neither believed that the masses were capable of governing themselves.

Jefferson was a scholar, lawyer, agrarian, architect, and philosopher. Hamilton was a successful lawyer and a great orator who, as pen to Washington during the Revolution, had filled the archives of this country with an impressive picture of General Washington. Hamilton was more brilliant than Jefferson, and possessed the ego that enabled him to assume leadership of any movement and spokesman for any group.

Hamilton hated, while Jefferson loved, the French Revolution. Hamilton was for a strong central government. He had favored a Constitution that provided life tenure for the president with power to appoint members of the Senate and governors of the states. All were to have high salaries. He was for a powerful standing army.

Jefferson was for the independence of the states—later known as states' rights. He planned an unpaid militia, was penurious in spending government funds, and was opposed to any ambassador to foreign courts or to any diplomatic establishment.

Hamilton desired that ambassadors live at foreign courts in a style similar to the courtly representatives of kings. He gave formal approval to the prevailing religious creed. He attended the Episcopal church. Jefferson was a dissenter and attended the Unitarian church.

Hamilton was a handsome, courtly gentleman who wore fine clothes and was every inch a Chesterfield. Jefferson combed his hair out of pigtail, discarded powder, wore pantaloons, and fastened his shoes with strings instead of buckles. He looked and acted the part of a country squire. Is it any wonder that these two, as Jefferson reported, "Were pitted against each other every day in the cabinet, like two fighting cocks?"

The Hamilton–Jefferson fight continued for ten years as a personal conflict. It then became a national affair of party proportions when the Republican party was born, and political aristocracy succumbed to a siren of democracy. Strangely enough, the management of that political encounter in New York was led by Aaron Burr.

Politics, religion, and family quarrels lead men to do the most atrocious deeds. These are the breeding places for feuds, duels, and wars. Possibly no one else has painted a better picture of the strife and bad blood that accompanied the overthrow of the Federalists and the enthronement of the Republicans than Thomas Jefferson, who wrote:

> *The passions are too high at present to be cooled in our day. You and I have formerly seen warm debates and high political passions. But gentlemen of different politics would then speak to each other, and separate the business of the Senate from that of society. It is not so now. Men who have been intimate all their lives cross the street to avoid meeting and turn their heads the other way, lest they should be obliged to touch their hats!*
>
> *All the passions are boiling over and one who keeps himself cool and clear of contagion, is so far below the point of ordinary conversation that he finds himself insulated in every society. The interruption of letters is becoming is so notorious that I am forming a resolution of declining correspondence with my friends through the channels of the post office altogether.*

Senator William Plumer wrote, "Burr . . . presides . . . with great ease, dignity and propriety. He confines the speaker to the point."

In February 1802, Commodore Truxton wrote to Burr:

I have seen many of your friends; you are toast-
ed daily. I had no idea that changes could become so
great in half a year. I sincerely anticipate the pleasure
of seeing you in possession of the first office under our
blessed constitution after March 3, 1805. I pray that
events may put you there before. I cannot be a hypo-
crite to effect the esteem of a man, or men, who I do
not believe have at heart those principles which are so
necessary to give character and consequences to our
beloved country. My friends in politics are aware how
cautious you ought to be just now. You are not in the
confidence of J [Jefferson]. You must take care of Al-
exander Hamilton.

In his election as president by a majority of the states
where the Federalists were in control, Jefferson was second
choice. This fact, together with the political venom that was
engendered by the prolonged fight in the House, aroused in
Thomas Jefferson hatred that followed him to his grave. Like
Hamilton, Jefferson was envious of Burr's talents and jealous
of the esteem in which Burr was held by the masses. Writing
about Jefferson in his biography of Burr, Nathan Schachner recorded, "An office which is palpably the gift of another excites
certain inner presentments."

Aaron Burr made it a rule never to answer a charge or to
heed a calumny. He paid little or no attention to the newspaper
critics. They little, if any, disturbed his serenity. His friends, however, often replied, especially to slander, lies, and disgraceful libels.
Burr went to Jefferson in January 1804 with a view of having
a mutual understanding so that a schism in the party might be
averted. Jefferson, however, was determined to replace Burr with
Madison as his successor in the presidency. Concerning the conference, Jefferson wrote in his diary, "Burr's conduct inspires me
with distrust."

During the New York gubernatorial election in 1804,

Hamilton went to Albany for a conference with party associates at which he addressed them at Lewis's Tavern. Concerning his address, the *Morning Chronicle* said, "General Hamilton addressed the meeting with his usual eloquence. The principal part of his speech went on to show that no reliance can be placed in Mr. Burr."

Concerning this election, Samuel P. Orth wrote:

> *Burr's following were held by their chief well within the precincts of decorum. But the Clintonians were fire-eaters. Their brands were fed with the oil of Federalism. Cheetham especially reveled in libel and gorged his spleen in hand bills and pamphlets whose lies were equaled only by their vulgarity. . . .*
>
> *There is a prevalent feeling that Burr was intent upon severing the Union, and by becoming Governor of New York planned to elevate himself to the Presidency of the northern republic composed of the states of New England and North Atlantic States. The persistence of this opinion reveals the ease with which nature is misled and how unfair history may become. The only foundation for such a slander is the wicked imagination of the unprincipled Cheetham and the zealous partisanship of Hamilton.*

Burr was nominated as an independent candidate. His supporters stressed that he was a single man who would not have a family at the public crib (a trough). They reviewed at length his Revolutionary War record; they carefully restated his stand against the British treaty; they renewed the public's acquaintance with Burr's record of integrity; they paraded at length Burr's ancestry: his father as a noted divine and a creator of Princeton University, and his mother as the daughter of the eminent theologian Jonathan Edwards.

As biographer James Parton wrote:

Up to this time there was scarcely a blemish on the character of Burr, and certainly no one but would have been delighted to associate with him and share his reflected glory. But politics, that demon that has ruined so many great men, it was now to choose for its object a shining mark! Burr carried the city by a small majority, but the poison of Hamilton's letters was far more effective up-state. Burr was defeated by more than seven thousand.

It was during this election, on April 23, 1804, that Dr. Charles D. Cooper wrote to Philip Schuyler:

General Hamilton and Judge Kent have declared, in substance, that they looked upon Mr. Burr to be a dangerous man, and one who ought not to be trusted with the reins of government. If, sir, you attended a meeting of Federalists at the City Tavern where General Hamilton made a speech on the pending election, I might appeal to you for the truth of so much of this assertion as related to him. . . . I could detail to you a still more despicable opinion which General Hamilton has expressed of Mr. Burr.

Hamilton had been personally warned by Burr that he must confine himself to the truth when he made statements concerning the integrity or honor of Burr. Hamilton's enmity outran his judgment. Within six weeks after the election Hamilton's fateful words fell into the hands of Burr.

Smarting under defeat, Burr directed William P. Van Ness to convey the Dr. Cooper letter to General Hamilton and point out the offensive passage. Van Ness also delivered a note that read, "You might perceive, Sir, the necessity of a prompt and unqualified acknowledgment or denial of the use of any expression which could warrant the assertions of Dr. Cooper."

Charles Biddle, who with Hamilton had dined at Richmond Hill during the pre-election days of 1804, says there was nothing in their mutual conduct to suggest any enmity between the two other than natural incompatibility concerning political questions; that Burr was really quite fond of Hamilton personally. He adds, however, that in his library Hamilton had labored incessantly to disparage Colonel Burr—to injure his cause, to bring about his defeat using one of the most effective weapons in history: his pen.

At the letter and at Burr's note, Hamilton stared long and earnestly. Apparently he forgot for a time the presence of his visitor. Tragedy lurked in the words Hamilton had uttered; now they returned to demand his attention—his decision. Finally Hamilton turned to Van Ness and said it was a matter that would require consideration, and that his answer would be shortly forthcoming. Two days later Van Ness received the response. It was lengthy and argumentative, saying;

> *The more I have reflected the more I have become convinced that I could not, without manifest impropriety, make the avowal or disavowal which you seem to think necessary. . . . I trust, on more reflection, you will see the matter in the same light with me. If not, I can only regret the circumstance, and must abide the consequences.*

Consequences indeed, and great they were! Previously both men had taken a part in like experiences. Hamilton's son had fallen in a duel only a short time before. There is a long list of similar engagements: Gates, Randolph, Swartwout, Thompson and, later, even Andrew Jackson was to kill his man. Further demands brought equally unsatisfactory replies. A formal challenge was issued and accepted. The necessary arrangements were made by two seconds. The date, July 11, and the place, Weehawken, just across the Hudson in New Jersey. Weehawken had been the scene of many duels. Now it was to become historic. The Hamilton–Burr duel served one good purpose: prominence of the principals gave nationwide impetus to a movement that eventually put an end to dueling.

Burr and Hamilton had met before under circumstances that involved the code. After Hamilton had published in 1796 his strange documents admitting his intimacy with Maria Reynolds, Senator James Monroe and Congressmen Abraham Venable and Frederick Muhlenberg visited Mr. Hamilton to learn as Hamilton published:

> *My real crime is an amorous connection with his wife, for a considerable time with his privity and connivance. . . . This confession is not made without a blush. I cannot be the apologist of any vice because the ardor of passion may have made it mine. I can never cease to condemn myself for the pang which it may inflict in a bosom eminently entitled to all my gratitude, fidelity and love. But that bosom will approve, that at even, at so great an expense, I should effectually wipe away a more serious stain from a name, which it cherishes with no less elevation than tenderness.*

Monroe's subsequent attitude and behavior caused Hamilton to ask his friend Aaron Burr to act as his second, and it appears that Burr was able to adjust that affair without pistols.

For a fortnight after choosing the date for the duel, the principals and seconds went about the business of putting their houses in order and engaged in their normal activities with never a word to the unknowing world in which they mingled. They met the Fourth of July around the same board, the Society of Cincinnati, of which both were members. Hamilton, president of the society, was hilarious and even boisterous, leaping upon a table to sing a song. In the eyes of his friends he was unusually reckless. Burr remained quiet, watching Hamilton's feverish display of enthusiasm; then, at an early hour, he retired from the festive occasion. The coming event appeared to have stirred one of the principals to unwonted action, the other to unusual quietude.

Burr had previously made his will, and on the tenth of July wrote to Theodosia advising what he had done. The letter advised "If I should die this year" that Theo take charge of specified papers. His devotion to his daughter was expressed at the end of this letter:

> *I am indebted to you, my dearest Theodosia, for a very great portion of the happiness which I have enjoyed in this life. You have completely satisfied all that my heart and affections had hoped or even wished. With a little more perseverance, determination and industry, you will obtain all that my ambition or vanity had fondly imagined. Let your son have occasion to be proud that he had a mother. Adieu. Adieu.*

To his son-in-law he wrote:

> *I have called out General Hamilton and we meet tomorrow morning. If it should be my lot to fall. . . . yet I shall live in you and your son. I commit to you all that is most dear to me—my reputation and my daughter. . . . Let me entreat you to stimulate and aid Theodosia in the cultivation of her mind.*
>
> *It is indispensable to her happiness and essential to yours. It is also of the utmost importance to your son. She would presently acquire a critical knowledge of Latin, English and all branches of natural philosophy. . . . If you should differ with me as to the importance of this measure suffer me to ask it of you as a last favor. She will richly compensate your trouble.*

Hamilton wound up his legal business. He appears to have devoted himself largely to writing for posterity what he was pleased to call his "Apologia," a remarkable document in which he said he was opposed to dueling as a religious and moral principle. While quite sure that his wife and children, as well as his creditors, required his continued life, he could not avoid the issue because:

> *It is not to be denied that my animadversions on political principles, character, and views of Colonel Burr have been extremely severe; and on different occasions, I, in common with many others, have made very unfavorable criticisms on particular instances of the private conduct of this gentleman.*
>
> *My religious and moral principles are strongly opposed to the practice of dueling, and it would even give me pain to be obliged to shed the blood of a fellow creature in private combat forbidden by the laws.*

So wrote Mr. Hamilton, apparently oblivious of his record, which is in great contrast to his apologies.

In 1778 Hamilton had challenged General Charles Lee for what he assumed was disrespectful behavior toward General Washington at the Battle of Monmouth. The choice fell upon Mr. Laurens, a fellow aide, who was to assume the responsibility for the fellow challenger. In addition to the Monroe challenge, which Hamilton had issued, but which he was so easily induced to cancel, there was a political quarrel with Commodore Nicholson where, again, Mr. Hamilton issued a challenge that his friends averted.

Hamilton was always stronger with the pen than with the sword, or even with the pistol, as his friends were later to learn. During the Revolution, while Hamilton was using his pen to glorify the deeds of General Washington, Burr was at the cannon's mouth.

With all the political aversion John Randolph exhibited for Burr, he has left a vivid picture of the contending pens that prepared the groundwork for the Hamilton–Burr duel:

> *I admire Burr's letters, particularly that signed by Van Ness, and think his whole conduct in that affair does him honor. . . . . In his correspondence with Hamilton, how visible is ascendancy over him, and how sensibly does the latter appear of it! There is apparent consciousness of some inferiority to his enemy displayed by Hamilton throughout that transaction, and from a previous sight of their letters I could have inferred the issue of the contest. On one side there is labored obscurity, much equivocation, and many attempts of evasion, not unmixed with a little blustering; on the other an unshaken adherence to his object, and an undeviating pursuit of it, not to be eluded or baffled. It reminded me of the slinking fox pressed by a vigorous old hound, where no shift is permitted to avail him.*

Eventually the day of reckoning arrived. Hamilton had sown to the wind. He reaped the whirlwind. His pen, the most caustic of record, was used with the assassin's intent. He was determined to remove Aaron Burr from his political pathway: remove the man whom he held responsible for the defeat of his father-in-law in the Senate; for the establishment of a third bank; for the defeat of the Federalists in 1800 when Burr was chosen vice president. Burr was within reach of the presidency; this must never become a reality. Aaron Burr should never become president if Alexander Hamilton could prevent it!

Never in the history of the United States has another pen been so persistent, so determined, and so cleverly wielded in becoming an instrument of destruction. Hamilton removed Burr from public life with his pen! He paid with his life for the murder of Burr's good name.

It was Hamilton's choice, and on the morning of July 11 he substituted pistols for pens. The distance was ten paces. At the appointed hour William Van Ness attended Burr; Nathaniel Pendleton was with Hamilton. The parties saluted, the pistols were loaded, and the two antagonists took positions. At the word both presented and fired. Burr remained erect. Hamilton raised himself convulsively, staggered, and pitched forward to the ground. Complying with William Van Ness's urgent demands, Burr retired. A surgeon from the barge approached. Hamilton was mortally wounded. He was transferred to New York, and lived thirty-one hours.

A friendly press exalted Hamilton. He was buried with military honors, within the shadows of the great interests he had served so well, in a little cemetery at the end of Wall Street. His burial place has become a shrine for those who then, as later, approved his course. He became a martyr to the unbridled liberties of his pen. Burr's chief mistake was giving him a crown!

It was a day when honor was more highly regarded than life. For years Hamilton and Burr had occupied the first places in the Union as orators and lawyers; now as political leaders. Hamilton was father of the Federalist party. In constructive leadership and in matters of state Hamilton was the brains of the administration of Washington and Adams. He typified aristocracy and oligarchy.

Hamilton's concepts of government were English. Burr sympathized with the rising tide of democracy in France. They represented two warring factions of society, each fighting for control of the government. Burr paved the way for the birth of democracy in the New World, first in New York, then in the Union—a tide that swept into power in 1800. Four years later Hamilton gave his all for its defeat, particularly the defeat of Burr. Hamilton's success in that struggle was accomplished largely by lying about Burr. This Burr must stop. But how? Let the historian Walter F. McCaleb answer.

> *Hamilton must cease his lying attacks. And how to silence Hamilton? It took a pistol shot, and the story of that encounter has been written all over our history. Possibly no single event has been so exaggerated, and certainly the dwarfed figure of Hamilton has been stretched until the canvas has cracked and torn. Presently we shall have a new portrait of him. I wonder whether we shall be able to recognize the man in his new frame?*

For ten years Burr served in the Senate; first as senator, then as vice president. When he retired the Senate unanimously approved his "integrity and ability." For thirteen years Hamilton vilified and denounced Burr. Hamilton's tireless energy and masterful intrigue destroyed Burr's good name. Hamilton reaped his reward! Eventually, Burr announced he should have recognized that the world was large enough for both. Burr had suffered the inevitable fate that awaits every man who takes human life!

Burr's friends decided that New York was too dangerous a place for him, and they secretly transported him to Philadelphia. Later he joined his friend Senator Pierce Butler on his feudal plantation on St. Simon's Island near Darien, Georgia. In September Burr surveyed the Spanish territory now a part of Florida, because to him it had long been apparent that this should belong to the Union.

Late in the month he returned by ship to Savannah. Here he was accorded an enthusiastic reception by a great concourse of people headed by a band. Such hospitality agreeably surprised Burr in view of the clamor from which he had so recently escaped in New York. From this expression of personal esteem he parted with regret to hasten to the arms of his daughter, her husband, and his little grandson, "Gampy." After regaining his composure he retraced his steps to Washington. At every step on his return he was received as a conquering hero. Even in Virginia many approved his killing of Hamilton. In this clash of ideals the South was on the side of Burr, to which a Southern senator gave the words: "the little Republican David hath slain the Federalists' Goliath!"

On October 31 Burr wrote to Theodosia, "Virginia is the last state, and Petersburg the last town in the state of Virginia in which I should have expected any marks of open hospitality and respect."

It was November 5, 1804, that Burr resumed his seat as vice president of the United States in the chair of the president of the Senate. His enemies glared at him as if he were a felon who had enraged their bitterest passions. His friends were happy.

Aaron Burr's lifeboat was ever tossed by contrary winds—some blowing cold and some hot; there was never a calm. The cordiality of the Senate pleased Burr; that of Jefferson surprised and amused him. It awakened his keenest speculation. Jefferson had long maintained an armed neutrality toward Burr. Now he was agreeable, courteous, and considerate. He even invited Burr to his secret counsels.

Why this change of front? Burr had not long to wait to solve this riddle. Jefferson was courting the good graces of the man who was to preside over the Senate at the death struggle of the judiciary that was the last stronghold of Federalism. Here, under John Marshall's guidance, as Jefferson viewed it, was an obstacle to the untrammeled expression of a free people.

In the Senate chamber the stage was set for the impeachment of Justice Samuel Chase. It was not the man but a precedent that was on trial. If Jefferson could unseat Chase, he might remove Chief Justice John Marshall. Thus empowered, he could pull down the temples of Federalism; he could destroy what was most antagonistic to his plans for democracy. Aaron Burr presided where the destinies of Jefferson's dreams were at stake.

Apparently it never occurred to Burr that his political destiny was involved in his decisions. While, however, they were approved by some of the best brains of the Union, they so enraged the president that he charged Burr with treason—not immediately, but just as soon as he could set the stage for the destruction of his political adversary.

The importance of Burr's decisions become more apparent when it is realized that they saved our national judiciary; that they preserved John Marshall as chief justice, where he presided longer than any successor. Marshall's decisions as chief justice established for America a bulwark of integrity and judicial honor that has preserved the Constitution. If Jefferson fostered the Bill of Rights, Marshall rescued and preserved it.

The refusal of Aaron Burr to do the political bidding of Thomas Jefferson preserved John Marshall as chief justice. Marshall construed the Constitution and established justice and liberty for the individual; he saved the republic. When America fully recognizes that Aaron Burr saved John Marshall, Burr will tower among our greatest patriots!

On the morning of Jefferson's inauguration John Marshall wrote, "Democrats are divided into speculative theorists and absolute terrorists. With the latter I am not disposed to class Mr.

Jefferson. If he arranges himself with them, it is not difficult to foresee that much calamity is in store for our country—if he does not, they will soon become his enemies and calumniators."

At about the same time Thomas Jefferson wrote, "The Federalists have retired into the Judiciary as a stronghold, and from that battery all the works of Republicanism is to be battered down."

If all the caustic political denunciation of a lifetime were gathered for one campaign, it probably would still represent only a fraction of the savage partisan warfare that was waged when political control of the government was transferred to the Republicans. It represented politics concentrated—political dynamite.

A new republic was in the making. No one believed it would survive in the hands of an opposing party. Few Federalists had expected it to live in their own hands. Each of the colonies had struggled for a particular form of government. When they endeavored to unite, each wanted its form adopted. There was distrust, strife, and criticism. Only the Revolutionary War forced upon them a common bond, and that was for defense. Out of the Revolution and the adoption of the Constitution and twelve years of Federalist rule came the Republicans with Jefferson and Burr at the helm of the ship of state. Out of Jefferson's envy and jealousy came the charge of Burr's perfidy.

The republic was born in an hour of peril. Our Constitution is a precious document, yet ten of the sixty-five chosen delegates did not attend and only thirty-nine signed the "worthless fabric," as Hamilton called it. Ignorance concerning its making and its construing is a challenge to the youth of America to learn many truths that have so long been hidden in our archives—truth covered by partisans Hamilton and Jefferson. "Let there be light."

With the coming of the Chase trial Jefferson assumed a more conciliatory attitude toward Burr. Years that had been barren of political favors suddenly bore fruit. Burr's stepson, J. B. Prevost, was appointed judge of the Superior Court of New Orleans. Mrs. Burr's brother-in-law, James Brown, was made secretary of the Louisiana Territory. James Wilkinson was appointed governor of the Louisiana Territory.

The Senate convened as a high court of Impeachment January 2, 1805, to give judicial consideration to the charges preferred by the House and to test the political power of the president—to see if he was in control of nine Federalists and twenty-five Republicans.

For this dramatic occasion the Senate chamber was especially decorated. The desks in front of the two rows of seats on either side of the president of the Senate were covered with crimson cloth. These were for the senators. Three rows of the seats of the gallery were elevated in a semi-circle above the well of the amphitheater. These were draped in dark green with flanking boxes for the ladies of officialdom who were welcomed to give social standing to an otherwise dull political contest. Beneath the gallery were tiers of seats occupied by members of the House who had come to convince the Senate of the serious political import of the eight articles of impeachment.

John Randolph was in charge of the political endeavor to impeach Chase. Luther Martin, bulldog of the Federalists, opposed it. The eyes of the republic were on Aaron Burr, because he was presiding and acting as arbiter at a national political fight between Federalists and Republicans. From the first rap of his gavel until the curtain rang down he added to the glamour and setting by quick, precise decisions that added luster to the records of the most historic trial ever before Congress while sitting as a court of impeachment.

In reporting the trial the *Washington Federalist*, a paper that had always assailed Burr, wrote, "He conducted the trial with the dignity and impartiality of an angel, but with the rigor of a devil."

Chase was acquitted on all accounts, although a majority voted "Guilty" on three of the eight articles. Jefferson's plan for destroying the Federalists' power, which John Adams had lodged in the packed judiciary, failed. Jefferson's assumed friendliness for Burr turned to rage. According to the president's view, as presiding officer of the Senate Burr should have influenced that body to vote for impeachment. If Burr had been more interested in politics than in the preservation of the republic, doubtless he would have complied with the wishes of Jefferson. His action preserved John Marshall and reaped the revenge of Thomas Jefferson.

"The attack upon Mr. Chase was a systematic attempt upon the independence and powers of the judicial department and at the same time an attempt to prostrate the authority of the national government before those of the individual states," wrote John Quincy Adams.

While the Senate met in executive session March 2, Burr informed the members that illness would prevent his remaining during the closing hours of the session, much as he would like to do so. Up to the moment that Burr began to talk the senators had lounged about in apparent weariness from their exhaustive labors; now all was changed. Every man sat erect. There was in the words of the vice president and in his manner something that commanded attention. Everyone recognized that he was listening to a great speech, the greatest they had ever heard. It moved them to tears—Burr's farewell address.

"Every gentleman was silent. Not a whisper was heard. The deepest concern was manifested," wrote Senator Samuel Mitchell. The vice president apologized for any offense that his conduct in the chair might have caused individual members. He reminded them that a prudent impartiality had been his purpose, and exhorted them to a constant observance of the rules of decorum that had hitherto dignified their deliberations. He bade them farewell with regret and with the assurance of unfailing respect and solicitude.

Burr, according to the *Washington Federalist*, said:

> *This House, I need not remind you, is a sanctuary . . . and if the constitution be destined ever to perish by the sacrilegious hands of the demagogue, or the usurper, which God avert, its expiring agonies will be witnessed on this floor.*

Senator Mitchell records:

> He did not speak longer than half an hour, but he did it with such tenderness, knowledge and concern that it wrought upon the sympathy of the senators in a very uncommon manner. There was a solemn and silent weeping for perhaps five minutes.
>
> For own my part, I never experienced anything of the kind so affecting as this parting scene of the Vice-President from the Senate in which he had sat six years as a senator and four years as presiding officer. My colleague, General Smith, stout and manly as he is, wept as profusely as I did. He laid his head upon his table and did not recover from his emotion for a quarter of an hour or more.
>
> And for myself, though it is more than three hours since Burr went away, I have scarcely recovered my habitual calmness. . . . He is a most uncommon man, and I regret more deeply than ever the sad series of events which removed him from public usefulness and confidence. . . .
>
> Burr is one of the best officers that ever presided over a deliberative assembly. Where he is going or how he is to get through with his difficulties I know not.

Burr's farewell address produced a profound effect upon his auditors. It was spontaneous and touched the hearts of friends and enemies alike. To Theodosia's inquiry concerning what he had said, he wrote, "It was the solemnity, the anxiety, the expectation and the interest which I saw plainly painted on the countenances of the auditors, that inspired whatever said."

The Senate adopted unanimously resolutions of thanks to Burr "for the impartiality, integrity, and ability with which he has presided in the Senate, and their unqualified approbation of his conduct in that capacity."

Up to this time there was scarcely a blemish on the character of Burr, and certainly no one but would have been delighted to associate with him and share his reflected glory. But politics, that demon that has ruined so many great men, it was not to choose for its object a shining mark!!! Burr carried the city by a small majority, but the poison of Hamilton's letters was far more effective upstate. Burr was defeated by more than seven thousand.

— James Parton

10
Secession, Disunion, or Expansion?

The fires of political antagonism that were kindled during the first days of Jefferson's term burned fiercely. No factor was more potent in serving Jefferson and pursuing Burr than De Witt Clinton's newspaper, the *American Citizen*, under the editorial direction of James Cheetham. In this campaign of malignant destruction the *Philadelphia Aurora* joined. Jefferson was convinced that if he were to be re-elected president by the Republicans, Burr must be destroyed.

New England and Virginia were ruled by petty oligarchies. In the former the clergy had always hated Jefferson, proclaiming that he was "untruthful, a backbiter, a sensualist and a demagogue." His espousal of the Payne cause had aroused not only the New England clergy but the most unworthy ally of his stormy days of 1798, James Thomas Callender, a Scot adventurer who had disgraced the press of Richmond. This vermin collected every vile story of Jefferson's past, even charging that he had a family of Negro children by a slave named Sally, that he had violated the sanctity of home of Major Walker, and that he had privately employed Callender to write "The Prospect Before Us."

Atrocious stories like these were reprinted in the New England press without any regard for the truth. Reference to them is made here only to reveal the depths of degradation to which the politicians of that day stooped. Another common practice was to resort to the expedient of declaring that the state would secede if the federal government followed any line of policy that was considered inimical to the interests of the clique, party, or organization in power in that particular state.

No one appeared to expect the Union to survive, especially the Federalists, now that the Republicans were at the helm of the ship of state. Concerning this situation Henry Adams wrote:

> *The struggle was full of interest; for if Jefferson had never failed to break down every opponent from King George the III to Aaron Burr, the New England oligarchy for near two hundred years were a fatal enemy to every ruler not of their own choice, from King Charles I, to Thomas Jefferson.*

But Jefferson was a master of political strategy. His lieutenants seized the story that was bursting about the ears of Aaron Burr, the toast "To the Union of All Honest Men," to which they added his lack of cooperation in the passage of the Judiciary Act. This aroused the Virginians, the Clintons, and the Federalists in a common cause, which under the direction of Jefferson contributed to the defeat of Burr in New York.

The churches of New England joined the bar in organizing and fostering an intolerant social system, whereas, Henry Adams says:

The minister put his three-cornered hat on his head, took his silver-topped cane in his hand and walked down the street, knocking at one door and another of his best parishioners to warn them that a spirit of license and French infidelity was abroad. . . . Any man once placed under this ban fared badly if he afterwards came before a bench of magistrates.

Today America marvels at the yawning gulfs that existed between New England and New York and, more especially, between New England and Virginia. Each was jealous of the other; each refused to be bound by the constrictions of the other or bound by Federal restrictions in the interest of the one that were felt to be to the detriment of the other.

William Ellery Channing wrote from Richmond:

I blush for my own people, when I compare the selfish prudence of the Yankee with the generous confidence of the Virginian. Here I find great vices but greater virtues than I left behind me. There is one single trait that attaches me to the people I live with more than all the virtues of New England—they love money less than we do; they are more disinterested; their patriotism is not tied to their purse strings.

To nearly all Federalists the party's overthrow was a calamity. To a few it meant disaster; to more it meant the destruction of the Union. To some it meant revolution and the end of the newly formed republic.

Of the six Federalist senators from the Eastern states, all but Alcot and Adams thought the dissolution of the Union inevitable.

In January 1804 the despair of Senators Plumer, Pickering, Tracy, and Roger Griswold led a group of prominent citizens to start a movement to dissolve the Union. Pickering wrote to George Cabot of Massachusetts recounting the dangerous situation and outlining the means that were to be employed to save New England from the overthrow with the rest of the Union. Cabot discussed the matter with Parsons, Fisher Ames, and Stephen Higgins, agreeing that there was ground for their complaint but frowning upon the proposed remedy, making it plain that it was the politicians and not the people who were taking Republican rule so seriously. He counseled:

> *If we were made to feel that a very great calamity was threatened, from the abuse of power by National Administration, we might do almost anything; but it would be idle to talk to the deaf, to warn the people of distant evil. . . . A separation is now impracticable, because we do not feel the necessity or utility of it.*

Like Hamilton, Cabot did not believe that the people were capable of governing themselves. He suggested that the only chance to bring about the dissolution of the Union was "a war with Great Britain, manifestly provoked by our rulers." Tapping Reeve wrote Tracy, "I have seen many of our friends; all believe we must separate, and that this is the most favorable moment." The opinion of Griswold was "that these men conspired to break up the Union implied no dishonesty, because the Republican majority by its illegal measures had already destroyed the Constitution."

Hamilton sympathized with the secession movement. His philosophy was that of Cabot, Reeve, and Ames: that the country should come to its senses and restore the government to the Federalists and sound principles. Then democracy and its wild dreams would die out.

All virtue, political desecration, and statecraft are lodged in the Federalist party; this was the teaching of Hamilton. He was quite sure that the Republican party was comprised of illiterates who were incapable of statecraft; their political theories he held in contempt. The Union might be preserved in the hands of its creators, but in the hands of the Republicans there was little or no hope for its future. Hamilton was intolerant of all Republican policies; they were to him as distasteful as French infidelity was to the New England clergy.

Besides, if there was to be a reformation of statecraft, Hamilton had not contemplated that the country was to be reformed in a manner that he would fail to approve; just at this time a little group of Burr's friends together with a larger number of Federalists had nominated him for governor of New York in defiance to Hamilton's entreaties.

The news of Burr's nomination reached Pickering and Tracy in Washington along with the answer to their disunion plans and probably served to sidetrack their political schemes. Thus they, too, cast their lot with those who were arbitrarily to renounce Hamilton's leadership.

About this time Rufus King returned from London to resume his place as a recognized leader among the Federalists. As candidate for the vice presidency he had revealed a more conciliatory spirit, had given the masses credit for being entitled to a voice. To him on March 4, 1804, Pickering wrote:

> *I am disgusted with the men who now rule, and with their measures. At some manifestations of their malignancy I am shocked. The cowardly wretch at their head, while like a Parisian revolutionary monster prattling about humanity, would feel an infernal pleasure in the utter destruction of his opponents.*

While Pickering was praying for the overthrow of the Union, he saw some faint hope of saving New England by electing Aaron Burr governor of New York. Concerning the approaching election of 1804, he wrote:

> *The Federalists in general anxiously desire the election of Mr. Burr to the chair in New York, for they despair of a present ascendancy of the Federalist party.*

Mr. Burr alone, we think, can break your democratic phalanx, and we anticipate much good from this success. Were New York detached, as under his administration it would be, from the Virginia influence, the whole Union would be benefited. Jefferson would then be forced to observe some caution and forbearance in his measures. And if a separation should be deemed proper, the five New England states, New York and New Jersey would be united.

Rufus King's reply was characteristic of the man: that Pickering's views ought to fix the attention of the real friends of liberty in this quarter of the Union, especially since things were coming to a crisis. But the delay tormented Hamilton, Cabot, Ames, Pickering, Griswold, and a host of other Federalists, because they were enduring the gloom of the prospective decadence of the republic with no likelihood of return to its creators.

After a hundred and fifty years, when the permanency of the Union is taken for granted, it appears pertinent that attention be called to the equally persistent prevailing opinion at its inception: that the United States was of only a temporary nature and that its overthrow was but a matter of time. Every national election during the entire history of this country, however, has produced politicians, who, being out of power, conceived it a patriotic duty to convince the voter that the only chance for perpetuity of this Union was to kick the rascals out and return to power the outs.

Politics, like religion, appears impervious to change by argument or time. The student who has concluded that Burr's dream of expansion was in any way unpatriotic may profit by reading the views of some of the leading Federalists who were groaning and grumbling because the Republicans enjoyed the comforts and emoluments of office.

The records reveal that Jefferson and Hamilton were familiar with the Miranda expedition; the latter even contemplated having a conspicuous part in that ill-starred project for achieving the independence of South America. If there were glory and romantic expansion for Texas, however, so far as these two were concerned it must never be achieved by Aaron Burr. General Eaton wrote Jefferson to suggest that he appoint Burr to some foreign embassy "to get rid of a dangerous man."

The stories of war were not just Western dreams. The Spanish army had crossed the Sabine River, which marks the border between Louisiana and Texas, and was camped at Bayou Pierre. General Wilkinson declined to drive them back because to attack the Spaniards was to start a war in which the people of Tennessee and Kentucky were likely to draft Colonel Burr to lead their armies in driving the despised Dons across the Spanish border. Jonathan Dayton wrote to General Wilkinson:

> *It is now well ascertained that you are to be displaced in the next session. Jefferson will effect to yield reluctantly to the public sentiment, but yield he will; prepare yourself therefore for it; you know the rest. You are not a man to despair, or even to despond, especially when such prospects offer in another quarter. Are you ready? Are your numerous associates ready? Wealth and Glory Louisiana and Mexico. I shall have time to receive a letter from you before I set out for Ohio. . . .*

Wilkinson's acts had made it plain to a number of his friends, including Aaron Burr, that he thought that the Spanish army, now on Louisiana soil, could be pushed back and the pursuit continued to the Rio Grande where the American Flag would be raised over that territory. But the wily Wilkinson changed his plans. Apparently this was because in the state of mind of the people of the Mississippi Valley Burr would have too conspicuous a part in a movement so close to the hearts of the West, and as always, in common with Jefferson and Hamilton, he would have none of that, regardless of the cost of time and the natural expansion of the United States.

Except at the hands of Number Thirteen Wilkinson, there was
never produced against Colonel Burr any evidence that he had ever
mentioned the subject even, during his Mississippi journey.
— Samuel H. Wandell and Meade Minnigerode
Aaron Burr, Volume One

11
The Alleged Conspiracy

Because the British Minister, Anthony Merry, disliked Jefferson, he turned to Vice President Burr, as did three Creole gentlemen from New Orleans. They were Messieurs Sauve, Derbigney, and d'Estrehan, who had come to Washington in an endeavor to secure for their people the rights of citizenship which they had confidently expected when Louisiana became part of the Union. They complained that they were being treated as conquered subjects. James Wilkinson was in Washington to receive his commission as governor of Upper Louisiana. He said disappointment with the Washington government could lead to a new government in Louisiana.

About this time President Jefferson wrote to Mr. Bowdoin, his minister at Madrid, "We want nothing of [Spain's]. . . . she has met our advances with jealousy, secret malice and ill faith. Our patience is on its last trial."

Either Mr. Jefferson was insincere concerning American hopes for expansion, or he believed we'd acquired title to the Florida and Texas lands when we purchased Louisiana. Andrew Jackson was sure Florida was ours and accordingly took possession at a later date. Burr felt the same way. Others who were demanding acquisition were: John Randolph of Virginia, John Adair and John Brown of Kentucky, John Smith of Ohio, Matthew Lyon of Vermont, Robert R. Livingston, and James Wilkinson. The West demanded Florida and Texas as our natural and acquired right.

All commercial transactions with the outside world had been paralyzed when Spain had closed the port of New Orleans. Tennessee and Kentucky were enraged. With the purchase of the Louisiana Territory, Spain diverted all trade with Texas and Mexico from New Orleans, and the stagnation of business that followed was charged to the administration at Washington. To add to the ill will toward Washington, for years Spain had spent fifty thousand dollars annually to finance the Indians in making wars against Kentucky and Tennessee. These new states became veritable massacring grounds. For a number of years Aaron Burr had been the one person in Washington who had shown a sympathetic interest in these vexing problems. Burr's visit to this territory was welcomed with enthusiasm.

On March 29, 1805, Aaron Burr wrote his daughter from Philadelphia "In ten or twelve days I shall be on my westward.... the objects of this journey, not mere curiosity, or '*pour passer le temps*,' may lead me to New Orleans, and perhaps farther." Burr rode to Pittsburgh on horseback, where he purchased a floating house, sixty feet by fourteen with glass windows, containing a dining room, a kitchen with a fireplace, and two bedrooms, roofed from stem to stern with a rooftop walkway the length of it. For this houseboat Burr paid one hundred and thirty-three dollars.

After waiting one day for James Wilkinson to join him in Pittsburgh, Burr started down the Ohio and on the second day overtook Matthew Lyon, formerly a congressman from Vermont, now living in Kentucky. After fastening their boats together they floated conjointly for several days. Burr stopped at Blennerhassett Island only to find its eccentric owner was in the East. Mrs. Blennerhassett induced her distinguished visitor to remain for dinner, after which he pushed off for Cincinnati. Here Burr conferred with Jonathan Dayton, Senator John Smith, and a number of old army friends.

At Louisville the houseboat was exchanged for a horse, which Colonel Burr rode to Frankfort, Kentucky, where he was the guest of Senator John Brown. At Lexington he met Senator John Adair, to whom Wilkinson had written, "I was to have introduced my friend Burr to you, but this I failed by accident. He understands your merits and reckons on you. Prepare to visit me, and I will tell you all. We must have a peep at the unknown world beyond."

Andrew Jackson entertained Colonel Burr at Nashville, Tennessee, and introduced him to the populace, who welcomed him with music by a band, dancing, and feasting. Here Burr was urged to head a movement against the hated Dons, which honor he put aside, saying the hour was not yet. To Theo he wrote, "I have been received with much hospitality and kindness, and could stay a month with pleasure; but General Andrew Jackson having provided us with a boat, we shall set off p.m. Sunday, the 2nd day of June."

General Jackson was enthusiastic about Burr's colonization plans in Louisiana. He gave him a houseboat, which he christened the Ark, and furnished ten state militiamen and a lieutenant to man it. With Jacksonian enthusiasm he bade them Godspeed as they departed down the Cumberland, Ohio, and Mississippi rivers. Four days were spent with General Wilkinson at Fort Massac. A prosperous community of planters greeted Colonel Burr at Natchez on June 17 with warm Southern hospitality.

The welcome on June 25 in New Orleans was by a delegation consisting chiefly of Spanish, French, and Creoles. These were the people who had sent a committee to Washington to ask relief from restrictions that had brought commercial stagnation and political disappointment to the Crescent City. Official Washington had given them a cold shoulder; only the vice president had given an attentive ear.

Judge John Bartow Prevost and Edward Livingston in turn entertained Colonel Burr in his home. Major John Watkins painted a dark picture of the results produced on New Orleans when Spanish authorities had ordered all commercial relations with Texas and Mexico to cease, as punishment for acceptance of American authority when Louisiana Territory became a part of the Union. No one liked the reign of W. C. C. Claiborne as governor.

Judge James Workman insisted that war with Spain was imminent. The Mexican Association had been organized and was awaiting hostilities when a new government with New Orleans as its capital would be organized. Daniel Clark, merchant prince of the city and entire territory, gave Burr four hundred dollars to further the cause, which his organization had championed. He also furnished horses, on which Burr and his party returned north.

Natchez detained Colonel Burr nearly a week on his return visit, after which he traversed the line between West Florida and the United States, crossing the Yazoo "through a vile country destitute of springs and running water." Then came the Tennessee, "a clear, beautiful, magnificent river," which he crossed "forty miles below Muscle Shoals." Burr returned to Nashville and to General Jackson on the 6th of August.

Nashville tendered Colonel Burr a second dinner, to which he came on the arm of General Jackson, the state's most distinguished citizen. The welcome was even more enthusiastic than the first. Burr wrote to Theodosia that he was "lounging at the house of General Jackson, once a lawyer, later a judge, now a planter, a man of intelligence and one of those prompt, frank, ardent souls whom I love to meet."

On August 31 Burr was the guest of John Brown at Frankfort. Then he doubled back to St. Louis, where he compared notes with General Wilkinson, who was to leave Burr with the impression that he had cooled off concerning their long-contemplated conquest of Texas, or all of the Southwest—dreams that were shared by some of the foremost men from Massachusetts to Tennessee.

Burr returned to Washington, where he called on the president, to whom he divulged his plans for the colonization of the Ouachita. Jefferson's attitude toward Burr was in great contrast to that which he'd displayed when seeking Burr's help in an endeavor to convict Justice Samuel Chase. Just as Burr had sensed the futility of his interview with Wilkinson, he realized that the president was closing the door of state against him, and that an organized political scheme was being hatched to thwart his Western colonization enterprise.

So Colonel Burr transferred his efforts to Harman Blennerhassett, to whom he wrote regrets that he had missed him on his former visit and suggested that he was wasting his talents in the wilderness. To Wilkinson he wrote the cipher letter that the wily general changed and presented to the grand jury in the trial at Richmond. In manufacturing this evidence Jefferson and Wilkinson are most ingloriously linked together. Wilkinson's changes amounted to forgery, but even so, was this worse than Jefferson's act in using Wilkinson as a witness in his endeavor to convict Burr after Wilkinson was a proven traitor—a fact with which the president was conversant?

Burr and Wilkinson had become seasoned soldiers in action in Canada against larger British forces, the former at Quebec and the latter at Montreal, and had endured forced marches through thick forest and traversing streams and lakes. While Burr had served as a brigadier major to General Matthew Arnold at Quebec, Wilkinson had become aide-de-camp to Arnold after the withdrawal from Montreal. Later, while Burr gained General Washington's respect, he never gained his confidence, whereas Wilkinson curried Washington's favor and was appointed quartermaster general for the Revolutionary Army—until incurring Washington's disfavor because of his incompetence. As vice president Burr had recommended Wilkinson as general of the western division of the army, an appointment the president made just prior to his attempt to convict Justice Samuel Chase. Along with evidence of military shortcomings, Wilkinson had also revealed that he was without integrity. His conduct had several times aroused ugly rumors. Other historians cite sources showing Wilkinson as sorely lacking military ability in more than one campaign.

In recommending him as major general, Hamilton had observed, since he was suspected of conspiracies, "He is apt to become disgusted if neglected; and through disgust may be rendered really what he is now only suspected to be."

As a result of Burr's invitation, Blennerhassett joined in the preparations for the development of the Ouachita Colony. Burr had paid five thousand dollars on the purchase price of forty thousand for four hundred thousand acres of land in northern Louisiana Territory. The land was a portion of the Bastrop Land Grant, which Baron de Bastrop had received from the Spanish Crown in 1797. Oddly enough, Bastrop afterward migrated to Texas, where he became an important factor in its colonization and development. Burr had purchased this land as a commercial enterprise and with the intention of continuing the development Baron de Bastrop had begun, which consisted largely of the erection of a sugar mill and the attendant agricultural improvements. The location of his colony was a part of Burr's scheme, as it was proven at his trial, to have with him a goodly number of Americans near Texas "if and when there was a war with Spain."

Prior to his purchase of the Bastrop land, and sometime in 1804, President Jefferson ordered a survey of the Ouachita River, the record of which confirms the impression that he, too, was acquainted with its prospective value.

Burr's colonization plans aroused enthusiasm among his friends but provoked the condemnation of his enemies. Joseph H. Daveiss, Federal District Attorney of Kentucky, summoned Burr before the court on a charge of having violated the laws of the Union. The date is memorable because James Wilkinson usurped the powers of the president and the Senate on this day by serving Spain when he conceived and approved the Neutral Ground

Treaty. Both occurred November 5, 1806. Judge Harry Innes, before whom Daveiss filed his charges, dismissed them for want of evidence.

A week later Daveiss filed another charge alleging that Burr was setting afoot an unauthorized expedition against Mexico. When these charges were presented to the grand jury, Henry Clay represented Colonel Burr, who declared under oath:

> *I have no design. . . . to promote a dissolution of the Union or a separation of any one or more states from the residue. . . . I do not own a musket or bayonet, nor a single piece of military stores. My views have been explained to the principal officers of the government, and, I believe are well understood by the administration and seen by them with complacency.*

The grand jury reported "Not a true bill."

The chief witness before the grand jury was John Wood, who had written columns in the *Western World* of Frankfort, Kentucky, where he had alleged that Burr's Western mission was for a traitorous purpose. On the witness stand Wood admitted that he possessed no "information that was to amount to evidence." Wood did disclose that he was the employed tool of the federal district attorney, and that it was his mission to foul the good name of Aaron Burr. Strangely, the court took no notice of this dastardly political outrage against justice, even when there appeared in an ensuing issue of the *World*, written by the same pen, the following:

> *On this extraordinary occasion, we are well aware that the field of conjecture will be traveled in every direction by the curious reader and inquisitive politician. With ourselves, we confess it has excited neither astonishment or surprise, being, as we before mentioned, well informed of the subject eighteen months before.*

Wood's charges, admission, and subsequent statement are typical of the evidence which was offered against Burr throughout Jefferson's attempt to hang him. Daveiss's middle name was Hamilton. He demonstrated that he was obsessed by desires and ambitions similar to those of his namesake. Although Judge Innes refused his plea in the first instance, on November 25, the court allowed him to read the following indictment:

> *United States of America, Kentucky District to wit: The grand jury of the United States in and for the body of said district, do on their oaths present, that a certain Aaron Burr, late of the city of New York and vice president of the United States, did with force and arms at the county of Fayette in said district, on the 25th day of November last, willingly and unlawfully, and from evil premeditation, that and there set on foot and prepare a military expedition against the dominions of the King of Spain in North America contrary to the laws of the United States in such cases provided, and against the peace and dignity thereof.*

Another indictment was filed in Jefferson County alleging that a similar misdemeanor had been committed. No mention of any treasonable act was made. About the same time, in spreading the charges of treason in New Orleans, Wilkinson took notice of a charge by the *Western World* that accused him of being associated with Burr. At this he wrote to Jefferson, "I have at times been fearful your confidence might be shaken by the boldness of the vile Calumnies leveled at me." To fortify his standing with the president, Wilkinson sent for this inspection "numerous public and private testimonials of Honor and applause," to which he added that he was suing this newspaper for defamation, and that the truth would come out.

In Frankfort, Kentucky, crowds filled the streets and jammed the courtroom. "Who are the witnesses?" was on every tongue.

Scarcely anyone believed that Daveiss had any evidence against Burr. For the third time this proved true. For three months, Joseph Street and Wood, the proprietors of the *World*, had made a strenuous endeavor to lead the public to believe that they possessed incriminating evidence. In this publicity campaign they had printed in the *Lexington Gazette*:

> *The editors of this paper are called upon by William Littell and certain of the amiable youth of Frankfort, to produce the proofs of what they allege about the conspirators. Fellow citizens we will do no such thing. . . . If you sue us for slander, we will plead justification. We will go into no newspaper war about it with William Littell, William Hunter, the two constellations of prostitution, or any of your hirelings, and our Federalist friends have pointedly advised us by no means to suffer our evidence to be made known before it is called for in the court.*

Later it developed that the *Western World* was owned by Joseph Hamilton Daveiss and his brother-in-law, Humphrey Marshall.

A small proportion of the public was credulous enough to believe that the federal district attorney possessed the evidence Street and Wood had locked up so securely that they even defied the people of Lexington to attempt to force its divulgence. This proved the trick of a political buffoon, for Street declared under oath that he could give no information relative to the charges since his knowledge was limited to hearsay. He stated that he knew of no one who could support the charges.

After John Wood had admitted under oath that he had written the paragraphs, he confessed that he had lied about the whole matter, and in "A full Statement," said he had changed his mind about Colonel Burr and that he was persuaded that Burr had no intentions antagonistic to the laws and the best interests of the

United States. All other witnesses placed themselves in the hearsay class. The grand jury was so enraged that after returning the indictment "Not the true bill," issued the following:

> *The grand jury is happy to inform the court that no violent disturbance of the public tranquility, or breach of the laws has come to their knowledge. We have no hesitancy in declaring, that having carefully examined and scrutinized all testimony which has come before us, as well as charges against Burr, and those contained in the indictment against John Adair, that there has been no testimony before us which does in the smallest degree criminate the conduct of either of these persons; nor can we, from all the inquiries and investigation of the subject, discover that anything improper or injurious to the interests of the government of the United States, or contrary to the laws thereof, is designed or contemplated by either of them.*

Again the people applauded Burr. They arranged for a grand ball in his honor, where their felicitations took the form of toasts to his health and happiness and enthusiastic approval for the enterprise in which he was engaged.

Concerning this trial, Henry Adams wrote:

> *A second time the scene of outraged virtue was enacted. Once more the witnesses vanished, Senator Smith saddled his horse and fled; Adair would not appear and the judge lent his weight to the criminal. Burr was discharged with enthusiastic applause, without a stain on his character.*

Henry Clay had represented Burr, "for whose honor and innocence he could pledge his own," but after the president of the United States had falsely charged Burr with attempting to divide the Union, like nearly every one else, Clay assumed that he possessed evidence for such a proclamation, and wrote to his father-in-law, Colonel Thomas Hart:

> *It seems that we have been much mistaken about Burr. When I left Kentucky, I believed him both innocent and a persecuted man. In the course of my journey to his place, still entertaining that opinion, I expressed myself without reserve, and it seems owing to the freedom of my sentiments at Chillicothe I have exposed myself to the strictures of some anonymous writer at that place. They give me no uneasiness, as I am sensible that all my friends and acquaintances know me incapable of entering into the views of Burr. It appears from the president's message to Congress, in answer to the resolutions to the House of Representatives, calling for information, that Burr had formed no less daring projects than to reduce New Orleans, subjugate Mexico, and divide the Union.*

In this conspiracy against Aaron Burr, Thomas Jefferson never produced any evidence to support his charges, which were political allegations made by one politician against another. When examined in light of the facts, Jefferson's charges did not emanate from patriotic desire but from political ambition. In his eagerness for evidence to verify his charges, the president swallowed the lies of Eaton and Wilkinson without hesitation or investigation. When he realized that he had no evidence with which to prove his charges and faced John Marshall with two discredited witnesses, he admitted, "We do not know of a certainty yet what shall be proved, but, we can satisfy the world, if not the judges."

Jefferson's mortification before the chief justice was no less embarrassing than was that of Joseph Hamilton Daveiss before Justice Innes and the grand jury. Only Wilkinson before the grand jury at Richmond surpassed both in depths of degradation, where John Randolph recorded, "Perhaps you never saw a human being in so degraded a situation as the person of Wilkinson before the Grand Jury."

The practice of indulging in false charges against a political adversary seriously jeopardizes freedom of speech in America. Jefferson's charges against Burr have long been accepted by the world as the truth, yet he acknowledged almost in the same breath that they would not be accepted "by the judges." Is there another case where false propaganda has so completely misled the people for a century?

The evidence offered to the court and juries in Kentucky was not less defective than the statement concerning Burr's preparation for his colonization venture, as told by the president's proclamation:

> *Whereas information has been received that sundry persons, citizens of the United Stated, or residents within the same are conspiring and confederating together to begin and set on foot and prepare the means for a military expedition against the dominions of Spain; that for this purpose they are fitting out and arming vessels in western waters of the United States, collecting provisions, arms and military stores and means; and are deceiving and seducing well meaning citizens, under various pretenses, are organizing and officering, and arming themselves contrary to the laws in such cases provided: I have therefore thought fit to issue this my Proclamation, warning and enjoining all faithful citizens. . . .*

Five days later in his annual message the president reiterated his charges, but since no specific allegations were made, they consisted of political propaganda he leveled at Aaron Burr. Hamilton had paid the price of his calumny, but it has taken more than a century for the lies of Jefferson to confront him—to damn him! Eventually truth prevails! Today Jefferson stands discredited for his attempt to hang Burr!

The people of Kentucky, Tennessee, and the West generally were in sympathy with Burr's plans for colonization of the Ouachita. Almost to a man they were agreed that there was to be war with Spain, and that Texas was to the prize of a show of arms. Burr's eventual plans for acquiring and settling Texas "if and when there was war with Spain" appealed to their imagination. Hundreds of their neighbors were already in that territory.

No one understood the desires of the West better than General Wilkinson; no one saw the picture clearer or understood the public mind better than the Spanish pensioner. During the months that the Spanish were camped on American soil at Bayou Pierre, any loyal soldier of America would have driven them back and pushed on to until our flag floated over Texas, but not Wilkinson—that would remove him from the payroll of Spain.

On August 20, 1787, James Wilkinson took a secret oath of allegiance to Spain. The document is recorded at Madrid as "Number Thirteen." Two years later he acknowledged receipt of seven thousand dollars for his treasonable services. Other payments that have come to light are as follows. Nine thousand six hundred and forty dollars came to his order in 1796 at the hands of Don Thomas Portel. The next acknowledgment was for "a mule load of gold." In 1804, after Wilkinson had complained that he had not received his pension for ten years, he acknowledges receipt of twelve thousand dollars and soon afterward of eight thousand more. These payments were made upon Wilkinson's representation that he would advise Jefferson against Livingston's interpretation that West Florida was included in the Louisiana Purchase. Later this "finished scoundrel," as John Randolph called him, demanded more than a hundred thousand dollars for services rendered in protecting Spain against an alleged conquest by Aaron Burr.

While Burr was consulting with the leading citizens of the Mississippi Valley in the summer of 1805, Jefferson wrote his minister, James Madison:

> *The first wish of every Englishman's heart is to
> see us once more fighting by their sides against France;
> nor could the King or his ministers do an act so pop-
> ular as to enter into an alliance with us. . . . I think it
> possible . . . they would give us a general guarantee of
> Louisiana and the Floridas.*

This was well understood by Burr, Wilkinson, and Jackson,
as it was by nearly every other forward-looking statesman of the
Mississippi Valley, but the president allowed the rich prize to escape. It was many years later that even he was to awaken to his
short-sightedness—a policy that doubtless was the result of his
enmity toward Aaron Burr and that prevented the United States
from annexing Texas for many years. When Jefferson was seven-
ty-seven years of age, he wrote to James Monroe, then president:

> *I confess to you, I am not sorry for the non ratifi-
> cation of the Spanish treaty. . . . The province of Texas
> will be the richest state in the Union. Florida, moreover,
> is ours. Every nation in Europe concedes it by right. We
> need not care for its occupation in time of peace, and in
> war, the first cannon makes it ours without offense to
> anyone. The treaty has the valuable effect of strength-
> ening our title to Texas. With Mexico independent of
> Spain, Texas would join the United States.*

Edward Everett Hale wrote:

> *I have read the manuscript correspondence be-
> tween Hamilton and Wilkinson with reference to the
> proposed attack on New Orleans. Wilkinson made a
> visit to Hamilton to adjust the details of the campaign.
> This mine was ready to be sprung on poor Spain, when
> the republic of the United States should make war on
> the French.*

"Except at the hands of Number Thirteen Wilkinson," say Samuel Henry Wandell and Meade Minnigerode, "there never was produced against Colonel Burr any evidence that he had ever mentioned the subject, even during his Mississippi journey."

Noland's alleged court martial was supposed to have occurred at Fort Massac, where Burr discussed his plans for acquiring Texas "if and when there was war with Spain." From Fort Massac Wilkinson wrote a number of letters to prominent men in New Orleans introducing Burr. Among these, one to the boundary land commissioner read:

> *Recommending my eminent friend, Colonel Burr, a man of a million qualities. Serve this gentleman; he is my friend. . . . Your great family interests will promote the interests of Colonel Burr and will be preserved by following his advice. Do as I advise and you will soon send to the devil that boastful idiot, W.C.C. Claiborne.*

For a century the average American has accepted Jefferson's charge that Burr was a traitor to his native land without so much as making endeavor to learn the truth. It would be interesting to know what the reaction of Edward Everett Hale would have been if the grand old man could learn by whom he was duped into creating his fictitious story of Nolan when he recorded:

> *Philip Nolan was as fine a young officer as there was in the "Legion of the West," as the Western Division of our army was then called. When Aaron Burr made his first dashing expedition down to New Orleans in 1805, to Fort Massac, or somewhere above on the river, he met, as the Devil would have it, this gay, dashing, bright young fellow at some dinner party, I think. Burr marked him, talked to him, walked with him, took him a day or two's voyage in his flatboat and, in short, fascinated him. For the next year bar-*

rack-life was very tame to poor Nolan. He occasion-
ally availed himself the permission the great man had
given him to write to him. Long, high-worded, stilted
letters the poor boy wrote and rewrote and copied. . . .
before long . . . His Excellency, Honorable Aaron Burr,
appeared again. . . . He asked Nolan to take him out
in his skiff to show him a canebrake or a cottonwood
tree, as he said—really to seduce him—and by the time
the sail was over Nolan was enlisted body and soul.

Then, as we follow Hale's fictitious story, as fascinatingly unfolded as was Eaton's, it appears that the author becomes suspicious
that there was an organized attempt to crucify Burr, for he records:

Only when the grand catastrophe came, and Jef-
ferson and the House of Virginia of that day under-
took to break on the wheel all the possible Clarences
of the House of York by the great treason trial of Rich-
mond, some of the lesser fry of that distant Missis-
sippi Valley introduced the novelty at Fort Adams of
court-martials on the officers. . . . and to fill out the
list, little Nolan, against whom, Heaven knows, there
was evidence enough: that he had been sick of the ser-
vice, had been willing to be false to it, and would have
obeyed any order to march any-whither with anyone
who would follow him had the order been signed, "By
command of his Exc. A. Burr" . . . . when the president
of the court asked whether he wished to say anything
to show that he had always been faithful to the United
States; he cried out, in a fit of frenzy,—
"Damn the United States! I wish I may never
hear of the United States again!"

Thereafter follows a tale that has touched the hearts of millions of our most patriotic Americans concerning this poor delud-

ed soul, whose sentence was "that you never hear the name of the United States again" and who was doomed to wander as a prisoner on unknown seas for more than half a century—lost to home, friends, and country, and all because, according to his creator, he had been "seduced" by Aaron Burr.

In the great hereafter, when the Master of Human Destiny shall place responsibility for the sins of Philip Nolan, who shall be first—Thomas Jefferson or Edward Everett Hale?

While Edward Everett Hale immortalized Philip Nolan in his *A Man Without a Country*, the real Nolan was quite a different character. In her 1932 University of Texas master's thesis, Theresa Maurine Wilson presents Nolan as a horse-trader in the Texas territory. While serving General Wilkinson as a scout, July 21, 1797, Nolan reported:

> *I shall take care to give [Carondelet] no information, unless such may be calculated to mislead him. Whatever discoveries I can make shall be carefully preserved for General Wilkinson, for the benefit of our government! . . . look forward to the conquest of Mexico by the United States; and I expect my patron and friend, the General, will in such event give me a conspicuous command.*

On June 24, 1798, Thomas Jefferson addressed a letter to Philip Nolan in New Orleans. In Nolan's absence the letter was replied to by Daniel Clark, who cautioned Jefferson that the utmost secrecy must be observed in any letters written to Nolan since "the slightest Hint" might be attended by "fatal consequences to a man [Nolan] who has it in his power to render important services to the U.S.; and whom nature seems to have formed for Enterprises of which the rest of Mankind are incapable."

Vice President Jefferson appears to have invited Nolan to come to Washington to give him information about the Texas Territory for which, November 12, 1799, Wilkinson gave Nolan a letter of introduction addressed to Jefferson in which Nolan is represented as "a Mexican traveler who could be of vast service to the United States."

After Nolan and his twenty-seven associates were captured in Texas in 1800, one of their number, Mordicai Rechards, testified that he believed Noland had other ends than capturing wild horses—"that he had maps of all the rivers, explored everything more attentively and had assured his men that there were mines in the country, and if the Spaniards killed one of his men he would take a commission as an English general [which he could have] and take possession of this country."

Noland's alleged court martial was supposed to have occurred at Fort Massac, where Burr discussed his plans for acquiring Texas "if and when there was war with Spain." (He was killed by the Spanish in the Province of Texas during summer of 1800 per General Wilkinson.)

Andrew Jackson and John Coffee were among the contractors who built the Burr houseboats. While inspecting this work in September, Burr for a third time visited the Jackson home. Of this visit the general wrote a friend, "Colonel Burr is with me. Would it not be well for us to do something as a mark of attention to the Colonel? He has always been and still is a true and trusty friend of Tennessee."

Burr's plans for colonization were bearing fruit all along the Ohio. Theodosia and her husband, Joseph Alston, were most enthusiastic. They had advanced large sums of money and guaranteed Blennerhassett's advances, who had recklessly assigned all his assets to Burr's credit. On December 9 the island was a hive of activity, packing the household goods and loading two hundred barrels of provisions onto boats. Bonfires and lighted torches added eeriness to the scene.

Word had come that the government was to stop the Burr expedition. It was a feverish situation when a disorganized mob of volunteers appeared, apparently inflamed more by the prospect of plunder than the supposed militia patriotism under the guise of which they alleged that they had come to apprehend all who should set out from Blennerhassett. They were instructed to arrest

Blennerhassett and Burr and see that they did not escape.

Edward Tupper, who became a brigadier general in the War of 1812, watched the boats being loaded at the island. He testified under oath that he saw "Blennerhassett kiss his wife good-bye; he saw two pairs of pistols; that no guns were leveled at him, and that he could not detect any warlike appearances." This evidence was lost by the prosecution, to be uncovered in an Ohio pigeonhole many years after Jefferson failed to hang Burr.

Colonel Phelps was sent by the governor of Ohio to intercept Blennerhassett and the supplies. Finding they had escaped, his men filled up on wine from the cellars and became so inebriated that they pulled the pictures from the wall and the curtains from the windows, and shot the ceiling full of holes. They wrecked the most beautiful home in the Ohio valley. Here was an act of war committed by drunken braggarts summoned to defend their country against an alleged act of rebellion.

Pittsburgh furnished a boatload of a dozen of the Bastrop colonists. They were led by Morgan Neville, son of the chief justice of Pennsylvania. The young men had scarcely set sail when they were arrested near the mouth of the Little Kanawah. When they put in at Marietta, Ohio, they were warned to push off lest they be arrested.

After bidding her husband good-bye when he departed from their home, Mrs. Blennerhassett went to Marietta, where she witnessed the threatening attitude toward young Neville and his party. It was at his request that Mrs. Blennerhassett joined his party and traveled with them to Bayou Pierre. This little houseboat contained more than one fifth of the "twenty thousand freebooters" who, as Wilkinson whispered to Colonel Cushing, were "plotting to overthrow the government and destroy New Orleans."

In his letter to the president Wilkinson wrote:

> *A numerous and powerful association, extending from New York through the western states, to the territory bordering the Mississippi, has been formed,*

with the design to levy and rendezvous eight or ten thousand men in New Orleans, at a very near period; and from thence, with the cooperation of a naval armament, to carry the expedition to Vera Cruz.

Agents from Mexico, who were in Philadelphia at the beginning of August, are engaged in the enterprise. These persons have been given assurances, that the landing of the proposed expedition will be seconded by so general an insurrection, as to insure subversion to the present government, and silence all operations in three or four weeks. . . .

It is not known under what authority this enterprise has been projected, from whence the means of its support are derived, or what may be the intention of its leaders, in relation to the territory of New Orleans. But it is believed that the maritime co-operation will depend upon a British squadron from the West Indies, under the ostensible command of American masters.

This information has reached the reporter through several channels so direct and confidential that he cannot doubt the facts set forth; and, therefore, he considers it his duty to make this representation by courier extraordinary, to whom he has furnished five hundred dollars.

The next day, October 21, a second courier was dispatched to the president, with direful forebodings, only a part of which follows:

Yet the magnitude of the enterprise, and the desperation of the plan, and the stupendous consequences with which it seems pregnant, stagger my belief and excite doubts of the reality, against the conviction of my senses; and it is for this reason I shall forebear to commit names, because it is my desire to avert a great public calamity.

This second letter went on at great length in the same vein. It appears as if the general was a bit disturbed lest the president realize that he was attempting to deceive him, and that his assumed uneasiness and great desperation were just a sham under which he was trying to hide his hypocrisy. Then, to put fear into another nearby source, he dispatched a messenger October 22 to Colonel Freeman, commander in New Orleans, ordering the completion of all fortifications and hinting mysteriously at causes "Too imperious to be resisted, and too highly confidential to be whispered, or even suspected."

Then was begun the long-delayed march to the banks of the Sabine. Of course the enemy who had been there a month before to dispute with him the boundary line between the United States and Mexico had wearied of waiting and retired, but that was a small import to the doughty general. It did not keep Wilkinson from going with flags flying, drums beating, and scouts reconnoitering in military manner, all of which was calculated to appease any rebellion against plans of this military-political schemer.

General Wilkinson discovered upon reaching the Sabine that the enemy had retired. Immediately he dispatched a courier to Cordero, the Spanish commander, suggesting that the two retire to Nacogdoches and Natchitoches respectively, that they might agree that the Spanish would not again cross the Sabine.

The Neutral Ground Treaty was the result of that conference. It was signed November 5, 1806. Since both parties to its conception were in the service of Spain, naturally it was to her advantage. While the president approved it, the terms were screened from the public until after the trial at Richmond.

Before departing from the scene of this shameful transfer of American rights, Wilkinson wrote to Colonel Cushing in New Orleans:

> *The plot thickens, yet all those concerned, sleep profoundly. My God! What a situation our country has reached! Let us save it if we can. I think the offi-*

cers who have families at Fort Adams should be advised to leave them there, for if I am not mistaken, we shall have an insurrection of whites as well as blacks.

This was written solely to frighten New Orleans into submitting all civil government to military control so that Wilkinson might not be interfered with in his attempt to catch Burr.

Wilkinson was a master showman. He dramatized every situation. The president's co-operation was his chief concern; Jefferson, however, was a willing conspirator in the plan to hang Aaron Burr. Together they had deceived nearly everyone in the Union; the tranquility of the masses was probably never so universally disturbed. Cincinnati was so nervous that when a vessel loaded with merchandise from Louisville arrived and a practical joker exploded a bomb on the waterfront, the militia was called out.

Daily sessions of the cabinet were held. Commodore Prebel and Decanter were sent to New Orleans. Eight warships were ordered to the troubled waters. Then, as if awakening to the situation, the cabinet reported:

Not a word on any of the movements of Colonel Burr, but total silence of officers of the Government and members of Congress and the newspapers proves that he has committed no overt act.

The president wrote:

Burr is unquestionably very actively engaged in Western preparations to sever that part of the Union. We learn that he is actively building 10 or 12 boats able to take a large gun and fit the navigation of those waters. We give him all the attention our situation admits; as yet, we have no legal proof of any overt act which the law can lay hold of.

We are all in a flurry here hourly expecting Colonel Burr
and all of Kentucky and half of Tennessee at his back to punish
General Wilkinson, set the Negroes free, rob the banks and take
Mexico. Come and help me laugh at the fun.

– Silas Dinsmoor, U.S. Indian agent
Private Letters

12
A Satirical Situation

After spreading an alarm of revolution in New Orleans, in-
stilling hatred and dissention from Louisiana to Massachusetts,
and planting in the minds of the people a plan for the dissolution
of the Union, Wilkinson turned his attention to Governor Claiborne, to whom, after marking it "Sacredly Confidential," he sent
the following letter:

> *You are surrounded by dangers of which you*
> *dream not and the destruction of the American Union*
> *is seriously menaced. The storm will probably burst on*
> *New Orleans . . . where I shall meet it and triumph or*
> *perish. There are spies in every nook and cranny; be se-*
> *cret, Oh, Claiborne, so act that no emotions may be be-*

*trayed. The plot implicates thousands and among them
some of your particular friends as well as my own.*

Anticipating the panic his letter would create, Wilkinson
waited until November 25 before making his entrance to the city.
This the would-be Napoleon of the West did with military pomp
and martial display. Yet he maintained a silence that was ominous.
Claiborne was so frightened that he wrote to President Jefferson
he had heard that Burr was in the Western states, and feared his
views and intentions "were political, and of a kind most injurious.
General Wilkinson and myself will, to the best of our judgments
and abilities, support and honor the welfare of our country."

Wilkinson was a melodramatic actor. When he met Claiborne
he locked the doors and endeavored to make everyone believe
that life would not be worth a pewter spoon if the facts reached
the public. With great gusto he read the letter from Burr, giving
his version to the forgeries he had written into it and stressing the
paragraphs that would best serve his present designs. The West
was to secede. New Orleans was to be revolutionized, Claiborne
murdered, and the banks robbed. Colonel Burr's agents were
known to him as a "Mr. Spence of the Navy, a Mr. Ogden and a
Dr. Bollman"; with these he had made contact and, of course, he
had not shown his hand.

Since Burr and his mighty host had been pictured as coming
down the Mississippi, Claiborne suggested that Wilkinson plant
his militia north of the city. Thus entrenched he might prevent the
capture of New Orleans, even capture Burr. Wilkinson refused.
He would retain military control of New Orleans. The city was
powerless to do more than protest, and rage!

Dr. Justus Erich Bollman and Samuel Swartwout were on
the high seas en route to Washington. Through an oversight Ogden remained. James Alexander, a youthful New Orleans lawyer,
applied for his release only to be arrested and taken with Ogden
to Fort Saint Philip. Edward Livingston's application for writs of
release was granted. This so upset Wilkinson that for once he lost

control of speech, and instead of saying that such writs could not be maintained against one charged with traitorous acts, he said, "The Traitor Bollman are applicable to traitors who are subjects of this writ," a rambling of the tongue without rhyme or reason.

Livingston persisted by pressing for an order against Wilkinson himself. In the uproar that followed court was adjourned and Judge Workman inquired if Governor Claiborne would support the civil authorities. He was an appointment of Jefferson's; he would do nothing. On December 26, Livingston again applied for an attachment, which was granted. In complete defiance of this order, Wilkinson informed the court that Ogden was not "in his power, possession or custody." Again, James Workman, judge of the County of Orleans, asked the governor to uphold the arm of the court in its controversy with the military. His reply was that he thought a prisoner claimed by civil authority should be surrendered. Since a thought not supported by a show of authority is nil when dealing with a Wilkinson, the civil authority was ignored.

Wilkinson proceeded to rule New Orleans with the autocracy of a despot. He opened private mail, suppressed the press, and arrested Workman, Livingston, and editor Bradford of the *Gazette*. While eating at Madame Nourage's private boarding house, General John Adair was "violently dragged from the table, paraded through the street," and taken to a swamp twenty-five miles below the city. Eventually, in company with Peter Ogden, he was shipped to Baltimore.

James Workman was a member of the Mexican Association in New Orleans. In his attempt to remove Wilkinson from oppressive authority of the city he gave Colonel Freeman a signed statement, which is now in the possession of the New York Historical Society:

> *Judge Workman informed me that he has been one of the persons who had long contemplated a plan to emancipate Mexico from the Spanish Government; and this plan was to raise an army at the expense of the*

adventurers under the auspices of the United States; that the first object would be to take Baton Rouge and Mobile and then march into the Spanish provinces west of the Mississippi; if they should succeed there, to erect an independent government under the protection of the United States.

That Colonel Burr had nothing to do with this project. He was mentioned as a proper person to command, and General Wilkinson was also named as a fit person to put at the head of the enterprise; that secrecy was enjoined to the associates lest the scheme should become known to the Spaniards, but not for any purpose whatever injurious to the interests of the United States.

This plan was contemplated at the time it was supposed the United States would inevitably be in war with Spain; when De Miranda's expedition was believed to have been sanctioned by the General Government. But so soon as this was disavowed all conversation whatever in relation to the proposed conquest of Mexico ceased.

Colonel Freeman communicated to General Wilkinson the substance of Workman's statement. He received his approval as to its provisions and its purposes. The details for its execution are contained in the document. A study of these leads to the inevitable conclusion that its members were as patriotic in the defense of America and as cautious in plans to emancipate Mexico as were the men who sat at the elbow of Mr. Jefferson. Envy and jealousy characterized Wilkinson's betrayal of Aaron Burr.

I never believed [Burr] to be a Fool. But he must be an Idiot or a Lunatick if he has really planned and attempted to execute such a Project as is imputed to him. . . . [Some of the Southern politicians] had no more regard to Truth than the Devil. At present I suspect that this Lying Spirit has been at Work concerning Burr and that Mr. Jefferson has been too hasty in his Message in which he has denounced him by name and pronounced him guilty. But if his guilt is as clear as the Noon day Sun, the first Magistrate ought not to have pronounced it so before a Jury had tryed him.

– Ex-President John Adams
Private Letters

13
Flees for His Life

Burr's parting words with the men who shared his dream of a home on the Ouachita were mingled with tears of regret at the situation in which all found themselves at Bayou Pierre. They had set out down the Ohio with light hearts and high hopes only to meet this tragic end. Notwithstanding the disappointment and the powerful influence that had encompassed the defeat of their purpose, every member of the party remained loyal to his chief—all save one; this was a soldier on furlough and thus amenable to the authority of General Wilkinson.

In spite of the facts that Governor Williams's soldiers were on guard, that Wilkinson's spies were on hand, and that Jefferson's agents were serving their political master, Colonel Burr spent his last night in the vicinity of Washington Town, the old territorial capital of Mississippi, on a visit with his men in their houseboats and with Madaline Price. The first streaks of the new day were showing in the east when, astride a good horse and accompanied by Chester Ashley as guide, the colonel departed from Windy Hill Manor; its master, Colonel Osmun, one of Burr's truest friends, furnished the guide and mount.

According to John Randolph, Colonel Burr was disguised "in a shabby suit of homespun with an old white hat flapping over his face." The going through the forest was difficult. Finally, having lost their way, they stopped at the village of Wakefield, Washington County, now in Alabama. Here they inquired of Nicholas Perkins, a lawyer, concerning the road to Colonel Hinson's plantation, to which they repaired, finding the colonel absent from home; Mrs. Hinson, however, gave them lodging. In typical Southern style she ordered the slaves to prepare a meal for the gentlemen and retired. Very soon thereafter Perkins arrived with the sheriff, Thomas Brightwell, who entered the house to arrest Burr. The night wore on, and when the sheriff failed to reappear, Perkins rode off to Fort Stoddert, a military post. Here he secured four soldiers, with whom he was returning to the Hinson plantation when he encountered Sheriff Brightwell, who, having been won over, was acting as guide for the escape of the fugitives.

Burr was arrested and imprisoned at Fort Stoddert, where he made friends so quickly that Commandant Edmund Pendleton Gains became alarmed and turned him over to Perkins and a detachment of eight soldiers, who started for Washington. They avoided all civilization and traveled as secretly as possible lest an outraged public should rescue their prisoner. The party waded great swamps, traversed trackless forests and swam flooding streams; yet the average distance covered daily was forty miles. Burr never complained of fatigue or illness. He was always a good sport. Perkins testified at the trial that he had recognized Burr originally by his flashing eyes. He received three thousand three hundred and thirty one dollars for apprehending Burr.

Lieutenant Gams complained that the citizens of Fort Stoddert and the Tombigbee River section made it so unpleasant because he was detaining Burr that he was compelled to turn him over to a more powerful military establishment or run the chance that Burr be rescued from his authority. To General Wilkinson he wrote:

> The plans of Colonel Burr are now spoken of in terms of approbation and sympathy. I am convinced if Burr had remained here a week longer the consequences would have been of the most serious nature. Burr frequently observed "my great offense and the only one laid to my charge was a design to give you the Floridas."

When Perkins and his prisoner reached the Chester District in South Carolina, the home of Joseph Alston, Burr's son-in-law, and were passing a tavern where a group of people were assembled, Burr suddenly jumped from his horse and exclaimed in a loud voice, "I am Aaron Burr and under military arrest and claim the protection of the civil authorities."

Perkins was a large man. After grabbing Burr around the waist, he literally flung him back into the saddle. Surrounding Burr's horse, one of the party led it while the others on either side whipped it into a gallop, and before the astonished citizens could recover their senses, the military squad with its prisoner was out of sight.

Not again to endanger the loss of this prisoner, Perkins placed Burr in a carriage and, after drawing the curtains, proceeded stealthily to Fredericksburg. Here he received orders from the president to take Burr to Richmond, Virginia, where the government was setting the stage for his trial on a charge of high treason.

It was just as the shadows of evening were falling across the almost deserted streets of Richmond on March 26, 1807, that this begrimed cavalcade cantered to its journey's end. From imprisonment by Rodney's illegal detention Burr had escaped, from the wrath and cunning of Wilkinson's gang armed with "dirks and pistols." By the aid of friends Burr's life was saved, but now he faced the organized political legion of Virginia and its master, Thomas Jefferson.

From Washington, almost six months before, Burr had departed with high hopes and amid the plaudits of his friends. All along the Ohio River valley they had cheered him on his way toward a dream of a peaceful home on the banks of the Ouachita. Here, surrounded by his friends, he no doubt planned to organize a group of ambitious Americans to wrest from Mexico the vast empire a part of which was one day to become the Republic of Texas, but the jealousy of Jefferson, fanned by the lies of Wilkinson, accomplished his defeat. For the fifth time Burr was arrested at the instigation of Jefferson. Chief Justice John Marshall wrote:

> *Since treason is the most atrocious offense which can be committed against the political body so it is the charge most capable of being employed as the instrument of those malignant and vindictive passions which may rage in the bosoms of contending parties struggling for power.*

With Burr in the grasp of the military, Jefferson proceeded to convict him in the public mind by writing:

> *Burr has indeed made a most inglorious exhibition of his much overrated talent. He is on his way to Richmond for trial. No man's history proves better the value of honesty. With that, what might he not have been.*

Wilkinson's frenzied fiction had found ready repose in Jefferson's ears. This fiction the president proceeded to propagandize until the nation was led to believe that the government possessed irrefutable evidence of Burr's guilt. Thomas Jefferson convicted Aaron Burr of treason by using the office of the president of the

United States to deliberately deceive the people so that he might hang a political opponent.

Was it not natural that the American people believed that Jefferson possessed evidence of Burr's guilt? Is it less than natural that this same people failed to observe that no evidence of Jefferson's charges was presented at the trial, and that the verdict of the jury was "NOT GUILTY"?

Jefferson's treatment of Burr just prior to the trial presents the strangest episode in the life of the author of the Declaration of Independence, where a great democrat becomes a tyrant, where a great scientist builds his structure of hate on the flimsiest pretense of a premise, where the father of the Bill of Rights tears to shreds every constitutional guarantee of personal liberty, and where a disciple of Truth substituted the doctrine that the end justifies the mean. It's a sad picture of Jefferson!

If the president had incontrovertible proof of Burr's guilt, in the light of his preachments of liberty, justice, and freedom, we should expect him to withhold judgment until evidence was presented before a court.

But no—in his eagerness to destroy the usefulness of Burr, Jefferson proceeded by his pen and by the use of the press to convict. Fortunately for the American judiciary and for personal liberty, at the time of this writing the people have not been so deceived by any other president!

Eaton's fantastic tale of Burr's plans to assassinate the president was supplemented by Wilkinson's wild rumors. Augmenting these were implications by the government, which were so damning, it was hinted, that for reasons of state the proof could not be released. These were magnified and multiplied until the name of Burr became an execration. His friends were amazed; Federalist Senator William Plumer wrote:

> *I am too well acquainted with the man to believe him guilty of all the absurdity that is ascribed to him. He is a man of first rate talents. He may be capable of*

much wickedness, but not of folly. I must have plena-
ry evidence, before I believe him capable of commit-
ting a hundredth part of the absurd and foolish things
ascribed to him. In fact the President of the United
States a day or two since informed me that he knew of
no evidence sufficient to convict him of high crimes or
misdemeanor.

The acrimonious warfare reached such high tide January 16, 1807, that John Randolph demanded that the president lay before the House evidence supporting the conspiracies mentioned in his message. Having no evidence, the president sidestepped Randolph's demand and replied bombastically, "Aaron Burr is the principal actor in a plot to disrupt the Union."

It later developed that the president's evidence consisted of that old canard about the seizure of Washington, which had originally been prepared for Marquis Yrujo's consumption, with which General William Eaton had entertained certain congressmen, alleging that he had it direct from Burr. The general's imagination had run wild; his lugubrious tongue had Colonel Burr turning Congress "neck and heels" out of doors, "assassinating the president, seizing the Navy and the Treasury" with the colonel as "protector of an energetic government." The ebullient Eaton even had Colonel Burr in charge of the Mexican government as a subdivision of his new contemplated empire. It was a wild daydream, but it was a bit stale in Washington.

Outside of Washington the president's statement created a sensation; in the Capitol, however, and to politicians, it was old stuff. Ex-president John Adams stated a consensus:

I never believed [Burr] to be a Fool. But he must
be an Idiot or a Lunatick if he has really planned and
attempted to execute such a Project as is imputed to
him. . . . [Some of the Southern politicians] had no
more regard to Truth than the Devil. At present I sus-

pect that this Lying Spirit has been at Work concerning Burr. However, regardless of everything else, if his guilt is as clear as the Noonday Sun, the first Magistrate ought not to have pronounced it so before a Jury had tryed him.

In desperation for evidence with which to convict Burr, the president had accepted Wilkinson's version and the garbled copy of Burr's cipher letter. This plunged both Wilkinson's version and Jefferson into a degrading situation. Only dire necessity could have forced the wily Wilkinson and the clever Jefferson to present a grand jury with a forged document. Not to be circumscribed by constitutional limitations, the president asked for the suspension of the writ of *habeas corpus*. To secure this he asked William B. Giles, the administration whip, to propose such resolution in secret session. Giles introduced the measure the January 23, and the Senate passed it with scarcely a dissenting voice.

The House was in a different frame of mind and refused the secret session by a vote of one hundred and twenty-three to three. A vitriolic debate ensued, where, strangely enough, Jefferson's son-in-law, John W. Eppes, surprised his colleagues by shouting, "Never, under this government, has personal liberty been held at the will of a single individual." The bill was defeated by a vote of one hundred and thirteen to nineteen.

Thus for the second time the plans of Wilkinson and Jefferson had gone wrong in their endeavor to hang Burr. First, General Wilkinson had failed in his attempt to catch Burr in his martial-law trap. Now the president had failed to have him at his personal mercy when Congress refused to suspend the writ of *habeas corpus*.

Fate takes charge of events at the unexpected moment. The president's plan for securely fastening a noose about Burr's neck failed just when Bollman and Swartwout arrived from New Orleans. Since they would have been in the clutches of the military if Congress had placed them at the mercy of the president—as a result of a suspension of the writ of habeas corpus—the path for disposing of Burr would have been cleared. The lengths to which Thomas Jefferson went in his attempt to hang Aaron Burr should never be forgotten by the Congress of the United States.

As a part of their political strategy, Jefferson and Madison had instructed the squad of soldiers who escorted Bollman and Swartwout from the boat to the military prison in Washington City to bring them before the president and secretary of state. In the office of the secretary and with a promise from his inquisitors not to use thereafter any information divulged, Bollman was baited for evidence against Burr. Acting as agents for the executive department of the government, Jefferson and Madison resorted to trickery in an attempt to fasten about Burr's neck their specially prepared noose. What was worse, at the first opportunity the promise of the inquisitors was forgotten.

From Bollman came a story that Burr planned to revolutionize Mexico and make a monarchy of it. He would seize the French artillery in New Orleans and the shipping in the harbor by force if necessary; but would avoid violence and protect the rights of the individual. After the amassed forces were conveyed to Vera Cruz, Bollman was to hasten to Washington to inform the government and to urge war with Spain.

As for Yrujo, Bollman was sure that he had been hoodwinked into believing that Burr was to revolutionize Louisiana, or Western States; this was to quiet the suspicions of Spain. Yrujo had offered Burr arms and money; but "Burr despised the dirty character of Yrujo, and never would accept either money or anything else from that quarter." Thus, Jefferson and Madison failed to learn anything that was detrimental to Burr, and certainly nothing treasonable.

Samuel Swartwout and Dr. Justus Erich Bollman had each received a copy of the cipher letter from Colonel Burr. Swartwout and Peter Ogden, son of Matthias Ogden, carried their copy overland. Having missed General Wilkinson in St. Louis, they followed him south to Kaskaskia and on to Natchez. From Natchez

Ogden went to New Orleans, while Swartwout called on General Wilkinson at the American headquarters to deliver the now-famous cipher letter.

Cipher letters, or code letters, were common in those days. Washington, Adams, and Jefferson had all refused to allow any important communication to be made by mail, and as Jefferson explained, "I am forming a resolution of declining correspondence with my friends through the channels of the post office altogether."

After entertaining Samuel Swartwout in the most hospitable manner and receiving from him, as he was to report, all manner of incriminating information concerning Colonel Burr's plans, Wilkinson permitted the young man to depart. For a time he went about the city at will, under the surveillance of Wilkinson's sleuths. Dr. Justus Erich Bollman had gone to the city by the water route. Thus it was that these two men were to become the chief conspirators, agents of Burr, in the estimation of General Wilkinson.

As to the contents of the Burr cipher letter, these can never be known since General Wilkinson altered parts to make the whole serve his purposes. The alteration began by omitting "Your letter postmarked thirteenth of May is received." General Wilkinson's translation, excluding the erased acknowledgment, follows:

At length I have obtained funds and have actually commenced. The Eastern detachments from different points and under different pretenses will rendezvous on the Ohio the first of November. Everything internal and external favors our views. Naval protection of England is secured. Truxton is going to Jamaica to arrange with the admiral on that station. It will meet us at the Mississippi. England, a navy of the United States, are ready to join, and final orders are given to my friends and followers. It will be a host of choice spirits. Wilkinson shall be second to Burr only; Wilkinson shall dictate the rank and promotion of his officers.

Burr will proceed westward first August, never to return. With him goes his daughter; her husband will follow in October with a corps of worthies. Send forthwith an intelligent and confidential friend with whom Burr may confer; he shall return immediately with further interesting details; this is essential to concert and harmony of movement. Send a list of all persons known to Wilkinson west of the mountains who could be useful, with a note delineating their characters. By your messenger send me four or five commissions of your officers, which you can borrow under any pretense you please; they shall be returned faithfully. Already are orders given to the contractor to forward six months' provisions to points Wilkinson may name; this shall not be used until the last moment and then under proper injunctions.

Our object, my dear friend, is brought to a point so long desired. Burr guarantees the result with his life and honor, with the lives and honor and the fortunes of hundreds of the best blood of our country. Burr's plan of operation is to move down rapidly from the Falls on the fifteenth of November with the first five hundred or a thousand men in light boats now constructing for that purpose; to be at Natchez between the fifth and the fifteenth of December, there to meet you; there to determine whether it will be expedient to the first instance to seize or pass by Baton Rouge. On receipt of this send Burr an answer. Draw on Burr for all expenses, etc. The people of the country to which we are going are prepared to receive us; their agents, now with Burr, say that if we will protect their religion and not subject them to a foreign Power, that in three weeks all will be settled.

James Wilkinson in 1797 portrait by Charles Willson Peale

The gods invite us to glory and fortune; it remains to be seen whether we deserve the boon. The bearer of this goes express to you. He is a man of invincible honor and perfect discretion, formed to execute rather than project, capable of relating facts with fidelity and incapable of relating them otherwise; he is thoroughly informed of the plans and intentions of Burr, and will disclose to you as far as you require and no further. He has imbibed a reverence for your character, and may be embarrassed in your presence; put him at ease, and he will satisfy you.

To the copy transported by Dr. Bollman was added this post-script: "Doctor Bollman, equally confidential, better informed on the subject and more enlightened, will hand this duplicate."

The acquisition of Texas had long been contemplated by Burr and Wilkinson. Their military association began with the expedition to Quebec. Wilkinson was recommended to the command of the Western Division of the army by Vice President Burr. Spanish tyranny had aroused the West to open rebellion, and this had led to the Burr–Wilkinson plans for its conquest "if and when there was war with Spain." And the discussion of war with Spain naturally led those interested to indicate who was most likely to become their leader. Preference for Burr was almost universal, and this aroused the political envy and jealousy of Wilkinson, and it prompted the betrayal of Burr.

Tennessee and Kentucky were the hotbed of the rebellion against Spain. General Jackson was not only in command of the militia of Tennessee, but was the outstanding soldier, the dominant personality, and the idol of the West. When Jackson gave Burr his endorsement and took an active part in the building of his houseboats for transporting his party to Louisiana, this not only aroused Wilkinson, but aroused Jefferson as well. Both fully realized if the American soldier ever crossed the Sabine that no one was wise enough to predict where he would stop; it might be with the territory of Texas, but more likely the Stars and Stripes would fly over Mexico City. Such honor and glory must never come to Aaron Burr, and it would not if Jefferson and Wilkinson could prevent it.

Thus, in planning the capture of Burr, General Wilkinson had declared martial law in New Orleans, where he arrested Swartwout and Bollman as agents of Burr. He sent them by ship to

Baltimore, where they arrived on January 22. Four days later they were transferred to Washington and by district attorney general Rodney placed under arrest on a charge of treason. On January 13 the prisoners applied for and obtained a writ of habeas corpus. Three days later they were discharged.

In the meantime James Alexander had arrived in Baltimore, where on February 6 he was discharged because of lack of evidence. General Adair and Peter Ogden followed on the seventeenth, to be discharged on the eighteenth, because "there was no proof of any nature whatsoever against them." For this arrest General Adair sued and obtained judgment against Wilkinson for false imprisonment. At the request of Thomas Jefferson, Congress reimbursed Wilkinson.

What a travesty that Wilkinson should be rewarded publicly by Congress for one of his many crimes, yet Burr was persecuted as no other man in public life in America, with never an attempt made to remove the stigma nor to return to him more than fifty thousand dollars that was taken from him and his friends as a result of the president's false charge!

In Washington things were going badly with the administration. Alleged conspirators were turned loose as fast as they arrived. Wilkinson was discredited. Members of Congress were beginning to inquire if he were a "Pensioner of Spain?" John Randolph had asked for evidence that Aaron Burr was not the victim of "two-fold" treachery by Jefferson and Wilkinson. Broom referred to the abuses "committed by a military officer at the head of the army. . . . in full view of the highest authorities of the Union." For his part he wished to live "under a government of laws, and not of men."

By this time it was quite plain that Jefferson's persecution of Burr was purely political. In presenting Burr before the bar of justice at Richmond the prestige of the president was at stake. In turning his attack on John Marshall in that same trial the prestige of the president was at stake. What a blow it must have been to Jefferson when Marshall emerged from the trial with honor and Burr with acquittal!

What would be the result if all your charges against General Wilkinson should be proven? Why, just what the Federalists and the enemies of the present administration wish. It would turn the indignation of the people from Burr on Wilkinson. Burr would escape, and Wilkinson take his place.

– Caesar A. Rodney, U.S. Attorney General
Trial of Aaron Burr

14
Why Rodney Stepped Aside

Reports of the trial of Aaron Burr were taken in shorthand by David Robertson, a lawyer. The examination of Colonel Burr was begun March 30, 1807. The trial continued through the spring and summer. The verdict of "Not Guilty" was rendered September 15. Robertson records, "It was the middle of June before the reporter was prevailed upon to undertake the publication." He was, however, familiar with the case from its inception, since he attended the preliminaries. In his introduction he observes:

> *In whatever view these trials are to be regarded, they must be deemed very interesting. But when we consider the celebrity of the party accused, the stations and characters of some of those implicated with him,*

the magnitude and extent of their supposed designs, the danger of the union of the states apprehended therefrom, the learned and profound doctrines which were so ably discussed by such eminent counsel, and the great talents of the court, this report cannot but be highly important and valuable. Perhaps no trial for treason has taken place in any country, in which more ability, learning, ingenuity, and eloquence has been displayed. All the important decisions on treason in England and in this country were actually examined and considered. . . . nor was less industry or judgment shown in arguing the application and effect of the Constitution of the United States, and the common law, if it existed at all as a law of the Union.

It is believed that this report will be amusing and interesting to all persons capable of reading and understanding; and that to the lawyer, politician and man of general information it will be particularly gratifying, as it will comprehend a valuable treatise on criminal law, and particularly high treason.

The report covers 1,135 pages. It is printed in two volumes. The first three paragraphs of Robertson's report are verbatim:

Colonel Aaron Burr, who had been arrested on the Tombigbee river, in the Mississippi Territory, on the 19th of February last, and brought to the city under a military escort on Thursday evening the 26th instant, remained under guard until this day, when he was delivered over to the civil authority, by virtue of a warrant issued by the chief justice of the United States, grounded on the charges of a high misdemeanor, in setting on foot and preparing, within the territories of the United States, a military expedition, to be carried on from thence against the dominions of the king of Spain, with whom the United States then were and still are at peace; and also of treason against the United States

Between the hours of twelve and one o'clock, Major Scott, the marshal of the district of Virginia, attending by two of his deputies, waited on colonel Burr, at his lodgings in the Eagle Tavern, and, after informing him in most respectful manner, of the nature and object of his visit, conducted him through the awfully silent and attentive assemblage of citizens to a retired room in the house, where he was brought before the chief Justice Marshall for examination. The counsel and a witness for the United States, the counsel for the prisoner, the marshal and his deputies, and a few friends invited by the counsel of Colonel Burr, were alone admitted. . . . Burr was admitted to bail in the sum of five thousand dollars.

Tuesday, 31st March, 1807: Present, John Marshall Chief Justice of the United States. Counsel for the prosecution, Caesar A. Rodney, Attorney General of the United States; George Hay, Attorney of the United States for the district of Virginia. Counsel for Colonel Burr, Edmund Randolph esquire, John Wickham, esquire.

Mr. Hay moved that the prisoner be committed upon two charges: first, for high misdemeanor in setting on foot within the United States a military expedition against the dominions of Spain; second, for treason, in assembling an armed force, with a design to seize the city of New Orleans, to revolutionize the territory attached to it, and separate the Western from the Atlantic States.

John Wickham contended that there was no evidence of treason committed by Colonel Burr; that there was no overt act; that the cipher letter was not delivered to Wilkinson by Burr, nor proven to be written by him—in fact, a decade after Sturm completed this work, Burr's signature was proven to be a forgery. He said it would be cruel to insist on bail in any considerable sum, since Burr had been brought to a place for trial where he had fewer friends than in any other part of the Union; besides, there was not a shadow of evidence to support the charge of treason.

Edmund Randolph, who had served as U.S. Attorney General under Washington, was then regarded, as he is today, as one of the most learned lawyers of all time. Randolph said he never before "had heard of a conjecture of an overt act of treason attempted to be proved from a supposed intention!" He declared that Burr had a right to resist oppression; that he had not fled from justice but from military oppression; that he had been acquitted in Kentucky and a Mississippi grand jury had refused to indict him.

In the trial report, counselor David Robertson wrote of Attorney General Caesar A. Rodney:

> When he considered the numerous and attentive audience, the public so strongly excited, the character charged, and the crime of which he was accused, he was more than usually embarrassed. He had never felt more for any person than the prisoner, who was not less than the late vice president of the United States, esteemed for his transcendent talents and whom he once considered his friend, and had treated him as such in his own house. . . . that it was incumbent on those who prosecuted to prove the probable cause to believe his guilt, and that a chain of circumstances showed, without doubt, that he was guilty; that he would endeavor to convince him by his manner of conducting the prosecution, that the Government was not influenced by malicious and vindictive passions to persecute him.

In view of the fact that the attorney general immediately retired from the case, attention is directed to his statement. Rodney was indeed in an embarrassing position; he did not "believe" Burr was guilty. Besides, he had learned that the chief witness was the

Thomas Jefferson in 1800 portrait by Rembrandt Peale

traitor whom the government should be hanging because he was proven guilty by the records. To add to his embarrassment, the people of Richmond openly charged that Wilkinson was a pensioner of Spain; and more embarrassing still, Andrew Jackson, the most powerful personality in all the West, charged not only that Wilkinson was the chief conspirator in this case but that the president was an abettor.

It was from this ugly situation that Rodney stepped aside from the prosecution and journeyed to Washington, where the president acknowledged that he was aware of the charges against Wilkinson but insisted that it would be necessary to cover up these charges for the present—at least until Burr was convicted. Rodney revolted at an attempt to convict Burr with such evidence as Wilkinson offered, and by a witness who was discredited by the public. The two quarreled over the situation, when Rodney inquired:

> *What would be the result if this should be proven? Why, just what the Federalists and the enemies of the administration wish—it would turn the indignation of the people from Burr to Wilkinson; Burr would escape, and Wilkinson would take his place.*

"The vindictive passions" of Thomas Jefferson prevailed. Rodney retired from the prosecution of Burr and never again appeared in court, where he would be "influenced by malicious and vindictive passions to persecute him."

Is there need for additional evidence why the man who was appointed U.S. attorney general while his father, Thomas Rodney, illegally held Burr in Washington Town, Mississippi, refused to prosecute Burr? All the officers of the territories of Louisiana and Mississippi, governors, judges and even the creator of martial law, James Wilkinson, were appointees of Jefferson. Of this situation Senator Albert J. Beveridge, biographer of John Marshall, has recorded:

> *When the [Mississippi] grand jury was dismissed, Burr asked to be discharged and his sureties released from bond. The Judge was Thomas Rodney, father of Caesar A. Rodney whom Jefferson soon afterwards appointed Attorney General. Judge Rodney out-Wilkinsoned Wilkinson; he denied Burr's request and ordered*

him to renew his bond or go to jail. This was done despite the facts that the grand jury had refused to indict Burr and that there was not legal charge whatever before the court.

President Jefferson appointed Caesar A. Rodney U.S. Attorney General on January 20. Fifteen days later came the refusal of Thomas Rodney to release Burr. The elder Rodney was at that time not only judge but also land commissioner of Mississippi Territory. In his biography of Caesar A. Rodney, J. Oliver Wolcott, secretary of the treasury, wrote:

Rodney's first appearance with the Burr trial was in the case of Bollman and Swartwout, who had been arrested and sent to Washington. This arrest was illegal, and without special legislation the men could not be held. Rodney applied to Judge Cranch, the warrant was issued but Rodney declined to argue the point.

Before Burr's indictment, a Major Bruff came from St. Louis, saying that "Wilkinson was a spy and a traitor." It was well known that Jefferson could not afford to have the general put on trial. He had, in spite of warnings, left the general in charge of the Western country. If he should be brought to court, the president would have to either support a man whose guilt would be very likely proven, or else admit his own negligence. It was necessary, therefore, to quiet Bruff. He was told that there might be an inquiry later, therefore the general was not indicted.

Burr was found to be not guilty. This angered Jefferson; for a time he thought of attacking Marshall as a judge, but the entire attack would have hinged upon General Wilkinson's testimony; if Wilkinson were discredited, Jefferson was in danger.

Burr had formed the no less daring projects than to reduce New Orleans, subjugate Mexico, and divide the Union. . . .

Hitherto we have believed our law to be, that suspicion on probable grounds was sufficient cause to commit a person for trial . . .

What loophole they will find in the case, when it comes to trial, we cannot foresee. Eaton, Stoddart, and Wilkinson, will satisfy the world, if not the judges, of Burr's guilt.

– Thomas Jefferson
Private Letters

The president of the United States . . . informed me that he knew of no evidence sufficient to convict [Burr] of either high crimes or misdemeanor.

– Senator William Plumer

15
Coming Events Cast Their Shadows

Into the spotlight at Richmond came Burr, pale with the terrors of incarceration. He was elegantly attired, his demeanor was composed, his bearing dignified, and his eyes flashing fire. Everyone observed his high forehead and his dominating personality. He quickly confounded his enemies, alarmed his traducers, and nullified the usefulness of a host of witnesses, some of whom had been catechized by the president.

In freeing Swartwout and Bollman, Chief Justice Marshall had said:

War must actually be levied. . . . To conspire to levy war, and to actually levy war are distinct offenses. . . . The first must be brought into operation by the as-

*semblage of men for a purpose treasonable in itself, or
the fact of levying war cannot have been committed.*

This was sound law; it was in accord with the provision of
the Constitution that clearly defines treason against the United
States to consist "only in levying war against them, or in adhering
to their enemies, giving them aid and comfort."

In that decision the chief justice inadvertently invited trouble
for himself by saying:

> *It is the intention of the Court to say that no indi-
> vidual can be guilty of this crime who has not appeared
> in arms against his country. . . . If a body of men be ac-
> tually assembled for the purpose of effecting by force a
> treasonable purpose; all of those who perform any part,
> however minute, or however remote from the scene of
> action, and who are actually leagued in the general con-
> spiracy, are to be considered as traitors.*

This extraneous observation by the chief justice resulted
eventually in Virginia being selected as the site of the Burr trial.
In his absence supplies for the Bastrop Colony were loaded on the
boats at the Blennerhassett Island. Here the militia had entered
the beautiful home to leave it plundered and wrecked. Here they
drank themselves into a state of inebriation. These agents of the
government were the real lawbreakers; this lawlessness occurred
in Woods County, Virginia, a state that was politically dominated
by Jefferson, Madison, and Monroe.

Unhappily for that political trio, Virginia was also the home
of John Marshall, whose throne Jefferson had attacked when he
instituted suit to remove Justice Chase. Vice President Burr had
just been sworn into office and was standing at the elbow of the
chief justice Marshall when the latter administered the oath of office to Thomas Jefferson as president. Marshall had proven himself a Federalist warhorse—and the very one that the president

would have preferred to have removed, rather than Justice Chase. Since Chase, however, was more vulnerable, he had been selected with the hope of establishing a precedent when action against Marshall was to follow. To the great surprise of the president, the Senate proved recalcitrant and demonstrated that it was less pliable in his hands than was the House when drawing the charges. Burr also had been a factor in the acquittal of Chase; thus both Burr and Marshall had become the objects of Jefferson's hatred.

As the trial proceeded at Richmond, the spotlight of the Nation was turned first on Burr, then on Marshall and eventually on Jefferson. In the light of evidence that was withheld by the prosecution, and in the light of additional evidence that has been uncovered and is here presented, some of it for the first time, it is established beyond question that President Jefferson possessed incontrovertible proof of Wilkinson's perfidy. But instead of hanging a known traitor, he chose to defend him that he might hang a patriot.

Personal enmity in Thomas Jefferson was stronger than a sense of personal justice. In his persecution of Aaron Burr, Thomas Jefferson made "liberty and justice" an abomination in the sight of God and man. As they stand revealed by the light of truth, Aaron Burr was a better patriot than Thomas Jefferson!

Continued reports of the evil deeds of Wilkinson had reduced his standing in the estimation of Jefferson. Wilkinson had been warned that he was to be removed from office. In desperation he decided that only services heroic in the eyes of the president would save his scalp. By turning traitor to the friend who had helped to get his appointment, by installing martial law in New Orleans, and in making an all-out effort to capture Burr, he reinstated himself with the president.

Wilkinson's service to Jefferson in his attempt to capture Burr placed that "Finished Scoundrel" beyond the reach of evidence when the stories of his long-suspected service as a pensioner of Spain became known. Awareness of Jefferson's intense hatred for Burr prompted Wilkinson to kidnap and "cut-off" the victim of their "two-fold" hatred.

It was General Eaton who had originally proposed to the president that he appoint Burr as ambassador to Spain to thus remove him from the political arena and at the same time rid himself of a politically dangerous enemy. When asked why he had not told the president of Burr's Washington conspiracy and his Western projects, Eaton replied, "The president apparently thought I was aiding Burr."

In view of Jefferson's subsequent action, it is no longer difficult to fathom his reason for paying Eaton ten thousand dollars for an old and long-before-rejected claim. If Eaton's affidavit proved worthless, so does a straw in the hand of a drowning man. The state of mind revealed by Mr. Jefferson in accepting the type of men and the quality of evidence introduced at Richmond in the personages of William Eaton and James Wilkinson clearly established why the clever Jefferson, while third in enlistment, became the leader in promulgating the stories of fiction and defamation. In his madness to hang Burr the president lost his usual discretion.

What crimes men do commit when inspired by envy and jealousy!

A vast dragnet was spread over almost the whole United States and drawn swiftly and remorselessly to Washington.
— Albert J. Beveridge
The Life of John Marshall

16
The Preliminary Trial

Chief Justice John Marshall had come from Washington to Richmond to receive Aaron Burr from the custody of the military, in whose grasp he had been held ever since his arrest, and to provide civil authority for his preliminary examination. It was March 30, 1807, that Burr was brought before Marshall in the Eagle Tavern. The room was so small that many of the curious crowd were denied admission.

Under the president's instruction Attorney General Caesar A. Rodney had been given orders that justices of the peace throughout the Union examine everyone suspected of having knowledge of Burr's plans, and that they be furnished with a free trip to the trial.

Concerning this building of a political machine for the manufacture of evidence, Albert Beveridge wrote, "A vast dragnet was spread over almost the whole of the Unites States and drawn swiftly and remorselessly to Washington."

While complying with the president's instruction, Rodney discovered that it was James Wilkinson and not Aaron Burr who was guilty of treason. Later, when the enormity of this situation dawned upon the attorney general, he stepped aside and refused to prosecute Burr.

Thus was forced upon George Hay, United States District Attorney General of Virginia, responsibility for the prosecution of Aaron Burr. Hay was a good lawyer. His prosecution of Burr, however, did not add to his laurels. Whether he was intimidated and confused by the president's demands or his heart was simply not in it has long been the subject of debate. His associates were William Wirt, young, aggressive and oratorical, and also Alexander MacRea, lieutenant governor of Virginia. The latter was added for political reasons and really embarrassed the prosecution more than he helped.

Marshall was given to repetition; Burr never repeated. He was concise and most convincing, although never oratorical; his conversational tone was commanding, almost irresistible. There were moments when he was hypnotic. Here again, at Burr's trial, these two faced each other, as they had done when Marshall administered the oath of office and Jefferson became president.

The trial was begun when George Hay introduced into evidence a copy of the record of the case of Swartwout and Bollman. These were depositions of Wilkinson and Eaton. Nicholas Perkins testified to his capture of Burr. When he finished, motion was made by Hay to commit the prisoner for the grand jury, and on two grounds: namely, high misdemeanor "in setting on foot, within the United States, a military expedition against the dominions of the King of Spain" and second, and vastly more important if proved, "for treason in assembling an armed force with the design to seize the city of New Orleans, to revolutionize the territory attached to it and to separate the western from the Atlantic states."

Burr was admitted to bail in the sum of five thousand dollars, and court was adjourned to convene the next day in the State Capitol, where it was hoped that there would be room for the great crowds. The jam, however, was so great that Hay moved for adjournment to the House of Delegates. The move was almost a demand on the part of the district attorney, who was determined to secure all the publicity possible, since conviction before the public was of greater political import than to secure conviction in court. Even the larger place was crowded to the limit.

The president had admitted that he had no evidence with which to convict Burr before the court but had publicly announced that he could convict him before the public. If a layman had been guilty of such endeavor it might have been attributed to ignorance, yet for a clever lawyer, a great philosopher, and the father of the Declaration of Independence, what motives other than enmity, jealousy, and determination to crucify may we ascribe?

When court finally opened in the largest room to be had in Richmond, it was evident that the mob spirit was in the air. Burr and his scattered friends sensed this, but by calm demeanor he added daily to their number. The malice of the prosecution was so obvious that it aroused the wrath of the Federalists; it even stirred the ire of many independent Republicans.

Burr was the most composed man at the trial.

Hay proposed to commit Burr for treason, chiefly on Wilkinson's cipher letter. To the district attorney this was proof positive of treasonable intent; to Wickham it was evidence of innocence of crime, and more, it was proof of a perfectly laudable enterprise— an expedition against the Spanish possessions, if and when the United States declared war.

Thirty years later Burr's endeavor proved worthy of a patriot when Sam Houston, with the support of President Andrew Jackson, attempted a similar mission and carved out of the Spanish territory the Republic of Texas.

The first great thrill of the opening session came when Burr

Chief Justice John Marshall in 1832 portrait by Henry Inman

arose to repel some observations made by Hay "of a personal nature." Burr pointed out that he was being persecuted merely on conjectures conceived by the infamous Wilkinson, who was feeding his fictions to the president. Burr recounted his incarceration by the military. He called attention to four former charges for this same offense in each of which he had been held guiltless—even praised while his persecutors had been roundly excoriated.

When Burr sat down there was a mild hum of approval. It was apparent that he had a few friends in the audience. Hay frowned, Wickham smiled. For the defense it was the first ray of hope.

For two days the legal battle raged. The prosecution made a great effort to induce Marshall to bind Burr over to the grand jury. The defense fought to have him released. Finally, on April 1 came the decision, comprehensive and of great length: concerning the misdemeanor, that the cipher letter and Wilkinson's deposition sufficiently constituted a *prima facie* case to warrant committing Burr for the grand jury's investigation.

As to the graver charge of treason, that was quite another matter. The Constitution of the United States expressly provided that: "Treason against the United States shall consist only in levying war against them, or adhering to their enemies, giving them aid and comfort."

Then the great jurist pointed out that the Constitution clearly stated that "no person shall be convicted of it Treason unless on the testimony of two witnesses to the same overt act, or on confession in open court."

Amplification of the constitutional provisions in the light of Blackstone and other English authorities was made by Marshall. He applied these to the evidence offered to support the charge. He pointed out that the sole evidence before the court to support the charge was the affidavits of Eaton and Wilkinson, consisting of rumors and conjectures, mere intention as against commission. In the examination of Colonel Aaron Burr "to determine whether the charges are supported by probable cause" he ruled:

> *An intention to commit treason is an offense entirely distinct from the actual commission of that crime. War can only be levied by the employment of force. Troops must be embodied, men must be assembled in order to levy war. . . . these are facts that cannot remain invisible.*
>
> *Treason may be machinated in secret, but it can be perpetrated only in open day and in the eve of the world. Testimony of a fact which in its own nature is so notorious ought to be unequivocal.*

From the general, Marshall proceeded to the particular:

The fact to be proved in this case is an act of public notoriety. It must exist in view of the world, or it cannot exist at all. The assembling of forces to levy war is a visible transaction, and numbers must witness it. It is therefore capable of proof; and when time to collect this proof is given, it ought to be adduced, or suspicion becomes ground too weak to stand upon. Several months have elapsed, since this fact did occur, if it ever occurred. More than five weeks have elapsed, since the opinion of the supreme court has declared the necessity of proving this fact exists. Why is it not proved?

The court paused, and from the entire audience of the great crowded room came a sigh of relief from the suspense while the momentous question was being so masterfully answered, for the chief justice had completely answered his own question before propounding it. The effect upon the lawyers, as well as the audience, was as if he had spoken in an open ground before a great mountain, where the echo was to resound: "Why is it not proved?"

The spirit of Jefferson hovered over the trial from its inception. When Marshall had raised this all-important question, it was as if he were saying directly to the president:

Sir, when you replied to John Randolph's motion in the House to lay before that body evidence supporting charges of treason, you said, "Aaron Burr is the principal actor to disrupt the Union." I, in common with all people of the country, supposed you knew what you were talking about!

And again the audience waited for the echo:

Why is it not proved?

Attorney General Rodney, acting under instructions from the president and his cabinet, and prior to Rodney's discovery of the treachery of Wilkinson, had printed thousands of affidavits as to Burr's alleged crimes. These had been broadcast all over the land with an appeal to all good citizens having knowledge of the facts to come forward and make affidavit to what they knew; or, what is more to the point, make affidavit to what they believed.

The false propaganda of Jefferson and Wilkinson quickly took root in the minds of the populace, where it bore fruit and at the government's expense. Is it any wonder that the crowds at Richmond were so large, or that from the beginning there was clamor for Burr's blood? Is it not even more remarkable that John Marshall was able to restrain the jury to a consideration of the evidence?

Jefferson was determined to hang Burr—remove him from political life. Marshall's decision spurred him to greater activity. He ordered the search for and manufacture of evidence on a scale that has never been equaled in the history of American jurisprudence. His agents literally swarmed down the Ohio and the Mississippi valleys prying, snooping, and corralling everyone who would aid the cause. It became a crusade. It was carried out in the manner of the Crusaders of the tenth century and with almost as much fanaticism as those religious enthusiasts.

Into Woods County went a messenger especially instructed to get depositions; some proved of value to Burr, but these were discarded. Jefferson and his agents were not seeking the truth. They proposed to prevent Burr from getting off with a misdemeanor charge, and if possible, hang him.

Wilkinson was cornered. His doctored cipher letter was incriminating. Martial law had given him mastery of New Orleans, but Burr escaped. How was he to assist his partner in convicting Burr? He had successfully duped the president, a co-partner in the crime. How could he outwit Marshall? Ah, that was the rub!

Nothing is so desirable to me as that after mankind shall have been abused by such gross falsehoods as to events while passing, their minds should at length be set to rights by genuine truth.

– Thomas Jefferson
Private Letters

17
The President is Enraged

Burr's freedom stunned the prosecution and enraged the president. Figuratively speaking, Jefferson's red hair stood on end. By fast courier he was advised of the escape of the accused. Angrily he wrote to James Bowdoin:

> *Hitherto we have believed our law to be. . . . that suspicion on probable grounds was sufficient to commit a person for trial. But the judges have decided that the conclusive evidence must be ready the moment of arrest, or they will discharge the malefactor. If this is still insisted on, Burr will be discharged; because his crimes have been sown from Maine, through the whole western states to New Orleans;*

we cannot bring witnesses under four months. The fact is, the federalists make Burr's cause their own, and exert their whole influence to shield him from punishment, as did the adherents of Miranda. And it is unfortunate that federalism is still predominate in our judiciary department, which is consequently in opposition to the legislative and executive branches, and is able to baffle their measures often.

Unfortunately, the learned Jefferson permitted his political prejudices to influence his judgment. He knew suspicion of a crime had never been sufficient to hold a prisoner after a preliminary hearing. His sophistry was the instrument of tyrants before the advent of the English common law. No one was better aware of this than the president. But it appears in the light of this fact, and other damaging statements emanating from his pen, that while he was a clever theorist, at times he was an unmitigated prevaricator.

What humiliation do we, who have worshipped at the throne of his democratic preachments, suffer! We shed tears of remorse at his unmasking! We witness democracy encompassed by envy and engulfed by political treachery. Strangely, on Jefferson's desk we witness the unveiling of Hamilton's bust! Politics does make strange bedfellows. Together here dwelt the two who pretended to hate each other. They were united in a common cause and motivated by a common ambition—to crucify Aaron Burr!

Regardless of a lack of evidence, since the chief justice had declined to hold Burr on a charge of treason, the judiciary in general, and Marshall in particular, must be made to feel the power of the president. This great preacher of democracy was revealing his true colors as a tyrant of autocracy. It was April 20 that Jefferson resumed his writings for the benefit of the public, whom he had completely deceived concerning Burr's guilt; and this notwithstanding, he had failed to produce any evidence to support his charges. He wrote:

That there should be anxiety and doubt in the public mind in the present defective state of proof is not wonderful; and this has been sedulously encouraged by the tricks of the judges to force the trial before it is possible to collect the evidence. All this, however, will work well. The nation will judge both the offender and the judges for themselves. If a member of the executive or legislative does wrong, the day is not far distant when the people will remove him. They will see then that one of the great coordinate branches of government, setting itself in opposition to the other two, and to the common sense of the nation, proclaims immunity to that class of offenders which endeavor to overturn the Constitution, and are themselves protected by the Constitution; for impeachment is a farce which will not be tried again. If their protection of Burr produces this amendment, it will do more good than his condemnation would have done.

Against Burr, personally, I have never had one hostile sentiment. I never indeed thought him an honest frank-dealing man, but considered him as a crooked gun, or another perverted machine, whose aim or shot you could never be sure of. Still, while he possessed the confidence of the nation, I thought it my duty to respect him in their confidence and treat him as if he deserved it; and if his punishment can be commuted now for the useful amendment to the Constitution, I shall rejoice in it.

While the president was fuming over Burr's having had the charges reduced to misdemeanor, the latter was calmly deliberating over his initial victory. He was not underestimating Jefferson's malignant hatred toward him. But Theodosia was not the stoic her father was; she was profoundly disturbed by his persecution. Burr reproved her as follows:

CHAPTER 17 • THE PRESIDENT IS ENRAGED

Your letters of the 10, and the preceding seem to indicate a sort of stupor; now you rise to a frenzy. Another ten days will, it is to be hoped, have brought you back to reason. You have read to little purpose if you have not remarked that such things happen in all democratic governments. Was there in Greece or Rome a man of virtue and independence, and supposed to possess great talents, who was not the object of vindictive and unrelenting persecution?

Hay wrote his Chief in Washington:

Burr lies utterly dormant. I do not understand that he pays any visits, and I believe he receives very few. The disposition manifested by the enemies of the administration to patronize him, and raise a clamor, seems to have gone off.

From the amount of work Burr did, he was far from dormant. He briefed the law of treason, mapped his case for any contingency, and left a record for defense against unsupported charges of treason that is unsurpassed in legal history. He associated with the leading families of Richmond. Virginia's social world gathered about in the friendliest manner. No one acted as though he were charged with the most heinous crime on the calendar. There were occasions when he was lionized as if he were still vice president and as if he were likely to become president. This, too, at the capital of the state that was always dominated by the Virginia legion, of which Jefferson was chief.

Nor was the prosecution asleep. Witnesses were summoned from Richmond to Boston, from New York to New Orleans, and a hand-picked grand jury was being selected. Concerning this, Colonel Burr wrote to Theodosia:

It is composed of twenty Democrats and four Federalists. Among the former is W. C. Nicholas, my vindictive and avowed personal enemy—the most so that could be found in this state. The most indefatigable industry is being used by the agents of the government, and they have money to command without stint. I could not only foil the prosecutors, but render them ridiculous and infamous, if I possessed the same means. The democrat papers teem with abuse against me and my counsel, and even against the Chief Justice. Nothing is left undone or unsaid which can prejudice the public mind, and produce a conviction without evidence.

When Richmond witnessed the resumption of the Burr trial on May 22, 1807, its population of five thousand suddenly doubled. There were frontiersmen from Louisiana, Mississippi, and Ohio territories and from the sixteen states of the Union. It was a motley array consisting of mountaineers from Kentucky and Tennessee, planters from the South, and many residents from every section of Virginia, the Carolinas, New York, Philadelphia, and even far-away Boston.

A hush spread over the great hall of the House of Delegates as John Marshall stepped to his desk. The clock on the wall revealed that it was post noon. It was a hot and excited throng that sought a vantage point from which to view the two chief actors—John Marshall in the seat of the mighty, and Aaron Burr, as prisoner at the bar.

Posterity is indebted to Winfield Scott, later hero of the Mexican War, for this word portrait:

Clad in black silk, elegant, distinguished, slim, eyes blackly brilliant, hair brushed neatly back and tied in fashionable powdered queue, speaking in even tones whose least syllable penetrated the stir and bustle of the courtroom, Aaron Burr was a figure to impress the rudest. On the bench next to the tall, loose-jointed Chief Justice sat an Associate Justice for that cir-

cuit, one Cyrus Griffin, conceived in anonymity and dedicated throughout the long proceedings to silences more utter than the frozen Antarctica.

No arguments were addressed to him by the opposing counsel; there is no sign of his presence in the two volumes of record except for a few faint words, modest in tone and thought, followed by a quick relapse into the caverns of discreet darkness. One wonders at his thoughts as he sat, day after day, a lay figure, while his towering colleague delivered path-finding opinions and the "oratorial thunder burst about him."

After John Randolph had demanded in the House evidence to support the president's statement that "Aaron Burr is the principal actor in a plot to disrupt the Union," the chief executive proclaimed that "suspicion on probable grounds was sufficient to commit a person for trial!"

Senator William Branch Giles, Jefferson's whip in the U.S. Senate, was selected as a member of the grand jury at the behest of the president, to whom Giles wrote that he bestir himself, for any lack of evidence would "implicate the character of the administration." Throughout the trial of Aaron Burr his life was subservient to the prestige of Thomas Jefferson. Members of that handpicked grand jury thoroughly understood that they were selected to serve the president rather than pass upon the innocence or guilt of the accused. The president had failed in an attempt to secure a writ of habeas corpus, only to have James Wilkinson fail to capture Burr and remove him by a military trail. Both were in desperate circumstances. The life of Burr was only a political pawn in the hands of James Wilkinson and Thomas Jefferson.

As the chief witness before the grand jury James Wilkinson came directly from the scene of his attempt to kidnap Burr, where seven men as his agents were promised five thousand dollars if they were successful, and who, despite being strongly supported by a federal judge and governor, had failed. Burr's escape from that political trap completely upset the plans of the Jefferson–Wilkinson alliance.

The Mammoth of iniquity escaped—not that any man pre-
tended to think him innocent ... Wilkinson is the only man I ever
saw who was from the bark to the very core a villain. .... [T]his
man stands on the very summit and pinnacle of executive favor.

– John Randolph
Foreman of the Grand Jury

18
The Handpicked Grand Jury

John Marshall delivered on April 1, 1897, the second of his series of opinions that have established the judicial highway of what constitutes traitorous action under the Constitution. The construction is both learned and legal. It is also far more humane than under the old English law.

"The hand of malignity may grasp an individual against whom its hate may be directed," but, perceiving that this had aroused the partisans of Jefferson, he endeavored to pacify their anger by calling attention to the fact that this was a quotation from Blackstone, with only an elucidation—"Treason is the only crime specifically defined in the Constitution; all others are left to Congress."

The chief justice further observed:

As this is the most atrocious offense which can be committed against the political body, so it is the charge which is most capable of being employed as the instrument of those malignant and vindictive passions which may rage in the bosoms of contending parties struggling for power.

After analyzing the affidavits of Eaton and Wilkinson, the court inquired:

Where is the evidence that Burr assembled an army to levy war on the United States? It is not before the Court. Why? The fact to be proved is one of public notoriety. The Supreme Court has declared the necessity of proving the fact, if it exists. If the troops had been assembled by Burr five months previous, it would be easy for the Government to secure the evidence and procure affidavits.

The grand jury was soon adjourned, and this was continued from day to day, as the star witness, General Wilkinson, had not arrived from New Orleans. On May 25 Hay moved to commit Burr for treason on the ground of new evidence. Burr's attorneys protested it had been previously agreed that this would not be done without notice; besides, this would compel the court to usurp the functions of the grand jury, now in session.

In an endeavor to excuse his failure to observe the agreement regarding giving notice about further commiting Burr, Hay said Wilkinson was soon to arrive "and I do not pretend to say what effect it might produce on the mind of Colonel Burr; but, certainly Colonel Burr would be able to effect his escape, merely upon paying the recognizance of his present bail."

Benjamin Botts inquired if he were trying the case in court or in the public press with a view of further poisoning the public mind. Burr reminded the prosecution that they had had six months in which to prepare for trial; now, by constant adjournments, they were admitting inability to go before the grand jury. Then, with much feeling, the colonel declared that when a democratic government "had aped the despotism of European autocracy, shanghaied his friends, robbed the post offices and utilized the functions of the courts, with the president of the United States shouting war, it was about time they had located this mythical creation of Wilkinson's imagination."

Thus was repeated over and over by Burr and his counsel the illegality of Jefferson's acts and those of this agents, until the prosecution began to question whether it were Burr, Wilkinson, or the president who was really on trial—for now the public was being acquainted with some phases of the malignancy of the prosecution of which it had little dreamed.

Finally, on May 26 Marshall overruled Burr's objections, declaring such motion was in proper form and could be used instead of presenting bills for indictment to the grand jury. Hay demanded Burr post additional bail, which Burr refused to do.

Additional instructions from Jefferson to Hay were:

> *It becomes our duty to provide that full testimony of the proceedings be laid before the legislature, and through them to the public. For this purpose, it is necessary that we be furnished with the testimony of every person, who shall be with you as a witness. If the Grand Jury find a bill, the evidence given in court, taken as verbatim as possible, will be what we desire. If there be no bill, and consequently no examination before court, then I must beseech you to have every man privately examined by way of affidavit, and to furnish me with the whole testimony. . . . Go to any expense necessary for the purpose, and meet it with the funds provided by the Attorney General for other expenses.*

In support of his motion to commit for treason, Hay produced his witnesses and announced that he would place them on the stand and read the depositions of the absent in chronological order. But Wickham insisted that a strict legal order must be followed, and that first, the overt act itself must be proved, and then Burr's complicity therein. Hay was blocked, so he outlined a great plot involving both treason to the United States and an attack on Spain, and demanded a free hand. Burr was in no mood to grant favors. Since he was on trial for his life, he could see no reason for so-called "courtesies."

Marshall ruled that the prosecution be permitted certain latitude in the introduction of its testimony, and immediately Hay offered Wilkinson's affidavit. Botts objected and insisted that the overt act be first proved, and that it be established that there had been war in Virginia, the site of the alleged treason. Referring again to the decision in the Bollman and Swartwout case, Botts insisted that evidence be offered that there had been a war before treason could possibly have been committed. Again he quoted, "In this country, as there cannot be a constructive treasonable war, plans and acts of associates can only come in when the former have executed and the latter have been visibly and publicly assisted."

After the defense had insisted that without an overt act no constructive treason could possibly exist, Marshall asked Hay why he had produced Wilkinson's affidavit when the Supreme Court had ruled that it contained no proof of the overt act.

In a desperate effort to prove that war had been waged on Blennerhassett Island, Hay called his witnesses. Peter Taylor, the gardener, told of his journey to warn Burr of impending mobs, of Blennerhassett's confused, rambling talk, of the assemblage of armed men on the island that fateful night of December 10 when Blennerhassett fled. Jacob Albright, a day laborer, unfolded his story of the leveled muskets at the breast of Tupper. Both admitted that Burr had not been on the island during these alleged acts of war against the United States.

Hay attempted to present an affidavit of Jacob Dunbaugh, a Fort Massac sergeant whom Captain Bissell had given a furlough that he might accompany Burr. It developed that Dunbaugh had been posted as a deserter, and to avoid the penalty, and at Wilkinson's suggestion, he signed this affidavit. This was the kind of evidence that was drummed up by Wilkinson in an endeavor to convict Burr. It purported to prove that there was a hasty deposit of warlike material, together with a large stand of arms in the Mississippi River just prior to the search of Burr's flotilla. Marshall supported a motion of the defense to the introduction of this affidavit.

Hay announced that until Wilkinson arrived he would have no further evidence to submit; then he demanded that Burr's bail be increased. To this Luther Martin replied, "The motion of the gentleman amounts to this: 'We have no evidence of treason, and are not ready to go to trial for the purpose of proving it; we therefore move the court to increase the bail.'"

To await the arrival of the chief witness, General Wilkinson, the court took another adjournment. Wilkinson was always coming in a few days, but it began to look as though he would never appear. His appearance in court was the chief topic of conversation. It was wagered that his arrival would so frighten Burr that he would abscond, but quite a different picture was painted by Washington Irving, then a youthful correspondent to the *New York Morning Chronicle*, which was published by his brother, Dr. Peter Irving (and which Burr had godfathered):

> We are enjoying a kind of suspension of hostilities; the grand jury having been dismissed the day before yesterday for five or six days, that they may go home, see their wives, get their clothes washed, and flog the negroes. [As for Burr,] he retains his serenity and self possession unshaken, and wears the same aspect in all times and situations.

Great crowds of witnesses loitered about town at government expense and by the orders of the president. At the beginning of the trial no one appeared who dared to express an opinion favorable to Burr. Now an occasional Burr exponent was heard. Chief among these was Andrew Jackson, who was convinced of Burr's innocence. He was equally positive that Jefferson was a demon bent only on Burr's persecution—determined to remove Burr from his political pathway. As for Wilkinson, Jackson said he was a "Pensioner of Spain," and of this, Jackson asserted, Jefferson was fully aware: "He is hiding that scoundrel beneath his official petticoat." As the trial proceeded, General Jackson grew more vociferous and outspoken. It was his practice to gather a crowd in the capitol grounds, even in front of the courtroom, where he proceeded to defend Burr and condemn Jefferson. Thus was passed the month of June while awaiting the arrival of Wilkinson.

While, however, the court and its witnesses awaited the arrival of Wilkinson, Burr was busily engaged in the preparation of his case. Like Napoleon in stature, Burr was a bundle of energy that was undaunted and unafraid, and regardless of the number times that he was charged with crime, accused, and tried, he was never afraid, never convicted. But he was never too busy to write to his beloved Theodosia: "From night to morning there are daily a thousand amusing incidents; things at which you will laugh, also things at which you will pout and scold."

But Burr did more than write to Theodosia and block the plans of the prosecution. When court convened June 9, in his suave, courteous manner he addressed the chief justice, who, it appeared, was a trifle weary of a multitude of technical objections. Very quietly Burr called the court's attention to Jefferson's message to Congress in which the president had spoken of a certain letter and certain other documents, all dated October 21,1806, that he had received from General Wilkinson.

During the recess of the session of the court Colonel Burr had slipped off to Washington, where he had applied to Robert Smith, secretary of the Navy, for these papers, only to be refused.

Now it had become necessary for the preparation of a proper defense that several of these documents be made available to him, and he therefore requested the honorable court to issue a subpoena *duces tecum* to the president of the United States to produce these papers in open court, unless—here he bowed with unusual courtesy to the opposing counsel—they would consent to submit them to the inspection of the defense.

Nonplussed, Hay stammered that if the court thought it material, he would endeavor to obtain such papers as might be material. Marshall returned the inquiry and asked Hay how he was to pass upon their relevancy when they were not before him.

Angered by this question, Hay replied that the court had no power to compel the president to attend by means of a subpoena. Marshall, too, was in a state of doubt as to bringing the chief executive of the nation before the bar, yet he would listen to the arguments. Court was adjourned, and Hay proceeded to write an impassioned plea to Jefferson to forward the papers lest this afford Burr a pretext for clamor.

During one of these intermissions, while awaiting the arrival of Wilkinson, as a matter of social relaxation John Wickham gave a dinner to which he invited Marshall and Burr. Wickham was a commanding social figure in Richmond; he was one of the distinguished lawyers of the South. Wickham and Marshall were intimate friends. The dinner was an expression of social courtesy. The food was as delicious as the wines and juleps were famous. Wit and wisdom flowed as freely as old vintages. Southern conviviality and hospitality abounded—save in the minds of the uninvited—Hay, Eaton, and Jefferson. To them it was conduct "grossly indecent, wanton insult; or, was it charity, hypocrisy or federalism?"

The personnel of the Wickham party was in great contrast to the multitude the president had corralled at government expense. Some of these were mountaineers arrayed in coonskin caps, woolen shirts, and homespun trousers, others wore deerskin coats and leggings; all were motivated by a common purpose—to crucify what to them was a false political leader.

When the arguments concerning the special papers Burr had asked for were resumed June 10, hot tempers outran the thermometers. Hay raised the question as to whether Burr had any standing in court. This was a proceeding to commit and not a trial after indictment; therefore, he was not entitled to any legal process.

Luther Martin replied:

> We applied for copies and were refused under presidential influence. In New York on the farcical trials of Ogden and Smith the officers of the government screened themselves from attending, under the sanction of the president's name. Perhaps the same farce may be repeated here.

Turning to the chief justice, Martin continued:

> This is a peculiar case, Sir. The President has undertaken to prejudice my client by declaring that "Of his guilt there can be no doubt" He has assumed to himself the knowledge of the Supreme Being. . . . He has proclaimed him a traitor in the face of that country, which has rewarded him. He has let slip the dogs of war, the hell-hounds of persecution, to hunt down my friend. And would this President of the United States, who has raised all this absurd clamor, pretend to keep back the papers which are wanted for this trial, where life itself is at stake? . . . Can it then be presumed that the president would be sorry to have the colonel Burr's innocence proved?

The courtroom reverberated with Martin's thundering voice. His normally red face darkened as he directed his attack against the sacrosanct person who as president would stoop to any depth to punish but would not allow the prisoner at the bar the protection that the Constitution had guaranteed. The spectators were amazed at what they heard. They had come expecting the greatest drama of a lifetime, but its presentation was surpassing expectations.

Martin's picture of the president stunned everyone, even the prosecution. In an endeavor to protect him and prevent his appearance before the court, prosecution counselor Alexander MacRea stammered and foundered about. He admitted that as a private individual Jefferson might be forced to respond to the subpoena as anyone else, but as the president of the United States, that was quite another matter, and as for these papers, these were "confidential communications." This amazing roar of forensic debate continued for three days; then on June 13 Hay came to court with a reply from Jefferson. He said that he was:

> *Reserving the necessary right of the president of the United States to decide, independently of all other authority, what papers, coming to him as President, the public interests permit to be communicated, and to whom, I assure you of my readiness under that restriction, voluntarily to furnish on all occasions, whatever the purpose of justice may require.*

Having hedged himself against judicial compulsion, the president authorized the production by Hay of Wilkinson's letter of October 21—but he would withhold those parts that were not material. And as for the Army and Navy orders, these should be specified by proper description.

On June 13 the court rendered a decision concerning its judicial power to compel the president to attend by means of a subpoena *duces tecum*, directed against the chief executive. The decision was comprehensive. Marshall said the point at issue was "Whether a subpoena *duces tecum* can be directed against the president of the United States, and whether it ought to be directed in this case."

The chief justice could not find in either the Constitution or the statutes any exception whatever to the right of the accused to compulsory process. However, there was the "The single reservation of the King," but there are many points of difference between the president and a king. Of these he mentioned two: "The King can do no wrong—that no blame can be attached to him; that he cannot be named in debate."

Apparently in the mind of chief justice there were other points of difference between the president of the United States and the king of England. An example of that difference was revealed when the great democrat, Thomas Jefferson, sought office—the authority he now would sacredly guard from tarnishment; still, it must be that he was subject to judicial authority. Therefore he directed the duces tecum against the president.

The prosecution was dumbfounded. Hay wrote the president, "There was never such a trial from the beginning of the world to this day." But Hay's spirits revived when the chief justice apologized for having said that the government "expected" Burr's conviction. While the truth, everyone was surprised when the cautious chief justice, John Marshall, had inadvertently confessed judgment for the prosecution.

The uncontrolled temper of Thomas Jefferson often led him into trouble. The habit of committing to paper his mental reactions while angered, especially his contempt for his adversaries, reveals a mental weakness not to be expected in the Sage of Monticello. Upon receipt of Marshall's decision, Jefferson wrote, "Luther Martin is an unprincipled and impudent federal bulldog." Then he inquired of Hay, "Shall we move to commit Luther Martin as particeps crimini with Burr or just summon him as a witness?"

How fortunate for Thomas Jefferson that the Constitution and the power of the chief executive prevented evidence of the Jefferson–Wilkinson co-conspiracy against Aaron Burr from being presented to the people as well as to John Marshall!

When Dr. Erich Justice Bollman arrived in Washington from New Orleans as a prisoner of Wilkinson's martial law, he was called before the president and James Madison, secretary of state, who emphasized that he could be of service to his country by revealing what he knew about Burr's activities in New Orleans. After being assured that any statement he made would be held in strict confidence and not thereafter divulged, Bollman talked freely.

The moment he was seated in the witness chair at Richmond, Bollman was confronted by what he had said, and by Mr. Hay's written instructions: "If Bollman should prevaricate, ask him whether or not he did not say so and so to Mr. Madison and myself."

Supplementing this, the president enclosed a sheath of blank pardons that he instructed Hay to fill at his discretion and to "distribute among the petty offenders, and even the gross offenders should ever be visible that the principal will otherwise escape."

Much to the surprise of Hay, when Bollman came to the witness chair he declined a proffered pardon. This followed a heated argument concerning the admissibility of his testimony. Now he refused to testify on the ground that his testimony might incriminate himself. But Hay's embarrassment was relieved by the arrival of General Wilkinson.

"The bets were against Burr that he would abscond should Wilkinson come to Richmond," wrote Washington Irving, "but he still maintains his ground and still enters the court every morning with the same serene placid air that he would show were he brought here to plead anther man's cause."

When the chief witness confronted the grand jury on June 15, objection was made to his taking to the stand any papers, even to refresh his memory, unless the court had first passed on their evidential pertinence. After tedious arguments and many citations of law, Marshall permitted the jury to inspect only such papers as represented an integral part of Wilkinson's story and which had been written by himself.

The pompous Wilkinson in resplendent uniform appeared bewildered, even flustered. He had expected Burr to be cowering, a trembling wretch, overwhelmed by conviction and awed by his presence. The tables were turned, and in this dilemma he wrote to Jefferson:

I was not aware of the importance attached to my presence, for I had anticipated a deluge of testimony would have poured forth from all quarters to overwhelm Burr with guilt and dishonor. Sadly, indeed I was mistaken, and to my astonishment I found the traitor vindicated, and myself condemned by a mass of wealth, character, influence and talents—Merciful God, what a spectacle did I behold—integrity and truth perverted and trampled under foot by turpitude and guilt, patriotism appalled and usurpation triumphant. Did I ever expect it would depend upon my humble self to stop the current of that polluted stream. Never, never.

What a pity the grand jury did not see Wilkinson's letter! But let Jefferson's propagandist continue:

In spite of myself my eyes darted a flash of indignation at the little traitor, on whom they continued fixed until I was called to the Book;—here, sir, I found my expectations verified—this lionhearted, eagle-eyed Hero, jerking under the weight of conscious guilt, with haggard eyes, in an effort to meet the indignant salutation of outraged honor; but it was in vain, his audacity failed him. His averted face grew pale, and effected passion to conceal his perturbation.

Fortunately Washington Irving witnessed this dramatic scene, of which he painted quite a different picture:

Wilkinson strutted into court . . . stood for a moment swelling like a turkey cock. But Burr did not so much as glance his way until the Chief Justice directed the clerk to swear him in; at the mention of the name Burr turned his head, looked him full in the face with one of his piercing regards, swept his eyes over his whole person from head to foot, as if to scan its dimensions, and then coolly resumed his former position, and went on conversing with his counsel as tranquilly as ever. The whole look was over in an instant; but it was an admirable one. There was no apparent study or constraint in it; no affectation of disdain or defiance; a slight expression of contempt played over his countenance. . . . Wilkinson is now before the Grand Jury with his mighty mass of words to deliver himself of, that he claims at least two days more to discharge the wondrous cargo.

Concerning the cipher letter which Wilkinson presented to the grand jury, John Randolph examined him over and over, and much to the general's embarrassment. Randolph succeeded in placing responsibility for the weird, fantastic tale of Burr's alleged acts of treason on the general, who admitted that he had made certain erasures, had altered and changed phrases that they might better implicate Burr. By both words and action Wilkinson impressed and convinced the jury of his villainy. He escaped indictment only by a vote of seven to nine and then as a result of the influence of the president. This was exerted through a Republican lawyer who was a member of the grand jury. Of Wilkinson before the grand jury John Randolph wrote:

The mammoth of iniquity escaped, not that any man pretended to think him innocent, but upon certain wire-drawn distinctions that I will not pester you with. Wilkinson is the only man I ever saw who was from the bark to the very core a villain. . . . Perhaps you never saw a human nature in so degraded a situation as in the person of Wilkinson before the Grand Jury, and yet this man stands on the very summit and pinnacle of executive favor.

The methods used in the selection of the grand jury give some idea of the quality of justice contemplated. Senator William Branch Giles, as political representative of the president, had advocated the suspension of the writ of *habeas corpus*, which, to Burr's way of thinking, could be done only if he supposed "that there was rebellion or insurrection, and a public danger of no uncommon kind."

Giles admitted that he had acted and spoken as Burr charged; but he insisted that he held no "personal resentments against the accused," and assured that he could act fairly as a juror, but offered to withdraw. Marshall observed, "If the gentleman has made up his mind and declared his mind, it would be best for him to withdraw."

Colonel Wilson Cary Nicholas, with considerable vehemence, demanded to know the objections to him. Burr replied that Nicholas "entertained a bitter personal animosity; however, further inquiry will be unnecessary if he retires, as Mr. Giles did."

The "animosity" had existed for years; and was well understood by all public men. He had been very much excited over Burr's Western journey. Besides, while endeavoring to get on the grand jury, Nicholas was a candidate for Congress. He knew that Jefferson's propaganda had convinced the public that Burr was a traitor; he had just received a letter from the president "beseeching" him to return to the Congress and promising him the Republican leadership of the House if he would do so. The letter also demanded Burr's conviction. Thus Nicholas was attempting to get on this jury that he might serve the president by assisting him in hanging Burr.

Another strange, incongruous situation: the president's son-in-law, Thomas Mann Randolph, had announced his retirement from the position Nicholas sought, because Nicholas would be in a better position to promote the policies of the president. It was another of the political duplicities Mr. Jefferson employed in his attempt to do legally what he did not desire to be held personally responsible for—Burr's murder!

Should the facts be less frankly told? What a picture of the immortal Jefferson, author of the Declaration of Independence, father of the Bill of Rights, founder of the University of Virginia and the greatest intellect to occupy the presidency until Woodrow Wilson!

Our most comprehensive biography of John Marshall is by Albert J. Beveridge, who wrote this thumbnail sketch of Thomas Jefferson:

> *From the moment he received the news of Marshall's decision to hold Burr for misdemeanor and accept bail upon that charge, the prosecution of this former associate became Jefferson's ruling thought and purpose. . . . Champion of equal rights for all men, yet any opposition to his personal or political interests appear to madden him. A personal antagonism, once formed, became to Thomas Jefferson a public policy.*

Two days after Marshall admitted Burr to bail, Jefferson wrote, "the Federalists make Burr's cause their own, and exert their whole influence to shield him." This came after the president had announced, "[we] will satisfy the world, if not the judges, of Burr's guilt."

One of the strangest revelations of history is the fact that while Jefferson never possessed evidence to prove his charges, he did so completely "satisfy the world" that after more than a century, fully ninety-nine out of every hundred persons think of Aaron Burr as a "traitor."

In research of the archives of the United States, England, France, and Spain that has covered a period of more than fifty years, no evidence tending to establish Jefferson's charge has been found. On the contrary, the evidence clearly establishes the fact that the charge was political—just an attempt by Jefferson to destroy the usefulness of Aaron Burr, to restrain Burr from interfering with the political ambitions of Thomas Jefferson. The baneful lust for power destroys every sense of justice.

No one understood this quite so well as John Marshall; he had before him evidence to this effect when he wrote into his decision:

> *As this is the most atrocious offense which can be committed against the political body, so it is the charge which is most capable of being employed as the instrument of those malignant and vindictive passions which may rage in the bosoms of contending parties struggling for power.*

Partisans on both sides found their fevers mounting daily. Public sentiment was fast veering in favor of Burr. Wilkinson had been a disappointment to the prosecution; he had enraged the defense, and had added materially to the number of partisans for Burr. Friends of Burr gathered about him boldly and declared that the trial had been purely political—an attempt to restore the waning prestige of the president. The guards who now accompanied Burr to and from the court each day were his friends. These had multiplied in number until the triumphal procession reached two hundred. They were self-appointed and breathed defiance at the government.

Samuel Swartwout met General Wilkinson on the street and deliberately shoved him off the sidewalk into the mud. Wilkinson escaped amid jeers. Wilkinson swallowed the insult; whereupon Swartwout published in the *Richmond Examiner* that he was "a traitor, a forger, a perjurer and a coward," all of which he ignored. Andrew Jackson "went wild with delight" and continued to proclaim to the crowds that gathered to hear him address them within hearing of the trial and on the court grounds that Wilkinson was obsessed of "craven villainy" and that Burr was innocent of Jefferson's charges.

We of the Jury say that Aaron Burr is not proved to be guilty under this indictment by any evidence submitted to us. We therefore find him not guilty.

– Report of the Petit Jury

19
Final Endeavor to Stain

The clerk had just read the list of the grand jury when Burr arose to address the court. Clad in black silk, hair powdered and queue tied in fastidious fashion, with extreme pallor of face contrasting his lustrous brown eyes, he presented a picture of elegance and a voice of charm that at once surprised and compelled attention. Burr spoke with such "impressive distinctness" that some of his auditors fifty years later proudly repeated his sentences. He inquired if any of the panel had been struck off and others substituted. It developed that this had been done; not, however, until the prosecution had turned loose "a torrent of abuse and prejudice such as was never excited against any man before a court of justice."

Colonel Burr had entered the room on the arm of his son-in-law, Joseph Alston, who was later to become the governor of South Carolina.

For a time Burr had been held in the penitentiary, but now he was under guard in the home of Luther Martin awaiting the pleasure of the prosecution. The more Richmond saw of Eaton, Wilkinson, Albright, et alia, the more its intelligence was insulted until its good people began to inquire if, after all, this were a prosecution for crime or persecution for political purposes!

It was the third of August 1807 that Burr's trial began before John Marshall, who was one of the twenty-six judges with whom John Adams had packed the federal courts. As chief justice, and because of his independence, Marshall had become the object of Jefferson's venom. John Marshall served as chief justice for a longer term of years than any of his successors. Only his bravery, intelligence, and sense of justice saved Aaron Burr from the malignant hatred of Thomas Jefferson. Only truth and time will reveal the Jefferson–Burr–Marshall political conspiracy in its true light.

At the side of John Marshall during the trial sat Judge Cyrus Griffin, who had nothing whatever to say. Before the trial was over the president resented his lack of service and protested that Griffin had failed to take issue with the chief justice on some of his rulings. But even the president's criticism failed to rouse the silent judge.

Eventually when twelve men had filled the jury box, all but two admitted that they were strongly convinced of Burr's guilt, and that their opinions were formed from the depositions of Eaton and Wilkinson, newspaper stories, and the president's proclamation and his propaganda.

After much time had been spent in examining the panel, Marshall enunciated the rule of procedure that "any deliberate opinion was sufficient cause to disqualify from duty; but light impressions that might yield to evidence would not be grounds for rejection." With this ruling to guide the inquisition, all the jurors who had been temporarily suspended were rejected for cause.

In anger Hay moved for a panel of from one hundred fifty to five hundred, and for once talked about expense. Burr replied that better results would be achieved if the court instructions were followed, to which Wickham added "that the first panel had contained too many members of Assembly and candidates for public office."

A second panel appeared on August 15. In the interim Hay wrote to the president that "The bias of Judge Marshall is so obvious as if it were stamped in his forehead. I may do him injustice, but I do not believe that I am, when I say he is endeavoring to work himself up to a state of firmness which will enable him to aid Burr throughout the trial without appearing to be conscious of doing wrong."

After it was apparent to everyone that a jury could not be found that had not made up its mind of Burr's guilt, Burr proposed that if he be allowed to select eight men out of the panel, he would permit them to be sworn in regardless of their opinions of himself. Hay was suspicious, but as he could find no objections to so fair and unusual procedure, he finally agreed to the proposition. Burr selected men at random; he even permitted Miles Bott to remain after he had said, "Colonel Burr ought to be hanged."

On the face of it the decision was a victory for the prosecution, but, as it proved eventually, was a factor in saving Burr's life.

When Eaton returned to the stand, he readily admitted, "Concerning any overt act which goes to prove Aaron Burr guilty of treason, I know nothing," but with Burr's treasonable intentions he claimed to be familiar. Under the ruling of the court he omitted his weird assassination story. Under cross-examination he admitted that the government had just paid him ten thousand dollars for an old rejected claim. His peacock parade from the stage excited little interest. For months he had frequented the saloons where he had spent much of his new wealth and where under the influence of liquor he had destroyed his effectiveness as a witness by his loose, rambling harangues.

Thomas Truxton was the second witness questioned by Hay. He related alleged conversations between himself and Burr concerning the conquest of Mexico, but insisted that this was contemplated only if, and when, the United States declared war against Spain. In his cross-examination Truxton said, "We were very intimate; there seemed no reserve on Burr's part, but I never heard him speak of a division of the Union."

MacRae asked, "Did he wish to fill your mind with resentment against the government?"

Truxton replied, "I was pretty full of it myself, and he joined me in opinion."

Peter Taylor, the gardener, returned to the stage to tell about warning Burr of Blennerhassett's wild talk and about the men on the island, some with guns, whether muskets or rifles he did not know; that they possessed powder and lead; that Burr, however, was not present on the island during the assemblage of men or during the flight. Thus during the first day was produced no evidence of treason; rather that Burr had not been present and did not have any part in the events.

Thus ended the prosecution's tale of terror, tragedy, and treason with which the country had been regaled for a year. Then the court heard the arguments of the defense for arrest of further testimony and in support of Burr's motion.

John Wickham made the opening address for the defense in support of the motion. He clothed his arguments with a wealth of well-reasoned logic, dressed in brilliant phraseology, built on a foundation of learned legal citations and flavored with wit. Littleton W. Tazwell, a member of the grand jury and a lawyer of some note, said, "It was the greatest forensic effort of the American bar."

Wickham argued that no person could be convicted of treason who was not personally present at the commission of the act charged. He admitted that there was an ancient English doctrine of constructive treason where the overt act of associates could be imputed to another, no matter how far distant from the scene, but in a profound argument he tore to shreds that doctrine, citing case after case and giving to each careful analysis. He pointed out obvious errors of the courts and explained the unsound reasoning that had led to such erroneous deductions. He stated that barbarous prejudices had been added to legal misconceptions to justify tyrannical and despotic acts.

It was to escape prejudice and unjust punishment that the colonists had fled to America. Was not the Constitution adopted to guarantee new rights for the individual? It is a new document, original in concept, and must be judged *per se* for the plain intent of the words employed. He argued that there was no common law in the United States derived from England, but a common law of the several states. Our Constitution created the offense of treason, and by exact wording limited the scope of the offense; overt acts of another cannot be ascribed to an accused when it is evident he could not be a party to the deed.

Burr was charged with the overt act while it was implied that it had been committed by others; thus the indictment was drawn in a defective fashion and should be dismissed. So far as being an accessory was concerned, Burr could not be convicted on this score until the principals had been found guilty; the whole proceeding, therefore, was premature. And finally, the facts had disclosed that there was no criminal assemblage on Blennerhassett Island, as charged, but only a peaceable assembling of citizens with such guns as were commonly carried in any Western country and all indispensable equipment of every man. There was no evidence of a military plot anywhere.

Marshall stopped Wickham to inquire if there were any reported cases in which it was shown that the presiding judge had the right to decide whether or not the evidence submitted to the jury was not proof of an overt act. Wickham replied that such right was inherent, that the jury might find the truth of the facts, but the judge must decide as a matter of law whether such facts so found constituted in law an overt act. This is the doctrine on which our courts have since predicated their decisions. It was founded by John Marshall.

Wickham asserted that force is necessary to accompany any levying of war. Only Albright had testified to forcible resistance to Tupper. Even if this evidence were true, it was insufficient. The Constitution expressly provides that two witnesses to the overt act are necessary. If the prosecution was seeking evidence from a credible witness, "Why was not Tupper called?"

The prosecution knew the answer to that question, but the answer was safely locked up in a pigeonhole in Ohio. Furthermore, there was no evidence that Tupper had acted on a warrant of authority, since that could not be presumed to have been issued from his office, as he was from Ohio and the island was in Virginia; and in any event, resistance to a process is a crime but not the crime of treason.

Wickham consumed two days in the delivery of this argument. It fills sixty-five pages of the printed reports of the trial. He covered every precedent, exhausted every argument, touched every scrap of evidence. When he had finished, the prosecution showed signs of panic.

After Hay had received permission to submit further evidence, Israel Miller testified that there were thirty-two men in Tyler's party, five rifles, and three or four pistols, and on the island there was one blunderbuss, two pairs of pistols, and one fusee, but nothing more. Purley Howe said he delivered forty boat poles, and that two men carrying rifles had ferried over to the Ohio shore for them. This was all the evidence Hay could supply.

Edmund Randolph followed Wickham, but added little to what his predecessor had advanced. When he had finished, Hay asked for time in which to prepare properly to "answer the elaborate arguments of the counsel for the accused; which having occupied two days for delivery must have been prepared with infinite labor and industry." The defense objected to a lengthy postponement, after which Marshall gave them three days.

Alexander MacRae opened the argument for the government, pleading that the Constitutional provisions were neither new nor novel but were identical to the English statute governing the same offense; hence English precedents and English decisions must control the interpretation of the law. He said in England words have been held sufficient to convict traitors who were personally far from the scene of the act. Burr, he thundered, was the principal, not an accessory; hence was legally present at Blennerhassett Island the night of December 10, though perhaps not in corporeal body.

William Wirt relentlessly hammered home Marshall's words:

> *If a body of men be assembled for the purpose of effecting by force a treasonable purpose all those who perform any part, however minute, or however remote from the scene of action are to be considered as traitors. Burr is the principal in this atrocious crime and not a mere underling.*

The speaker pointed out that the Constitution made no distinction between the principal and the accessory; however, that distinction is recognized in the English common law, which the defense had attempted with much labor to prove inapplicable.

Apparently even Wirt was to recognize that the fine points of law were more difficult for him to comprehend and present to a jury than the frailties of human nature; abruptly he turned to Harman Blennerhassett, who had lost his home and fortune and his opportunity to enjoy these because he had listened to the glamorous tale of Burr, of courts, honors, and dreams of conquest. To the paradise that Blennerhassett had created on an island in the Ohio, Wirt directed the attention of his listeners, painting a picture of beauty and loveliness that has lingered in literature where, according to Wirt's theory, Burr was responsible for the blight. Some of Wirt's phrases are worth repeating:

> *A man of letters, who fled from the storms of his own country to find quiet in ours. . . . carried with him taste and science and wealth; and lo! the desert smiled. Possessing himself of a beautiful island in the Ohio, he rears himself a place and decorates it with*

every romantic embellishment of fancy, and to crown the enchantment of the scene, a wife who was said to be lovely even beyond her sex. In the midst of all this peace, this innocent simplicity and this tranquility, this feast of mind, this pure banquet of heart, the destroyer comes; he comes to change this paradise into hell.

To this flight of fancy this able creator of word paintings added, "Is this poor gentleman the principal and Burr only an accessory?"

If only facts had not destroyed this fancy and fiction; if Eaton and Wilkinson had but delivered evidence instead of fiction; and if Jefferson had been actuated by a desire for justice instead of vengeance, then Burr might have been convicted of treason, and have paid with his blood, which these three so ardently desired!

Wirt's speech was even longer than Wickham's sixty-five pages; it covers sixty-seven pages of the printed reports. Benjamin Botts followed Wirt, whose oratorical pageantry had entertained and impressed both jury and audience. In reply, Botts said:

I cannot promise you, sir, a speech manufactured out of tropes and figures, sportingsleeping Venuses with voluptuous limbs and wanton nakedness; on the contrary, I am compelled to plod heavily and meekly through the dull doctrines of Hale and Foster.

After the audience had recovered from that amusing thrust, Botts inquired how it could be possible on Blennerhassett, where "every witness, every officer approached, and even the agents of the Government admit, that with the possible exception of Blennerhassett and Tyler, all are ignorant of Burr's purposes," that "a treasonable assemblage where those involved meditated no war on United States and would have shrunk in horror from the very thought of it?"

Next Botts inquired why so heinous a crime was manufactured by the administration out of such fantastic dreams as Eaton and Wilkinson painted, unless it was an attempt to bolster up the waning prestige of the president? Botts closed by reminding the jury of the damning devices, frauds, and chicanery that had been employed to hang Burr. He, too, played to the gallery and on the heartstrings of the jury.

Hay closed the case by making a veiled attack on Marshall in which he referred to the case of Fries that had been heard before Justice Chase:

> For *which conduct, with other causes, he was afterwards impeached, the censure which the judge drew upon himself was not on account of his opinions, however incorrect they might be, but for his arbitrary and irregular conduct of the trial; which was one of the principal causes for which he was afterward impeached. He attempted to wrest the decision from the jury, and prejudge the case before hearing all the evidence in it; the identical thing which this court is now called upon by these gentlemen themselves to do.*

Charles Lee emphasized the attack on Marshall as an example of the disgraceful depths to which the prosecution would stoop in threatening his impeachment. Immediately Hay denied any such intention, and Marshall courteously accepted his apology. Notwithstanding all of which, no one could find any other reason for the threat nor any other grounds for attack.

Luther Martin's speech filled one hundred and eighteen pages. It was the longest and the most impassioned. His invective was cutting, his logic ponderous, his rhetoric exalted, his sarcasm withering, and his censure of the president abusive. Marshall's reasoning in the Bollman and Swartwout case was severely criticized, but pure motives were ascribed to his intentions. He, however, cautioned him that the clamor for Burr's life was bloodthirsty;

that these were manifestations of jealousy and not justice and had caused all this furor—this dastardly attempt to crucify Aaron Burr. His peroration was to the beautiful relation that had always characterized the lives of Theodosia and her father—a poem to the home.

The arguments finished, Marshall took two days to write his decision. It is the longest he ever delivered, at forty-seven pages. His compliments to the counsel are illuminating, particularly since the decision is based largely on the reasoning of the defense as presented by Wickham:

> A degree of eloquence seldom displayed on any occasion has embellished a solidity of argument and a depth of research by which the court has been greatly aided in forming the opinion it is about to deliver.

The pernicious doctrine of constructive treason was annihilated, until it held no place in American law and mores. He declared:

> The present indictment charges the prisoner with levying war against the United States, and alleges an overt act of levying war. That overt act must be proved, according to the mandates of the Constitution and the Act of Congress, by two witnesses. It is not proved by a single witness. The presence of the accused had been stated to be an essential component of the overt act in this indictment, unless the common law principle respecting accessories should render it unnecessary; and there is not only no witness who has proved his actual or legal presence, but the fact of his absence is not controverted.
> The counsel for the prosecution offer to give in evidence subsequent transactions at a different place and a different state, in order to prove—what? The overt act laid in the indictment? That the prisoner was one

of those assembled at Blennerhassett's Island? No, that is not alleged. It is well known that such testimony is not competent to establish such a fact. The Constitution and law require that the fact should be established by two witnesses; by establishment of other facts from which the jury might reason to this fact. This testimony, then, is not relevant. . . . The jury have now heard the opinion of the Court on the law of the case. They will apply the law to the facts, and will find a verdict of guilty or not guilty as their own consciences may direct.

Whereupon the jury retired to consider its verdict and soon returned with, "We, the jury, say that Aaron Burr has not been proved to be guilty under this indictment by the evidence submitted to us. We therefore find him not guilty."

The defense protested that the verdict was unusual, informal, and irregular. Burr demanded that the marshal of the court be ordered to send the jury back with instructions to alter it to proper form, or to make the correction.

Colonel Carrington, foreman of the jury, said it was their intention to return a verdict of acquittal, but if it were informal, the jury had agreed to alter it. Another juryman by the name of Parker contradicted this statement and insisted that he would not consent to any alteration of the verdict.

Marshall ruled that the verdict was one of acquittal, and directed the entry on the journal of "Not Guilty."

Every schoolboy knows the Constitution provides that "No person shall be convicted of treason unless on the testimony of two witnesses to the same overt act." The government had searched the Union for evidence and, failing to find it, made an attempt to convict Burr with fiction and propaganda.

Eaton's story proved only fiction. Wilkinson's reconstructed cipher letter reacted against him until the jury would have hanged him if the president had not intervened.

If the grand jury had known that the attorney general had

stepped aside because the president persisted in suppressing evidence that James Wilkinson was on the payroll of Spain, Wilkinson would have been hanged and Burr freed, just as Caesar A. Rodney had predicted.

Jefferson's suppression of the evidence against Wilkinson so that he might convict Burr constitutes a crime against justice that has no equal in the annals of the presidency.

The liberty of the press is most precious heritage. This is guaranteed by the Constitution. Its perpetuity was jeopardized when the press of this country neglected to tell the truth about Jefferson's attempt to hang Burr. Have the shades of Hamilton and Jefferson prevented the press from printing the facts about the conspiracy against Aaron Burr?

[At the New York Genealogical and Historical Society there is a slim soft-back titled The Aaron Burr Expedition. *It contains letters written by Silas Brown to his father that constitute first-hand testimony that would have convincingly refuted the charges of conspiracy. Excerpts from the book, including both letters and the reason that the testimony was never introduced at the trial, appear below. – H. H. Anderson, Jr., 2001]*

Letter from Pittsburgh, October 1, 1806
Silas Brown came from upstate New York and was concerned in the expedition led by Col. Burr in making a settlement on a large tract of land down the Ohio River.

Letter from Natchez, March 7, 1807
32 men and 4 boats were with Col Burr initially. He sent Brown and others to Blennerhasset Island with orders to bring 14 to 15 boats down the River. The Ohio Militia had seized 11 boats and issued a warrant of arrest for Blennerhasset to appear in Federal Court. Brown and the group took the remainder of the boats and ran the falls downstream entering Kentucky Dec. 27, 1806.

[Purportedly a note came from Burr with instructions to

"put our arms in order and that he will join us." Brown's comment is that "do not believe Burr ever wrote the note although it resembled his handwriting."]

Governor [William C. C.] Claiborne [Louisiana] searched our boats and was happy to find no arms. Our friend the Governor is quite different from Governor Tiffin of Ohio. Jan. 22, 1807 the latter called us fugitives.

[President Jefferson must have been aware all along (about the plans for the expedition and that there were no arms)—see Eaton's deposition. Gen Wilkinson then arrested Bollman, Swartwout and Ogden in New Orleans. Brown believes that Wilkinson was guilty of intrigue, and that the accusers of Burr were fully aware of his [real] plans.]

[What makes Silas Brown such a convincing writer, aside from the fact that he writes with complete objectivity, is that he speaks as an eyewitness and with meticulous detail. At length he describes the terrain, the rivers, and how they compare with his home state; he presents a comprehensive analysis of commerce in the region, e.g., the role of cotton and how it has already enriched the plantation owners.]

<u>Sept. 10, 1807—Silas to his father, Ephraim, from 140 miles outside of Natchez</u>

In July the fever attacked me and was so severe that it disqualified me for any kind of business till the first of September. . .

Since I began this letter I have been summoned to attend the great trial of Aaron Burr and others, at Richmond (Virginia) who are indicted for high treason and misdemeanors. . . . . in consequence of a debilitated state of health, I have declined going. My affidavit is taken* and sent to Richmond. . . .

As to the character of Comfort Tyler [who was arrested and taken to Richmond] and Israel Smith. . . . if the motives of every man concerned in the expedition had been as pure as theirs, we should have met with much less trouble and difficulty. . . .

<u>Oct. 26, 1807—Silas to his father recalling what happened the previous year</u>

Our little fleet consisted of 4 boats and 32 men. . . . I returned [to Blennerhassett Island] . . . . night of Dec 10 [1806] . . . . The men having had the information that the Kanahawa Militia and Wood County Mobs were to be at the island early the next morning for the purpose of exhibiting their true patriotism and taking us with force and arms. . . .

Arrived at mouth of Cumberland River, in Kentucky, the 29th of Dcmbr., at which place was Col. Burr. The whole body of men, including those with Col. Burr, did not exceed 100. . . . You say I "very much criminate Wilkinson and Eaton." 'Tis true—and where is the man who knows the late unprincipled conduct of Wilkinson in the affair of Burr who will not criminate and look upon him as a man whose assurances can never be confided in?

[Brown relates that he was summoned to appear at Burr's trial in Richmond, but that he had been ill for several months (the symptoms appear to have been malaria) and could not travel; he did provide an affidavit the fate of which is not known. He comments with rancor, "in the eyes of the public he [Burr] is Guilty."

Was the affidavit introduced in the trial? A search of the indices for Parton, Wandell, and Abernethy's biographies shows no Silas Brown. Sturm's search of the multi-volume court records yielded no evidence that that Brown's affidavit was ever introduced by the defense as evidence. Note that Dennis Lauchman has a booklet entitled Two Letters of Andrew Brown, *of Knox, New York, written to his son. It does not appear in Silas Carpenter's* The Trial of Aaron Burr *or* Reports of the Trial of Aaron Burr, 1808, *although without an index a comprehensive search presents a challenge. The same applies to J. J. Coombs's* The Trial of Aaron Burr for High Treason *which contains copies of the court records.]*

<u>November 19, 1807</u>

[Brown rebuts some of the criticism about Burr, his father's discourse on slavery in the west, and so forth in letters from his friend and his father. He further comments that Comfort Tyler of Onondega persuaded him to join the expedition; that it has an honorable purpose and is not hostile to the government.

When he went to Blennerhasset all was peaceful and there were no military stores. Governor Tiffin lied to President Jefferson (about the expedition) and set the Militia and a mob on them.

Burr's expedition did not exceed 100 persons. Wilkinson sent two gunboats and a bomb ketch to Natchez to block the river and laid an embargo on all vessels to New Orleans. Wilkinson went to Sabine River and stated, "I will play the Devil."]

[It is unfortunate for Colonel Burr that Silas Brown could not appear, as his testimony would have been a powerful defense in corroboration of his case.]

If those whose province and duty it is to prosecute offenders against the laws of the United States shall be of the opinion that a crime of a deeper dye has been committed, it is at their choice to act in conformity with that opinion.

— Chief Justice John Marshall

20
Reverberations of the Trial

Courtesy pervades the Southland, even the jails. Colonel Burr found it flowering with friendship and thoughtful kindness from the day of his arrival in Richmond. When his accusers succeeded in having the accusation changed from misdemeanor to a charge of high treason, he was again committed to jail. Through the instrumentality of the Virginia bar he was transferred from a dirty, unsanitary jail to a suite of three comfortable rooms in the third story of the penitentiary. Today this new abode would be called an apartment.

To Colonel Burr's place of detention visitors came in droves. At times it presented the appearance of a levee. Servants came "with notes, messages and inquiries, bringing oranges, lemons, pineapples, raspberries, apricots, cream, butter, ice" and many other articles—presents from the ladies of Richmond. In preparation for the comfort of Theodosia friends provided a house. The jailer was all civility. On the evening after Colonel Burr's arrival at the penitentiary he inquired, "I hope, sir, that it will not be disagreeable to you if I lock the door after dark?"

"By no means," replied the prisoner. "I should prefer it, to keep out intruders."

"It is our custom, sir," continued the jailer, "to extinguish all lights at nine o'clock. I hope, sir, you will have no objections to conform to that."

"That, sir," said Colonel Burr, "I am sorry to say, is impossible, for I never go to bed till twelve, and always burn two candles."

"Very well, sir, just as you please," replied the jailer. "I should have been glad if it had been otherwise; but as you please, sir."

Toward the close of July Burr received word that Theodosia was coming. To her he wrote:

> Remember, no agitations, no complaints, no fears, or anxieties on the road, or I renounce thee. . . . I want an independent discerning witness to my conduct and to that of the government. The scenes which I have passed and those about to be transacted will exceed all reasonable credibility, and will hereafter be fables, unless attested by very high authority. I repeat what has heretofore been written, that I should never invite anyone, much less those so dear to me, to witness my disgrace. If absent you will suffer solicitude. In my presence you will feel none whatever may be the malice and the power of my enemies, and in both they abound.

Later he wrote facetiously:

> I am informed that some of the good people here have provided you a house, and furnished it, a few steps from my town-house, whither I shall move on

Sunday; but I will not, if I can possibly avoid it, move before your arrival, having a great desire to receive you all in this mansion. Pray, therefore, drive directly out here. You may get admission any time from four in the morning until ten at night. Write me by mail from Petersburg, that I may know of your approach.

Written in Theodosia's own handwriting on the last letter mentioned was, "Received on our approach to Richmond. How happy it made me." She reached Richmond on this same day, where she remained until the end of the trial for treason.

John Barney, who was afterwards a member of Congress from Maryland, was Burr's amanuensis at Richmond during the trial; he lived in close association with Burr during the trying days. Barney had long known the vice president, of whom he wrote:

In 1803 I witnessed the dignity, impartiality and winning grace with which Aaron Burr presided in the Senate of the United States during the trial of Judge Chase, impeached for partiality and injustice toward John Fries, indicted under the Alien and Sedition Law.

I attend his trial at Richmond, when he himself was indicted for treason. His prominent counselor was Luther Martin, of Baltimore, my father's layer, neighbor and friend. Martin's daughter, Marie, afterwards celebrated as Mrs. Richard Raynal Keene, invited my sister and myself to dine with Colonel Burr. He was then living in a house standing alone, around which was a patrol of guards.

The dinner was superb, abounding in all the luxuries which Virginia's generous soil yields in lavish abundance. Twenty ladies and gentlemen of rank, fortune, and fashion graced the festive board. Burr was esteemed as a persecuted martyr. Distress, in every shape and form makes an irresistible appeal to a woman's sympathy; her tears often flow for the suffering of a criminal who expiates his crime on the gibbet.

On this occasion Burr's fascinating flatteries were lavished indiscriminately on the sex in general. Man he had ever found treacherous—woman always true to sustain him in adversity, solacing in affliction, and giving a charm to life without which life itself was not worth possessing.

The grand jury finding a true bill, he was forthwith removed to the state prison. There we followed him; he received us in his usual bland, courteous manner; apologized for being introduced in his bed-chamber— his drawing-room being then deranged by the fitting up of his ice-house, which was in fact his chimney-corner. Iron gratings prevented his egress, but allowed free circulation of light and air. I felt and took pride in becoming his amanuensis. Each day as I rode along the streets my curricle was freighted with cake, confectionery, flowers, redolent with perfume, wreathed with fancy bouquets of endless variety.

The trial was tedious and prolonged. I traveled to the borders of North Carolina, lingered for a while at the noble mansion of Lady Skipworth. On my return, I found the persevering Attorney General George Hay fatigued and worried.

"Would that I could only hang upon a gate, and have a little negro swing me to and fro all day. The law's delay—the special pleadings of the bar, its interminable controversies have worn me out and exhausted me. I shan't be able to hang Burr, but will be content to hang myself on a gate."

Thus spoke George Hay, than whom never lived a purer patriot, or upright, conscientious man.

While Burr was insisting upon his right to a more ample vindication at the hands of the jury, Theodosia wrote to her half-sister:

> *I have this moment received a message from court announcing to me that the jury had brought in a verdict of acquittal, and I hasten to inform you of it, my dear, to allay the anxiety which, with more than your usual sweetness, you have expressed in your letter of the 22d of July.*
>
> *It afflicts me, indeed, to think that you should have suffered so much from sympathy with the imagined state of my feelings—for the knowledge of my father's innocence, my ineffable contempt for his enemies, and the elevation of his mind, have kept me above any sensation bordering on depression.*
>
> *Indeed, my father, so far from accepting of sympathy, has continually animated all around him; it was common to see his desponding friends filled with alarm at some new occurrence, terrified at some new appearance of danger, fly to him in search of encouragement and support, and laughed out of their fears by the subject of them.*
>
> *This I have witnessed every day, and it almost persuaded me that he possessed the secret of repelling danger as well as apprehension. Since my residence here, of which some days and nights were passed in the penitentiary, our little family circle has been the scene of uninterrupted gayety. Thus you see, my lovely sister, this visit has been a real party of pleasure. From many of the first inhabitants I have received the most unremitting and delicate attentions, sympathy, indeed, of any I ever experienced.*

It was a precept of Burr's that the inevitable be accepted without repining, that it was weakness to mourn and wisdom to enjoy, and after suffering losses, to hold fast to what was left, and enjoy it.

After the trial Wilkinson informed Jefferson that he was coming to Washington to pay his respects. He wrote:

> *You are doubtless well advised of the proceedings here in the Burr case—the Grand Jury actually made an attempt to present me for Misprison and Treason—I feel myself between "Scylla and Charybdis," the Jury would Dishonor me for failing to do my duty, and Burr and his Conspirators for performing it.*

Wilkinson had exposed the president in his true light—as protector of a traitor and as persecutor of a patriot. Marshall's fearless construction of the Constitution and of the statutes aroused popular distrust, even open hostility; it turned the limelight of publicity from Burr to Marshall. Accordingly, Marshall wrote his associates on the Supreme Court for their opinion of the law of treason as presented in the case of Aaron Burr.

Marshall was the object of the most vindictive criticism from a partisan press that was subservient to the wishes of the president. This he felt keenly, and he was deeply concerned that his decisions have the approval of the full court. He wrote:

> *I am aware of the unwillingness with which a judge will commit himself by an opinion on a case not before him, and on which he has heard no argument. . . . I am sure there would be a strong repugnance to giving contradictory decisions on the same points.*

Thus, with caution, common sense, and fearlessness founded upon the law and the Constitution, John Marshall paved the way for a wholesome respect for the Supreme Court. The vitriolic outbursts of the agents of Jefferson in their condemnation of the judiciary surpasses the comprehension of the present generation.

Only a Jefferson would have created such a situation, only a Burr would have withstood it, and only a Marshall would have endured it and survived!

The president ordered Hay to press for trial on the indictments for misdemeanor, not that he expected to convict Burr, but that his malice and resentment might be appeased. Possibly, if the search were continued and more evidence were manufactured, if more lucrative positions were offered as bribes for more evidence, someone might be induced to testify against Burr and Marshall. It made little difference who, if only Marshall could be impeached! Jefferson wrote, "The Chief Justice is occupied in hearing testimony intended for use, not against Burr, but against himself."

Marshall delivered the last of his opinions in the Burr trials on October 20. Again the government asked that Burr be held for treason and misdemeanor. This time the charge was that the enterprise had been directed solely against Spanish territory. For a fourth time Marshall refused to commit Burr for treason. He recorded that it would "be improper to commit the accused on the charge of treason."

Possibly this unjust and repeated persecution of Burr was permitted that the chief justice might escape impeachment, for Marshall knew that Jefferson was determined to remove him from office if he could find a way. Burr had faced the charges of three grand juries in Kentucky and Mississippi; a fourth grand jury not only refused to indict but added as a "grievance" that "the late military arrests made without warrant must sap the vitals of our political existence and crumble this glorious fabric into dust."

Examination of the charges against Burr before Marshall was begun on March 30. For seven months the inquisition persisted. In committing Burr for the fourth time Marshall said, "Unless it is perfectly clear that the act was innocent, he must grant the motion." He had concluded that Burr's purposes were to settle the Ouachita lands and to invade Mexico, if opportunity offered, perhaps, only in event of war with Spain.

Whether this was so or not, he would let the jury decide and would make no comment that might, in one way or the other, influence their judgment. He, therefore, would commit Burr and Blennerhassett "for preparing and providing the means for a military expedition against Spain."

In disgust Hay announced he would advise the government to desist from further prosecution.

Marshall's closing words in this decision read:

> *If those whose province and duty it is to prosecute offenders against the laws of the United States shall be of the opinion that a deeper dye has been committed, it is at their choice to act in conformity with that opinion.*

Thus the chief justice revealed he full well understood that the president held him responsible for the escape of Burr. Marshall entertained no illusions as to the influences the president would bring to bear in an attempt to impeach him: Wilkinson had reinstated himself with Jefferson by his so-called evidence to the grand jury. Eaton was bribed with ten thousand dollars out of the public treasury, and others had appeared whose motive in coming was prompted by the promise of a federal job.

A careful examination of this situation leads inevitably to the conclusion that Marshall was coerced into holding Burr for the fourth time, that he might avoid impeachment. Again he placed Burr under bond, this time in amount of three thousand dollars. Once more Burr was a free man; he went to Baltimore. But if he thought he was to be permitted to enjoy his liberty and go about unmolested, he was mistaken.

How well the president had succeeded in poisoning the public mind is attested by the mob of twelve to fifteen hundred that greeted Burr in Baltimore. Its advance agents formed under his window and played the "Rogue's March." The excitement that pervaded the city was intense. Speeches were made and the following handbills were distributed:

AWFUL!!!!

The public are hereby notified that "four choice spirits" are this afternoon, at three o'clock, to be marshaled for execution by hangman, or Gallows Hill, in consequence of the sentence pronounced against them by the unanimous voice of every honest man in the community.

The respective crimes for which they suffer are thus stated in the record.

First, Chief Justice M. for a repetition of his X.Y.Z. tricks, which are said to be much aggravated by his felonious capers in open Court, on the plea of irrelevancy;

Secondly, His Quid Majesty [Burr], charged with the trifling fault of wishing to divide the Union, and farm Baron Bastrop's grant;

Thirdly, the chemist [Blennerhasset], convicted of conspiracy to destroy the tone of the public Fiddle;

Fourthly, and lastly, but not least, Lawyer Brandy-bottle, for a false, scandalous, malicious Prophesy, that, before six months, "Aaron Burr would divide the Union."

N.B. The execution of accomplices is postponed to a future day.

Luther Martin demanded the protection of the law. Police were sent to the Evans Hotel by the Major. Burr and Swartwout were escorted to the stagecoach and made their escape to Philadelphia.

The mob paraded, shouting and huzzah-ing, led by a fife and drum corps. Midway in the throng was a cart on which was displayed an effigy of Chief Justice Marshall; following was another with an effigy of Aaron Burr and his defender Luther Martin. While making "as much noise as if they were about to destroy the city," these avowed agents of justice and liberty were followed by two troops of mounted police, who apparently witnessed the acts of the riotous throng with approval; not one attempted to disperse the crowd or prevent the execution of effigies.

Though this outbreak from the public proved Jefferson's statement that "we can satisfy the world, if not the judges," the president was far from being ready to accept the decision of Hay to "desist from further prosecution." Neither was he going to accept the verdicts of courts and juries of Burr's innocence. Jefferson wrote to Albert Gallatin that he had a rumor that Burr had sailed to New Orleans, and that he desired Gallatin to warn Claiborne and the colonel of the militia in that territory, for "I presume that a writ may be obtained from Ohio grounded on the indictment, by which Burr may be arrested and brought to trial."

In his message to Congress on the state of the nation, the president urged that Marshall be impeached, saying it was his duty to transmit the record of the Burr trial, and that:

> *Truth and duty alone extort the observation that wherever the laws were appealed in aid of public safety, their operation was on behalf of those only against whom they were invoked. From the record you will be able to judge whether the defect was in the testimony, or in the laws, or whether there is not a radical defect in the administration of the law? And whenever it shall be found the legislature alone can apply or originate the remedy.*

The president emphasized that:

> *The framers of the Constitution certainly supposed that they guarded as well their government against destruction by treason as their citizens against oppression under pretense of it; and if the pliability of the law as construed in the case of Fries, and its wonderful refractoriness as construed in that of Burr, show that neither end has been obtained, and induce an aw-*

ful doubt whether we all live under the same law. The right of the jury too to decide the law as well as fact seems nugatory without the evidence pertinent to their sense of law. If these ends are not attained it becomes worthy of inquiry by what means more effectual they may be secured.

Jefferson's cabinet protested against these radical recommendations. Some sentences were stricken from his message. However, Congress was asked to impeach Marshall. This was frustrated only because its attention was absorbed by an impending war with England.

The new provision concerning treason was written into the American Constitution to protect its citizens against the insane mass psychology which may be injected into the public mind through the propaganda of such men as Thomas Jefferson—men who when they become enraged at a political enemy lose all sense of justice. Concerning this, Francis M. Finch wrote that it was "to protect the people against the horrible and dangerous doctrine of constructive treason which had stained the English records with blood and filled the English valleys with innocent graves."

After recording the astonishing amount of innocent blood that the tyrants of Europe had spilled by charging a political enemy with treason, Albert Beveridge observes:

Even in England, so harsh had been the rulings of the courts against those charged with treason, so inhuman the execution of judgments upon persons found guilty under these rulings, so slight the pretexts that sent innocent men and women to their death, that the framers of our fundamental law had been careful to define treason with utmost clearness.

Even today the people of the United States are almost wholly ignorant of the innocence of Aaron Burr. They do not know that Thomas Jefferson never produced any evidence to prove his charges; that he admitted he did not have the evidence; that Jefferson used public funds with which he bribed a false witness; that Burr was before grand jury after grand jury before he was indicted; that the grand jury that eventually indicted him was hand-picked; that this jury rendered its verdict without observing the instructions of the court; that Jefferson persisted in persecuting Burr long after he was advised by his personally selected attorneys to desist; and that Caesar A. Rodney, the attorney general of the United States, refused to prosecute Burr.

Next to Aaron Burr, John Marshall suffered most from the malignant poison injected into the minds of the Union by Thomas Jefferson. It is almost past comprehension how very little the American people know, after more than a hundred years, about the results of Jefferson's false propaganda against Aaron Burr and John Marshall. As the agent of the president, William Thompson wrote a series of letters to John Marshall. These were originally printed in the *Richmond Inquirer*, but were copied in a partisan press and thus spread over the nation.

Thompson wrote, "Let the judge be impeached," that he was a "wavering irresolute spirit," that his conduct had been inspired by "power illicitly obtained," that he had earned "infamy and detestation," and that his entire life was that "of a sly, bigoted politician, who has worked against the people." In his defense of Jefferson and his tirade against Marshall, Thompson continued, "Common sense and violated justice cry aloud against such conduct; and demand against you the enforcement of these laws, which you refuse to administer."

This arraignment of Marshall was submitted to Jefferson before it was published. In conclusion Thompson wrote:

> *Could I be instrumental in removing you from the elevation which you have dishonored by your crimes, I would still trace you. . . . for screening a criminal and degrading a judge by the juggle of judicial face.*

Morally guilty, traitors at heart and in fact. . . . Such a criminal and such a judge, few countries ever produced. . . . you are forever doomed to blot the fair page of American history, to be held up, as examples of infamy and disgrace, of perverted talents and unpunished criminality, of foes of liberty and traitors of your country.

This is the reward that John Marshall received at the instigation of Thomas Jefferson for intelligently and bravely construing the Constitution; for refusing to permit Aaron Burr to be convicted and hanged without evidence of his guilt, and with evidence of his innocence safely locked up in the archives of the government!

Perhaps no one will read of Jefferson's attempt to hang Burr without a desire to learn more about the man who prevented that crime. Marshall and Jefferson were cousins. The mother of Jefferson was Jane Randolph, the daughter of Isham Randolph, while the mother of Marshall was Mary Randolph Keith, daughter of Mary Isham Randolph, whose father was Thomas Randolph, the brother of Jefferson's maternal grandfather. Thomas Jefferson was the great-grandson, while John Marshall was the great-great grandson, of William Randolph and Mary Isham.

Other members of the Randolph family at the Burr trial were Edmund Randolph and John Randolph.

Marshall was a frontiersman, soldier, legislator, politician, and secretary of state before becoming chief justice, in which position he served thirty-four years, longer than any successor. In 1835, Joseph Story wrote, "Marshall still possesses his intellectual powers in very high vigor; but his physical strength is manifestly on the decline. . . . What will spread over the nation when he is gone!"

An implacable enemy in life, the *Richmond Inquirer* admitted at his passing:

It would be impossible to over praise Marshall's brilliant talents. . . . he was as much beloved as he was respected. . . . There was so little of "the inso-

lence of office," and so much of the benignity of the man, that his presence always produced the most delightful impressions.

The *Whig and Public Advertiser* added, "No man has lived in this country, save George Washington, who united such warmth of affection for his person, and so deep and unaffected a respect for his character, and admiration for his great abilities."

Less is known about Marshall than of other great Americans. What has been written leaves him largely among some of the mythical characters who created this nation. In construing the Constitution, Marshall revealed its true intent and character, adding a quality of mercy and justice.

[I] never did harm or wished harm to a human being.
— Aaron Burr
Private Letters

21
Driven from Home

As a result of the president's charges of treason, Burr and his associates in the Bastrop colonization scheme and his defenders at Richmond were robbed of fifty thousand dollars. No attempt was ever made to restore this loss. When John Adair secured a judgment against Wilkinson for false imprisonment on a similar charge, Congress promptly indemnified him.

After Rodney learned that Wilkinson was a "Pensioner of Spain," he stepped aside and declined to prosecute Burr. After Hay learned that the public was aware of Wilkinson's treachery, he wrote the president, "My confidence in him is shaken, if not destroyed. I am sorry of it, on his account, on public account, and because you have expressed opinions in his favor, but you did not know then what you will know soon."

Propaganda and false charges by Thomas Jefferson formed the basis of most of the so-called "evidence" presented before John Marshall. Echoes from this propaganda created such resentment in the Senate that an attempt was made to expel John Smith from its membership because of "His participation in the conspiracy of Aaron Burr against the peace, union and liberties of the United States."

When the mob surrounded the Evans Hotel in Baltimore some politically minded Republicans threatened to leave the hostelry if Burr were not removed from the "tainted quarters." When Burr reached Philadelphia, a temporary refuge was found in the home of George Pollock. An old friend, Charles Biddle, found him "concealed in a French boarding house, pale and dejected." Biddle was so shocked at the change that he wrote, "How different from what he had been a short time before, when few persons in the city were not gratified at seeing him at their tables where he was always one of the most lively and entertaining of the company."

All this, too, was the result of the president's false propaganda!

For a year Jefferson had hounded Burr. For seven months he had used all the power of the presidency to hang him. At Baltimore Burr was hanged in effigy and escaped tar and feathers only by fleeing to Philadelphia. The wrath of the mob was inspired by the president of the United States when he wrote, "Burr's guilt is placed beyond question." How could Burr escape being "pale and dejected"?

Grand jury after grand jury refused to indict him until one was handpicked from politicians, office holders, and men selected under the direction of the president. Then followed a petit jury, all of whom admitted that they had been convinced of Burr's guilt by the accusations of the president; yet, this jury returned a verdict of "Not Guilty."

Of what value was an acquittal to Burr, when the president immediately forced another indictment? Burr was given freedom and liberty, but of what value were these inalienable rights so long as Jefferson was president? "Life, liberty and the pursuit of happiness" were to Aaron Burr but hollow mockery until after the presidential influence of Thomas Jefferson ceased. Jefferson endeavored to suspend the writ of *habeas corpus*, instituted martial law, and attempted to nullify the guarantees of the right of trial by a jury that he might hang Burr, and he did all this knowing that Burr was innocent of his charges.

Friends arranged that he see Theodosia before making his escape from tyranny and persecution. This proved the last meeting of father and daughter, although both endured four years of unbelievable suffering by virtue of this forced separation.

On board the *Clarissa Ann*, a British packet, June 7, 1808, and registered as H. E. Edwards, Aaron Burr escaped to England. One port of call at Halifax was made. Here he received letters from Sir George Prevost, a relative of Burr's deceased wife, and a passport certifying that "Mr. Edwards was the bearer of dispatches to the Right Honorable Robert Stewart Castlereagh," at whose offices he was to present himself on reaching London.

On July 13 Burr reached Falmouth; three days later he was in London. His presence in England created a sensation—at least in the mind of the American minister William Pinckney, who wrote to Madison:

> *Burr arrived in England by the last pack. . . . It has been suggested that his object was to engage in some Enterprise against the Spanish America under British auspices, the plan is of course defeated (at least for the present) by late Change in Relations of G. B. & Spain.*

Since troops were assembling under the command of Sir Arthur Wellesley, later known as Duke of Wellington, ostensibly for action in South America, Pinckney assumed that Burr expected to participate, knowing quite well that the American government would approve his assumption that Burr was planning a rupture between the United States and Great Britain. Burr was even charged with being responsible for a change in the British cabinet's attitude toward Pinckney.

Nothing was further from the facts, but neither Jefferson nor Madison was interested in the facts in any matter concerning Burr. The records afterward revealed that Colonel Burr was not permitted to have opportunity to discuss international affairs with those in British authority, and that his visits never reached further than the anteroom of the ministry.

Burr's visits did reach a point of courtesy later when, on August 10, in making out his declaration as an alien concerning this presence in England, Burr said, "I am personally known to Lord Mulgrave and Mr. Canning to whom the motives of my visit have been declared. The reasons have long been known to Lord Melville."

If scant courtesy were his reception with the British Foreign Secretary, George Canning, and with Cook, Castlereagh, and Mulgrave members of the cabinet, his reception with the military and in social circles was surprisingly successful. Burr's courtly manners, brilliant mind, and unusual wit were badges of entree to the best society.

Jeremy Bentham had long been admired by Burr, and after the two had enjoyed a week together at the former's country residence, Barrow Green, the association was continued at Bentham's townhouse, Queen's Square Place, London. Apparently it was an association of kindred spirits where mutual interests in immoral philosophy by brilliant intellects were cemented by a common bond.

William Godwin, too, chose to make Burr an intimate associate. He introduced him to the essayist Charles Lamb, and to William Cobbett. These men were so favorably impressed with Burr that they tried to induce him to stand for Parliament.

Of these newfound friends none was to impress Burr so favorably as Bentham, of whom he wrote to Theodosia:

> *I hasten to make you acquainted with Jeremy Bentham, author of a work entitled* Principles of Morals and Legislation; *and of many other works of less*

labor and research. You will recollect to have heard me place this man second to no one, ancient or modern, in profound thinking or logical or analytic reasoning.

The mutual friendship between Burr and Bentham resulted in Theodosia's picture being given to Bentham, who in turn sent Theodosia a copy of each of his books.

The enmity of Jefferson and his political family followed Burr to England, where it quickly aroused suspicion and ill feeling in the English cabinet. Burr wrote to Theodosia, "I have no longer the slightest hope of the countenance of the ministry for anything which might be proposed," and to Bentham he said, "I am the object of suspicion and alarm." Apparently Burr still dreamed of acquiring at least that part of Mexico, which eventually was added to the domain of the United States and which was larger in square miles than the original thirteen states—the great state of Texas.

The blight of Jefferson's ill will was not limited to Burr; it destroyed the usefulness of nearly everyone who supported him. After many years Swartwout returned to public favor sufficiently that he was appointed collector of the Port of New York. Bollman attempted to practice medicine in New Orleans, but public sentiment drove him to Europe. It was while Burr was on the continent that Bollman wrote:

> *Americans shun me, and Clark himself, anxious to make peace with his enemies, avoided me; wished me not to call on him, and came to see me by stealth. Only Judge Workman, now practicing as a lawyer, is interested in the old cause. His looks are steadfastly turned to the South.*

Next to Burr, the condemnation and influence of Jefferson was felt most by Theodosia. She wrote that "The world begins to cool terribly around me. You would be surprised how many I

The "cabinet portrait" of Aaron Burr by John Vanderlyn is estimated to have been painted during Burr's tenure in Paris in 1810–11.

supposed attached to me have abandoned the sorry, losing game of disinterested friendship. Frederick Prevost alone [her older half brother] is worth a host."

Sick and despondent because of the treatment of her father, Theodosia had entered into a state of melancholia on account of separation from him. She had suffered her greatest heartbreak when her husband, Joseph Alston, in common with nearly every-one else, had accepted as true the statement of the president that

Aaron Burr, portrait by John Vanderlyn 1810–11. Note how Vanderlyn "straightened" Burr's fabled aquiline nose, which in reality was crooked.

her father was a traitor. Although Alston was quick to recognize that the charge was false, he was destined to learn that in his hour of wavering the love of his wife was lost, and that the injury was beyond repair. To question the honor of her father was to Theodosia an error unpardonable.

Even Andrew Jackson accepted Jefferson's charge seriously for a time, but, quickly discerning the truth, soon declared Burr was innocent and that Jefferson was motivated solely by "malice and jealousy." Yet the public accepted Jefferson's charges so nearly universally that when Jackson ran for the presidency, he ignored Burr, because to do otherwise was impolitic.

In questioning the honor of her father even for one moment, Alston deprived himself of Theodosia's love. His act in her eyes was equivalent to questioning her virtue; thereafter Theodosia possessed only her son and the cherished dream in Mexico, and that was fast becoming a mirage. In despair she wrote:

> *I cannot part with what had so long lain near my heart, and not feel some regret, some sorrow. No doubt there are many other roads to happiness, but this appeared so perfectly suitable to you, so complete a remuneration for all the past that I cherished it as my comfort. My knowledge of your character, however, consoles me greatly. You will not remain idle. The situation in which you are placed would excite apathy itself, but your mind needs external impetus. When shall I receive the Journal? Good Heaven, how it will delight me!*

The Journal was a diary in which father recorded solely for his daughter those indignities he suffered as well as the frailties of nature in which he indulged. His critics have magnified and paraded these vulgar crudities that had marked his domestic life by their absence. Later, during his European odyssey, Burr explained to Theodosia that he was recording only trivial things because those worthwhile would be remembered and recounted. If the diary had reached Theodosia, she would have understood that it was also written as a means of retaining his sanity. But, alas, the diary, too, was denied to her.

To add to Burr's distress, word came that Theodosia was fatally ill. Immediately he haunted the offices of the best practitioners in London in an endeavor to alleviate her suffering and if possible find a cure for the disease that had also removed her mother from earth: cancer. In his eagerness to have his daughter with him Burr, wrote to Alston:

> As to money I have transferred over to Theodosia the sum which had been destined for my expense (say four or five hundred guineas); this will pay her passage to this place, and maintain her in the way I propose she shall live for four or five months. If she survives, I shall return her to the United States.

But Alston refused to allow her to come to England; instead, he required that she should return to their South Carolina home from New York, where she had gone for treatment. This so enraged the father that he berated Alston:

> You promised before marriage, and I now claim renewal of that promise: You may do anything; say anything; and write anything. After four experiments, all nearly fatal, I would not have made a fifth with a dog.

Becoming weary with British indifference to international affairs, Burr went to Oxford, where his enthusiasm for Bentham elicited so little interest that he wrote:

> The Prevost speaks of Bentham with reverence and, probably prays for him. I presume he thinks that he will be eternally damned, and I have no doubt he expects to be lolling on Abraham's bosom with great complacency hearing Bentham sing out for a drop of water.

The new year was begun in Edinburgh, where for a month he was guest of literati and aristocracy. Among those who acted as host and companion were Lord Justice Clark, Alexander McKenzie, and Francis Jeffrey, the founder of the *Edinburgh Review*. Sir

Walter Scott expressed pleasure at Burr's literary criticism. Here Burr was wined and dined by lords, dukes, marquises, admirals, generals, editors, judges, and the elite of Scot society. Concerning his Edinburgh reception, Burr wrote, "I lead a life of utter dissipation, driving out every day and at some party every night, wasting time and doing many silly things."

Apparently the Lord Justice Clark thought Burr was preparing to enter Parliament; he wrote, "Burr has made a very considerable sensation in the cabinet, and Cobbett is deeply impregnated with the magnitude of his talents as a statesman and a soldier." Then to Burr he wrote, "They [members of the cabinet] have been consulting how it is possible that you should be brought into the Parliament."

Apparently the siren voice of preferment reached Burr's ear; he returned and lingered for a time, listening to these friendly attempts to inveigle him into British citizenship, but his day-dreaming of a life in England was rudely ended when a bookseller threatened him with arrest for an old book account. The books had been seized at the port of entry, and Burr had not received them. Yet the laws were such that Burr must assume payment of the debt; and if he failed to do so, he could be arrested and thrown into prison.

To avoid this embarrassment, but more especially to avoid embarrassment to Bentham, with whom Burr was living, he moved to 35 James Street, where he lived under an assumed name. Here he met Madame Prevost, with whose beauty and amorous desires he found mutual relaxation for several weeks. Originally the bookseller had secured only a warrant of arrest for debt, but now, according to Burr's diary:

> *At one o'clock came in without knocking, four coarse-looking men, who said they had a state warrant, signed Liverpool. They took possession of my trunks, searched every part of the room for papers, threw all the loose articles into a sack, and away we went to the Alien Office.*

Three days later Burr was released, and due apology was made; but it was now quite plain that the British Government had decided to get rid of him. On April 14, 1809, he received a notice that read "Lord Liverpool expects that you leave town this day and the kingdom tomorrow."

After defying the order, Burr agreed to leave in due time and to place of his choice. Eleven days later he and his secretary departed for Sweden. The American government was so embittered that Burr was now driven from England; in fact he was trailed from country to country, a wanderer on the face of the earth.

On receipt of passports Burr boarded his Britannic Majesty's packet, the *Diana*, observing with some bitterness that "Mr. Jefferson, or the Spanish juntas, or probably both, have had influence enough to drive me out of this country."

England's treatment of her father awakened in Theodosia a sentiment that is to live and contribute to the immortality of both. It read:

> *I witness your extraordinary fortitude with new wonder at every new misfortune. You appear to me so superior, so elevated above all other men, I contemplate you with a strange mixture of humility, admiration, reverence, love and pride that very little superstition would be necessary to make me worship you as a superior being: such enthusiasm does your character excite in me. . . . I had rather not live than not be the daughter of such a man.*

Stockholm received Burr cordially. He was equally at home with the lowest as with the highest. He was entertained by Colonel and Professor Calm, the historian and geographer Catteau-Calleville, and Baron Muck. Burr was made to feel at home in the society of nobles. Of his presentation to the Swedish Regent, he wrote, "You would laugh to see Gamp with his sword and immense three-cornered hat."

Burr held long consultations with Swedish lawyers, with whom he discussed Swedish laws. He observed that their lawyers are only teachers of law; there is no legal profession:

> *Only think of a people, the most honest and peaceable in the world, and not a lawyer! No such animal, in Sweden! But again I must remind you that this Journal is only a memorandum to talk from. The most interesting and amusing incidents are not recorded at all, because I am sure to remember them.*

The Swedish legal system so fascinated Burr that he made an exhaustive study of it with a view of publishing a volume on the subject. Burr was always a student. He devoted himself assiduously to drama, history, military science, moral and social economics. The famous painter Carl Frederik von Breda pronounced Burr a connoisseur and associated with and directed him in his research in Sweden.

Burr's indifference to criticism is revealed by the following record in his Journal: "August 20, 1809, It was not until yesterday that I learnt that I have been the subject of newspaper discussion for several weeks. What is said about me I have neither heard nor inquired."

After four months spent in museums, archives, and art galleries, and in conference with philosophers, literary men, savants of the law, and scientists, Burr was ready for new territory for research. He addressed a letter to John Quincy Adams asking for a passport to Russia, where Adams was then the American minister. Since no reply came, it is easy to conjecture that Adams, too, was taking orders from Jefferson. But Burr went to Denmark and to Copenhagen, where the favorable exchange rate materially relieved his depleted purse.

At the little town of Altona near Hamburg, Germany, Burr encountered a colony of Americans who treated him so coolly that he wrote in his Journal:

*I find a great many Americans here, all are hostile
to A.B.—what a lot of rascals they must be to make
war on one they do not know; on one who never did
harm or wished harm to a human being. Yet they, perhaps, ought not to be blamed, since they are influenced
by what they hear. I learn that A. B. is announced in
the Paris papers in a manner in no way auspicious.*

Burr applied for a passport to Paris, but the French minister
was slow in acting. Finally he issued a passport to a little frontier
town with instructions to apply there for papers to enter Paris.
Later this Frenchman wrote:

*At the height of his glory and power Bonapar-
te was so suspicious that the variest trifle sufficed
to alarm him. . . . I recollect Colonel Burr, formerly
Vice-President of the United States, who had arrived
at Altona, was pointed out to me as a dangerous man,
and I received orders to watch him very closely, and
arrest him on the slightest ground of suspicion if he
should come to Hamburg. Colonel Burr was one of
those in favor of whom I ventured to disobey the orders I received from the restless police of Paris.*

*As soon as the minister of police heard of Burr's
arrival in Altona, he directed me to adopt toward him
those violent measures which are equivalent to persecution. In answer to these instructions I stated that
Colonel Burr had conducted himself at Altona with
much prudence and propriety; that he kept very little
company and he was scarcely spoken of. Far from regarding him as a man who required watching, having
learned that he wished to go to Paris, I caused a passport to be procured for him which he was to receive
in Frankfort, and I never heard that this dangerous
citizen had compromised the state in any way.*

At Gottingen, December 11, 1809, Burr met the famous mathematician Karl Friedrich Gauss, director of the Astronomical Observatory. Learning that the emperor had given his assent to the independence of Mexico, Burr exclaimed "Why the devil didn't he tell me this two years ago?"

An ulcerated tooth drove Burr into the arms and under the influence of a female dentist, concerning which he wrote in his Journal, "A lip which was bitten by a venomous animal on Friday last has swollen and is very painful. The origin of the thing is so ridiculous that I wished to hush it up; for the bite was given in a paroxysm of great good humor."

Burr's stay at Weimar in January 1810 is all too briefly told in his Journal when one contemplates the names recorded and remembers that his wardrobe was worn and his poverty obvious. His reception and welcome in the inner circle of the great amazes one. On the day he met Goethe, Burr observes that "This day would make about 200 pages if written out" and that he met Frau von Stein, lady of the court, and Princess Caroline, and that he dined in state with Charles Augustus, the Duke of Saxe-Weimar. To the glorious figures of the royal family Burr was introduced, and apparently all were as charmed as he.

Notwithstanding that he was an outcast from America, despised and persistently pursued wherever he went, Burr's personality and talents were recognized by Wieland the poet, Wilhelm the brother of the great naturalist, Alexander von Humboldt, and others of equal note.

From Weimar and a lady of court Burr departed most unceremoniously. Having discovered that he was desperately in love with Mademoiselle de Reizenstein, and that his infatuation was reciprocated, Burr dared not do otherwise than flee. He took his departure without a word of farewell to his newly made friends. He did not even inform the duke. On arrival at Erfurt he wrote in his Journal that he had escaped "a sorceress, and if I were President of the Secret Tribunal, she should be burnt alive tomorrow. Another interview and I might have been lost, and my hopes and prospects blasted and abandoned."

Nowhere else in the archives concerning Aaron Burr is there to be found another record of his being completely upset; and nowhere else may be read such intemperate language as here fell from his lips. Plainly Burr could easily have enjoyed the luxuries of such an association, but he would not. The ease and glamour of court life were not to the choosing of Aaron Burr.

The next day he was in Gotha as the guest of Ernst I, Duke of Saxe-Coburg. Here he met Lindenau, director of the observatory, and Galletti, the historian. At Frankfurt he learned that he was forbidden to come to France; he, however, did not hesitate but went on to Mayence. Here he was detained under police surveillance pending instructions from Paris. Fortunately for him some members of the Holland branch of the Burr family lived here, and with them he awaited his passport, which did not arrive until February; but on the sixteenth he reached the French capital. Immediately he asked for an audience with the minister of foreign relations, Duke de Cadore, and, having received permission, called and submitted his plans.

The archives of France are considerable cluttered up by plans that Burr allegedly submitted, but after all have been examined for evidence that Burr's mission was inimical to American interests, it becomes apparent that his object was the independence of Spanish America and nothing else—no treasonable designs upon the territory of the United States.

There are whisperings of a treasonable nature from the State Department. These were at the instigation of Madison. In the various depositories of Madison papers may be found charges and innuendoes that Burr's mission was of traitorous design. Mr. Madison asked Joe Barlow to confirm his suspicions "verify accusations against Burr." Since this agent did not reach France until the latter part of 1811, and did not report until September 26, 1812, his report is puzzling. He reported that France and England seem to like Burr's project of dividing the United States between them and that the plan was rather applauded by Napoleon; yet the records disclose that Barlow failed in his attempt to see Napoleon, just as Burr had failed. This is a good example of the kind of rubbish one encounters concerning Burr's plans, as well as his activities in state affairs while he was just "trying" to see Napoleon. One enemy of Burr's warned the State Department that Burr was entirely unworthy; then failed to identify himself, but signed as a "Citizen of the United States."

A tedious examination of the archives of France forces the inevitable conclusion that the allegations against Aaron Burr that repose there were by those who furnished the so-called evidence before John Marshall at Richmond. They bear the same earmarks. Without exception they were by enemies of Burr; they were made by agents of Jefferson.

On March 21, 1810, however, Burr submitted to Napoleon through the French Ministry an informative letter. It was addressed to Duc d'Otrante, who at the time was chief of police. It read:

> *Mr. Burr, from the United States of North America, having some months ago seen published in the Moniteur the expression of His Majesty's assent to the independence of the Spanish American colonies, came to Paris to offer his services to accomplish that object and others connected therewith. He asks neither men nor money. He asks only the authorization of His Majesty.*

Since no reply had come from his original request for opportunity to discuss the matter, this was a more definite statement of the objects sought. But it, too, failed to bring the desired interview.

After six months waiting for an answer from Napoleon and several conferences with deputy Louis Roux, Burr wrote, "I have no reason to believe that my business advances, or that I shall do anything here."

When Burr made his descent of the Mississippi to New Orleans, one of his conferences was with the Creoles who were disappointed with the new government at Washington and by the treatment that they had received, charging that they did not enjoy the privileges of American citizens. They had prepared a memorial addressed to Napoleon, which Burr advised that they suppress, promising to come to them "in another manner."

Burr planned, as the records now prove, that he would one day attempt to add the territory of Texas to the domain of the United States. The evidence which John Marshall summed up at trial in Richmond was that this would be "in the event of war with Spain."

Now that it was apparent that nothing could be accomplished by remaining in France, Burr asked for a passport to America. Not only did Napoleon decline to issue one, but Burr was held as a prisoner. On June 24, 1809, Theodosia wrote to Dolly Madison, wife of the president, to inquire:

> *Why then is my father banished from a country for which he has encountered wounds and dangers and fatigue for years? Why is he driven from his friends, from an only child, to pass an unlimited time in exile, and too at an age when others are reaping the harvest of past toils? . . . To whatever fate Mr. Madison may doom this application, I trust it will be treated with delicacy; of this I am more desirous as Mr. Alston is ignorant of the step I have taken in writing you.*

When one is reminded that the recipient of this letter, Dolly Madison, was a widow, Dolly P. Todd, when she was introduced to James Madison by Senator Aaron Burr; that she was conducting an exclusive boarding house in Philadelphia when she had gone to Senator Burr for legal advice, which was received and paid for with thanks; and that she was now the First Lady of the land by virtue of such circumstances; is it not a sad commentary upon a lack of gratitude that Theodosia never received acknowledgment of this letter?

While awaiting an answer from Napoleon, Burr met John Vanderlyn, whom he had sent to Paris for his education in art.

Vanderlyn was now a famous landscape and portrait painter, and acquainted with men and women of culture and influence to whom Burr was introduced. It was through the influence of this group that Burr eventually escaped the political web of the Virginia legion and its American master.

Subsequent to making application for a passport, Burr frequented the offices of Duc de Rovigo, the minister of police. On September 13, Burr was advised that his passport had been granted, only to learn twelve days later that the emperor had neither granted the passport nor made any answer to his requests. The minister of police suggested he see the American consul in Paris. This he did, only to learn that the consul was none other than Alexander MacRae, an attorney for the prosecution at Richmond. Burr's Journal contains the laconic record, "What a prospect!"

When Burr called on MacRae he suggested that he see Jonathan Russell, American charge d'affaire, who informed him that "It is the duty of the Consul, not mine," whereupon Burr wrote "If the latter answers insolently, the only revenge I will take, for revenge, you know, is not my nature, is to publish his letter."

MacRae's answer, dated October 29, 1810, said his knowledge of the circumstance under which Mr. Burr left the United States rendered it his duty to decline to give Mr. Burr either a passport or a permis de sejour. To this he added that if Burr felt aggrieved to see Russell.

So, like a shuttlecock, Burr was bandied between these two agents of the American government who apparently were quite happy to contribute to Burr's defeat in his attempt to return to America and to further persecute the object of their chiefs vengeance.

This time Burr wrote that he was ignorant "of any statute or instruction which authorizes a foreign minister or agent to inquire into any circumstance other than those which tend to establish the fact of citizen or not."

Aware that he possessed the trump card, Russell replied on November 4 that:

The man who evades the offended laws of his country, abandons for the time the right to their protection. This fugitive from justice, during his voluntary exile, has a claim to no other passport than one which shall enable him to surrender himself for trial for the offenses for which he stands charged. Such a passport Mr. Russell will furnish to Mr. Burr, but no other.

Thus was transferred from America to France the continued persecution of Aaron Burr.

At this time Burr was so destitute of funds that he walked twenty miles to save coach fare. His meals were of bread, cheese, and potatoes. There were days when his sole diet was potatoes; he could not afford coffee or tea. He lived in an attic room without fire, but even under these circumstances he bought a book for Theodosia and toys for her son, saying, "I never spend a lire that I do not calculate what pretty things I might have bought for you and Gampille, hence my economy."

Eventually came word from the Duc de Rovigo that the passport would be issued. Having received two thousand francs from Edward Griswold, Burr was very happy in anticipation of this return to America; but alas, his authority for departure proved but a promise, and more days of waiting followed. It was during this gloomy period that Burr read in the American newspapers that Napoleon was paying him two thousand pounds sterling annually.

In the midst of the disappointments in Paris word came from Theodosia that all their friends in America had deserted them. John P. Van Ness "is like the rest of the world. When I was in New York, W.P. [William P. Van Ness] was doubtful whether it would be safe to visit me. John Swartwout is true, invariably and nobly conspicuous as the sun. He retrieves the character of man."

After reporting that no word had come from Dolly Madison, Theodosia wrote she had appealed to Albert Gallatin for help, but that no response had come from him. She was so amazed at the treatment of her father in Paris that she wrote:

> *Go to New York; make your stand there. If you are attacked, you will be in the midst of the tenth legion. Civil debts may be procrastinated for a time by confinement to the limits. There you can take your breath; openly see your friends; make your arrangements and soon I think you will be able to throw off monetary shackles, and resume your station.*

Brave words, but it was under another twelve months before her father was to see New York.

Some powerful French friends secured another promise of the passport. Among these were the Duc de Bassano, who had been so impressed with Burr's knowledge of art that he had interested M. Denon, the director of fine arts. Together they had raised money for his passage and secured Russell's promise of a certificate of citizenship.

A number of mutually interested investors sent Burr to Amsterdam as their agent to purchase stock in the Holland Land Company, which owned millions of acres of virgin land in the United States. Just now there was a demand for these holdings; they afforded what appeared to be an opportunity for making some quick money. While on a visit to Bremen, Burr was taken ill and forced to return to Amsterdam for treatment. Here on June 14 he met an American, Combes, captain of a four-hundred-ton ship, who appeared most "anxious to serve me. Says he has often kept awake whole nights about me, though he had never seen me. Will fit up a cabin to my own caprice, and appears to think he can never do enough."

Burr's credulity was always getting him into trouble; his confidence in his fellow man often rendered him as guileless as a child. He had gone to Amsterdam primarily to make money out of his dreams that Holland Company stocks were a veritable gold mine, and by investing for friends he too expected to win a fortune. In anticipation of this easy money he wrote to Theodosia:

Now, if I can get a passport to Bremen and Amsterdam, I will send you a million francs within six months; but one-half of it must be laid out in pretty things. Oh, what beautiful things I will send you. Gampillus, too, shall have a beautiful little watch, and at least fifty trumpets of all different sorts and sizes. Home at 10, and have been casting up my millions and spending it. Lord, how many people I have made happy!

But like millions of others who have counted their counted their chickens before they were hatched, Burr was doomed to disappointment. With physical ills and still another hitch in the issuance of the passport, he again wrote to Napoleon reciting the treatment he had received in France and reminding him of the hospitality he had always accorded to the agents of his Majesty while they were in the United States. In this long memorial Burr advised Napoleon that "at a period when administration of the government of the United States was hostile to France and Frenchmen, they received from me efficient protection."

The action of Burr and his recorded mental reaction just at this period arouses a suspicion that Jefferson's persecution had driven him almost to distraction; notwithstanding his desperate need for money with which to return to America, he spent much of it for baubles for Theodosia and little Gampy.

"Americans have entered into a combination against A. B.;" according to the Journal, and "every man who speaks to him shall be shunned as unworthy of society; no master of vessel or other person shall take any letter or parcel for him, or other like benevolent things; all of which amuses me." Doubtless it would have been more nearly correct had Burr said "crazes me"!

Nevertheless, on July 17, 1811, Burr received a letter from Captain Combes saying that he was sailing on the twenty-third. With all the promises and influence brought to bear, Burr still did not possess the precious passport. But Bassano was not perturbed; he was just a trifle jubilant as he murmured "cherchez la femme!" Then he explained:

*The person through which I could have commu-
nicated to Mr. Russell that he should not have refused
a passport to Mr. Burr was in the country. I wrote to
her yesterday to return. She arrived at the moment that
your note was received. I shall have the passport in the
course of the day, and I shall forward it immediately to
the Duke [Rovigo], and I am convinced that you will
receive it tomorrow to transmit to Mr. Burr.*

Immediately Burr was off for Amsterdam as fast as he could
travel, only to learn that the ship was detained at Trexel, an island
in the North Sea. Now it was Combes who was in trouble. He had
spent some of the deposits made for passage, which was being
demanded. He was being sued for the return of the money. Still in
port September 8, Burr wrote:

*Combes demands of me 450 guilders immediate-
ly, or that he should break up the voyage and sell the
ship; by which I understand that, if I do not pay the
450, he will go off without me. . . . I have not 1/3 of
the sum he demands nor have I any hope of getting it.*

But by the sale of personal things the money was raised,
only to have the captain increase the fare to 480 guilders, then to
500. To raise this money Theodosia's watch was sold, and presto!
Burr's baggage was placed aboard the *Vigilant*. It was September
14, and the record reads:

*I feel as if I were already on the way to you, and
my heart beats with joy. Yet alas! that country which
I am so anxious to revisit, a land which will perhaps
reject me with horror. . . . My windows look out over
the ocean; that ocean that separates me from all that is
dear. With what pleasure I did greet it after three years
absence. . . . There seems to be no obstacle between us,*

*and I almost fancy that I can see you and Gampy, with
the sheep about the door and driving "the great ram
with a little stick."*

Many Dutch passengers wanted aboard, and to accommo-
date these there were delays for other passports. One morning to
Burr's surprise they were under full sail; the sea breeze was in his
nostrils; eagerly he strained his eyes for the western horizon—
surely over there lay Theodosia, little Gampy, and home! It little
mattered now that the ship accommodated, badly, "fifty-four passengers, of whom a majority were women and children; thirty-one
sailors, thirty-three hogs, and about a hundred other quadrupeds
and bipeds."

Burr's thoughts were of the Virginia legion whose venom
he had escaped in Paris, then of the sleuths he probably would
encounter when the *Vigilant* docked. But his musing was rudely
interrupted when an armed vessel, the British frigate *Le Desiree*,
lying just out of Holland waters, seized the *Vigilant* and took her
to Yarmouth roads as a prize. The flag of truce had been ignored,
and October 16 Burr was in London. The *Vigilant* was detained
for trial. There was, however, another ship sailing for Charleston.
Burr wrote, "But how to pay and how to get my baggage in time
are grave questions."

Jeremy Bentham was visited with never a word of the plight.
Appeal for assistance financially from friends was avoided by Aaron Burr, if there was another way; instead he sold the cambrics he
had collected in France especially for Theodosia. Then there was
the little matter of another passport, which must be secured in
some way if he were ever to leave London. These are but a small
part of the troubles that Aaron Burr encountered on his Odyssean
wanderings as an exile from home.

After months' delay a favorable decision was rendered for
the *Vigilant* on January 4, 1812. The good news came; Combes,
however, was sailing for New Orleans—the one port to which
Aaron Burr could not go, where Wilkinson and his revenge still

ruled. In the meantime the American government had prodded Russell in Paris—even transferred him to London. Here he was charge d'affaires, and no doubt had a hand in Combes's decision to re-charter this voyage, for he warned him not to transport Burr to the United States. Again the vengeance of Jefferson found its favorite mark.

After another six months during which the sleuths of the American government hounded his every move, Burr discovered a Captain Potter who for thirty guineas agreed to take him—only his alias now was Monsieur Arnot. Again Burr was forced to part with his precious cambrics, for which he received ten pounds. On March 21 Robert Morris, then in London, loaned him ten pounds while the last of the beautiful collection for Theodosia was parted with for still another ten pounds. Strangely, five pounds came from seltzer water.

On the twenty-fifth Burr's baggage was aboard the *Aurora*, but he must raise twenty additional pounds if he was to depart for America. John Reeve was his only hope, and to him he told of his dire need for this amount. Notwithstanding, Reeve had already advanced ten pounds. He listened in silence, and without a word "drew a check on his banker for twenty pounds, and how I did gallop across the park to get my twenty pounds." By good fortune a delay in sailing gave time for adieu to Bentham and the Godwins.

When the *Aurora* sailed March 26, 1812, only Captain Potter knew the identity of M. Arnot, whose presence if discovered would wreak vengeance of all the agents of Jefferson; but the skipper declared that while he feared war was impending between England and the United States, he was not afraid to return Burr to his native land. Evidently the freedom of the seas released Burr also from fear, since he wrote in his Journal, "If the British hang or roast every American they can catch, and seize all their property, no war would be declared by the United States under the present rulers."

Burr proved a prophet. The war of 1812 was not to the liking, nor was it affected by the Virginia dynasty. The West was eager for expansion, and up to the time Jefferson and his agents had destroyed Burr's influence, he was regarded as the most likely leader in a movement to foreclose our title to Florida and Texas, rights for which he and Andrew Jackson fought valiantly.

Wearily plodding through the streets of London, Burr suddenly faced Combes, from whom he demanded his passage to America, only to have the captain laugh in his face. This was like the indignities he had suffered while awaiting an opportunity to see Napoleon. Concerning his experience Burr wrote:

> It is a melancholy fact, my friend, that Europe is fast, very fast, rebarbarizing, retrograding with rapid strides to the darkest ages of intellectual and moral degradation; all that has been seen, or felt, or heard or read of despotism; all other, past or present, is faint or feeble; in its freedom and ease compared with that which now desolates Europe. The science of tyranny was in its infancy, it is now matured.
>
> Within the last fifteen years, greater ravages have been made on the dignity, the worth, and the rational enjoyments of human nature, than in any former ten centuries. All of the effort of genius, all the nobler sentiments and finer feelings, are depressed and paralyzed. Private faith, personal confidence and the whole strain of social virtues are condemned and eradicated. They are crimes. And you, my friend, even you, with all your generous propensities, your chivalrous notions of honor, and faith and delicacy, were you condemned to live within the grasp of the tyrant, even you would discard them all, or you would be sacrificed as a dangerous subject.

*In all history there is no record of a greater or more passion-
ate communion and understanding between father and daughter.
She was not merely the child of this loins; she was the paragon
he had slowly and laboriously created with his brain. She was the
living justification of his very existence.*

– Nat Schachner
Aaron Burr

22
The Exile Returns

It was Boston Harbor that witnessed Burr's return on May 5, 1812. In his Journal he describes himself as "a grave, silent, strange sort of an animal" because, to disguise his identity, he had allowed his whiskers to grow. So returned this exile who for four years had roamed over Europe, had endured unbelievable hardships and had enjoyed incredible splendors.

No tale of fiction would reach like depths of despair or mount to such heights of achievement—one day without food and asso-ciating with the commonest of earth, and the next the guest of the king and his court. Wit and wisdom to command the attention of the intellectuals, yet possessed of a democracy that found favor with the bourgeoisie of the earth. Versatility of accomplishments had Aaron Burr.

The collector of customs at Boston was a son of General Dearborn, but Burr ran the gauntlet and secured his baggage as M. Arnot, notwithstanding the extreme vindictive spirit of those under whose surveillance he passed unrecognized. He wrote letters to Theodosia and Samuel Swartwout, the latter in New York. He came and went unrecognized from his Cornhill Square boardinghouse, expecting some one to exclaim, "You are Aaron Burr!" but his disguise was too complete.

In the Boston directory he found a number of familiar names. To Jonathan Mason he wrote, "I pray you not to conjecture aloud who may be the writer; he wishes to remain incognito a few days. . . . If you will take the trouble of calling . . . you will find an old acquaintance who wishes a half hour's conversation with you." Mason did not call.

On May 19th Burr received a letter from Samuel Swartwout assuring him that he still had many friends and no enemies, that business prospects were not propitious and that two old creditors who have judgments are inexorable. Burr added, "Nothing will satisfy them but money or approved security, neither of which are in my power. The alternative is to be taken on execution and go the limits [jail]."

For five years Burr had been trying to escape jails and prisons; naturally, if his return to New York meant to go to jail, that placed him in another serious predicament. While considering this situation, a letter from Theodosia, written a year before, reached him. She counseled that "He face his old debts; see his friends and resume your situation." He decided to follow her advice.

In response to a request Benjamin Fessenden called. He had been an ensign in the Westchester campaign. He introduced Burr to President Kirkland of Harvard, who purchased some of the books he had brought back from Europe. This paid his board bill and enabled him to secure passage to New York. This time his alias was Mr. de Gamelli, and he sailed on the sloop *Rose*. Burr reached New York June 7, 1812, four years to the day from the time he had departed to escape from his enemies and their persecution, the fury of which John Marshall described so aptly as "the instrument of those malignant and vindictive passions which may rage in the bosoms of contending parties struggling for power."

Jefferson was no longer president, but what of Madison?

Madison had been the choice of Jefferson and the Virginia legion, the Virginia dynasty which had autocratically and murderously fought to destroy Burr that they might perpetuate political power. Fortunately for Burr, Madison was engrossed in his trouble with England.

James Wickham wrote from Richmond that the bail in Ohio had been paid and that other suits had been dismissed, adding "glad to hear that after so many sufferings Colonel Burr has the prospect of being restored to his country and permitted again to employ his talents to advantage."

His presence had been disclosed to a Boston newspaper and was copied in the New York Columbian: "Colonel Burr, once so celebrated for his talents and latterly so much talked of for his sufferings, arrived in Newburyport from France and England, and passed through this town on his way to New York."

The *Columbian* announced that Aaron Burr had returned to New York and that he had resumed the practice of law at 9 Nassau Street. After the expressions of surprise and some excitement had died out, there followed a consensus that his punishment had been too severe; for even his enemies were beginning to regret its excesses regardless of past beliefs and antagonism. The day his small sign was put up at least five hundred friends and well-wishers, prospective clients, and some merely filled with curiosity called.

Robert Troup, who had been so free with his harsh judgments, loaned Burr his law library until his son should need it. With ten dollars borrowed from a friend he was ready to return to his professional practice. His office took on such momentum from his former standing that in twelve days the fees had amounted to two thousand dollars and in the employment of his energies there came peace and a degree of comfort.

Aaron Burr was a human dynamo, excessively charged and happiest when busy. In great enthusiasm he wrote to Theodosia, from whom by return mail he was to receive two tragic letters announcing that her son was dead:

> *A few miserable days past, my dear father, and your late letters would have gladdened my soul; and even now I rejoice at their contents as much as it is possible for me to rejoice at anything, but there is no more joy for me; the world is blank. I have lost my boy. My child is gone forever. He expired on the 30th of June. My head is not now sufficiently collected to say anything further. May heaven, by other blessings, make you some amends for the noble grandson you have lost.*

The other letter was from Alston:

> *That boy, on whom all rested; our companion, our friend, he who was to have redeemed all your glory, and shed new luster upon our families—that boy, at once our happiness and pride, is taken from us—is dead. Poor Theodosia! She has endured all that a human could endure; but her admirable mind will triumph, she supports herself in a manner worthy of your daughter. We have not been able to form any definite plan of life. My present wish is that Theodosia should join you, with or without me, as soon as possible. I recognize your claim to her after such separation; but change of scene and your society will aid her. I am conscious in receiving at least that tone of mind which we are destined to carry through life with us.*

With the passing of "Little Gampy" half of the light of the world went out for Aaron Burr. The sturdy little boy for whom Burr had gone without food in France that he might purchase toys for him was dead. Only his mother, Theodosia, remained! And for her life was held by such a silken thread; the cancer was fast sapping her vitality.

Colonel Timothy Green, a retired lawyer and friend of the family, was dispatched to Charleston to bring Theodosia to her father. Her husband, Joseph Alston, was governor of South Carolina. He arranged that Captain Overstocks, commander of the *Patriot*, whose hatches were stocked with the spoils of months of privateering, should convey his wife to New York. The letter of authorization indicated that Theodosia's health was the mission of the *Patriot*, a ruse that guided the vessel through the British blockade at Cape Hatteras, where a challenge brought abroad a British officer. After examining Alston's letter, the challenger waived Captain Overstocks and his precious charge for a safe journey.

The *Patriot* had sailed from Charleston on December 30, 1812. Theodosia carried with her the private papers, letters, and documents her father had consigned to her care during his exile—papers which today would shed light upon many subjects that must remain dark. These together with Theodosia were lost in what the ship encountered off Cape Hatteras, one of those terrible storms for which that region is noted. The last person who saw her and the captain of the *Patriot* was the British agent who wished them a safe voyage; the morning after the terrible gale witnessed a deserted sea. The ship that ran the blockade had succumbed to the might of the storm.

Long weary days of waiting dragged themselves into weeks and no word came to the bereft husband or to the disconsolate father. To each other they wrote frantic notes of their suffering. Alston wrote:

> *Forebodings! wretched, heart-rending forebodings distract my mind. I may no longer have a wife; and yet my impatient restlessness addresses her a letter. Tomorrow will be three weeks since our separation, and not yet one line. Gracious God! for what am I reserved?*

With the reading of this letter Aaron Burr's heart died and with it the final flickering hope that Theodosia would yet arrive. He had walked the Battery at the south tip of Manhattan by day and long into the nights awaiting her arrival; ever peering for a topsail of the *Patriot*, longing for the arrival of his beloved Theodosia.

As the months rolled on, notice came of the terrible storm that had swept out of the Bermudas and wrought destruction through the Caribbean and northward, leaving a trail of misery even to New York. From Alston came the heartbroken cry:

> *My boy—my wife—both gone! But there are compensations, even for me, who has been deemed worthy of the heart of Theodosia Burr, and who has felt what it is to be blessed with such a woman's love, never will I forget my elevation.*

"Hope died more slowly in Burr's breast," wrote Nathan Schachner. He continued:

> *Perhaps she had been captured, and taken to some foreign port by a vagrant privateer. But as the weeks became months, even that poor consolation was gone. The second half of Burr's life was now dust and ashes. In all history there is no record of a greater or more passionate communion and understanding between father and daughter. She was not merely the child of his loins; she was the paragon he had slowly and laboriously created with his brain. She was the living justification of his very existence.*

The heart of Burr was buried with Theodosia. After the deaths of his daughter and grandson Burr moved about as if in a dream; his spirit was enshrouded in grief too bitter to discuss, too tender to expose, and too sweet to share. Thereafter his daily

The *Nag's Head* portrait, allegedly of Theodosia Burr Alston, was attributed to John Vanderlyn when "re-discovered" in the 1860s.

communion was with these departed spirits for whose existence he had assumed responsibility.

After a time he was engrossed in his profession, where for a quarter of a century clients continued to flock to a man who enjoyed the reputation of never having lost a case he personally conducted. The shades of Hamilton with all the blight of his powerful friends continued across his path, but this did not humble his power, nor could it quench his spirit.

Hamilton failed to conquer Burr in life, and after he was dead his friends carried on the fight, but their endeavors were limited to political realms, where the aristocratic ambitions of Hamilton and his friends gradually gave way to democracy and the voice of the people.

Burr and Hamilton had been consulted in the famous Medcef Eden case, which concerned the estate of a rich New York brewer who died in 1798. Eden was survived by two playboy sons who had been relieved of their fortune by dishonest usurers and scheming creditors. Hamilton had declined to take the case, giving as his reason that nothing could be salvaged, and even if he were successful it would involve some of his friends. One of the Eden brothers had died; but the other was in such desperate straits that he appealed to Burr to recover his property, which consisted chiefly of realty that had advanced enormously in value. In undertaking the struggle for the return of title to his client, Burr took into his home the Eden family, consisting of father, wife, and two daughters, all of whom he fed, clothed, and provided for during the many years that the case was dragging its way through the courts.

Cleverly, Burr avoided the valuable property in the city and devoted his efforts to a farm of little value, which was located on the north end of Manhattan Island. The suit for title alleged that fraud, usury, and coercion were practiced in the original assignments and foreclosures.

The case was not vigorously contested. After winning in the lower court, the appeal was taken to a superior court, where it was approved. Following the precedent, writs of ejectment were served by the score and there was fast scurrying for defense of titles.

Martin Van Buren, who was later to be president, took part with Burr, and for years the two fought through one court after another, winning suit after suit. The appeals continued for many years since the owners possessed great wealth, while Burr was almost penniless. Eventually the father died. By him Burr had been nominated as guardian for his two daughters, but when victory came, the costs had mounted to such proportions that they absorbed much of the proceeds to maintain the family and pay the enormous expenses that had eaten up a large portion of the judgments. Burr, however, and his clients were rewarded; he had earned a slight competency for old age. The two girls had enjoyed a good home and were well educated, and each possessed a small estate.

Originally when the two girls came to live with Burr, their father and mother had readily assented to his supervision of their education with the result that they were carefully trained in reading, sports, sciences, and the arts. Both were educated in a manner to conform with Burr's plan for educating Theodosia, which had not only taught them to think but had included refinement and culture.

Charles Burdett joined the group. The trio were educated that they might occupy almost any position in life. Their studies included the classics, modern languages, navigation, astronomy, the violin, and the flageolet. Afterward, Burdett reported:

> *We were placed under a private tutor, subject to Mr. Burr's strict control; nothing was neglected. Studies were regulated by system; health was cared for by incessant injunctions to take air and exercise. We were domiciled in Albany; where a room was devoted to Burr's sole use on his frequent trips on legal business to the capital, for it was his wont to review the studies that were pursued during his absence.*
>
> *These girls eventually came to be his secretaries and exercised a greater influence over his later life than anyone who had ever been connected with him, except by ties of consanguinity. He was perfectly wrapped up in them and they were the only human beings who ever filled the void caused by the death of Theodosia Alston. They reciprocated his affection as strongly as it was bestowed. They loved and honored him. His word was their law.*

Charles Burdett was born in 1814, two years after Burr returned from exile. He was a member of the Eden family when they came to live with Burr; he became Burr's son by adoption. He, too, was educated by Burr and under Burr's supervision. He attended Dr. Hazelin's school at Cooperstown, was a cadet in Captain Partridge's military academy, and entered the Navy. Out of this association he wrote, "Burr's ideas of education differed from those of every other person with whom I ever came in contact; he made me iron!"

The founder of the Norwich University, Alden Partridge, inquired of Burr concerning a protégé, receiving the following reply:

> *The young woman about whom you have made inquiries is 21 years of age. She possesses no single one of those talents which are commonly called useful in a female, i.e. she can neither darn a stocking or make a pudding—though in common justice I ought to add that she is eminently useful to me as a private secretary and reader; and, she is well qualified to assist in the education of her children, should she ever become a mother. She has been educated wholly under my superintendence, the principle aim of which has been to form her manners, to teach her knowledge of the world, the duties, disabilities and privileges of her sex; to appear to advantage in society, to do the honors of her own house with grace and dignity, in short to be the friend and companion of a man of sense, of education and taste.*

James Parton wrote that she said, "I never ask and never answer an impertinent question. I was brought up in the 'Burr' school." Mr. Parton further observed, "All of which she related with pride and bearing that confirmed every word she said."

Thomas Jefferson wrote that "all men are created equal" and are "endowed by their Creator with certain unalienable rights: life, liberty and the pursuit of happiness:" Yet these are just what Jefferson denied to Burr—robbed him of what he fought through the Revolution to secure, not only for himself but for every American.

Since it was Jefferson's false propaganda that robbed Burr of justice, liberty, and the pursuit of happiness, is it not the solemn duty of everyone who believes in justice to examine carefully the archives of America that he may know the truth and restore to Aaron Burr his good name?

Is an act sacrilegious that restores honor and virtue to its rightful owner because in so doing it convicts another who has long been esteemed as statesman?

The eminent biographer Walter F. McCaleb, who has probably done as much research concerning Jefferson's charges and persecution of Burr as any living American, recently wrote to the author:

> Aaron Burr typifies the highest type of an "American." He loved his country, fought for it valiantly. He envisaged its coming and sought with all the energy and intelligence he possessed to lay the foundations for the mightiest republic in the world. He it was who first saw the need of building the walls of the nation upon the margins of the Atlantic and Pacific oceans. That was the dream which lay at the bottom of his "conspiracy."

There! You see? I was right! I was only thirty years too soon. What was treason in me thirty years ago, is patriotism for another now.

– Aaron Burr

23
Thirty Years Too Soon

Aaron Burr was one public citizen who saw the good and ignored the evil in men. Once, when rebuked for aiding men who had disgraced themselves by becoming slaves to liquor, he replied, "They may be black to the world, I care not how black. They are ever white to me." Even after he had lost political standing with the masses, he was the brains of an intellectual group that wielded a large influence in national politics. It was his voice that first championed in New York, through this intelligentsia, the cause of Andrew Jackson for the presidency. This was in recognition of Old-Hickory integrity, and because:

A certain junta of actual factitious Virginians have had possession of the government for twenty-four

*years, consider the United States their property and
by bawling "support the administration" have so long
succeeded in duping the republican public.*

In this letter, which was written to his son-in-law, Joseph
Alston, who during the years of 1812 to 1814 had been governor
of South Carolina, Burr painted this picture of Monroe:

> *Naturally dull and stupid; extremely illiterate;
> indecisive to a degree that would be incredible to
> anyone who did not know him; pusillanimous, and,
> of course, hypocritical; and has no opinion on any
> subject, and will always be under the government
> of the worst men; pretends, as I am told, to some
> knowledge of military matters, but never command-
> ed a platoon, nor was ever fit to command one. "He
> served in the Revolutionary War!"—that is he acted
> a short time as aide-de-camp to Lord Stirling. Mon-
> roe's whole duty was to fill his lordship's tankard,
> and hear, with indication of admiration, his lordship's
> long stories about himself.*
>
> *Such is Monroe's military experience. I was with
> my regiment in the same division at the same time. As
> a lawyer Monroe was far below mediocrity. He never
> rose to the honor of trying a case of a hundred pounds.
> This is a character exactly suited to the views of the
> Virginia junta.*

Burr recognized that good government was to be had only by
changing the clique who ruled in Washington, the political Virginia junta who had held the reigns of power for twenty-four years.
He realized that it would take the strong character of Andrew
Jackson to eliminate the degrading system of preserving a political combination that had proven it was more interested in the
spoils of office than in serving the nation.

In this letter to his son-in-law, Burr continues:

> *If there be a man in the United States of firmness and decision and having standing enough to afford even a hope of success, it is your duty to hold him up to the public view. That man is Andrew Jackson. Nothing is wanting but a respectable nomination made before the proclamation of the Virginia caucus, and Jackson's success is inevitable.*
>
> *If this project should accord with your views, I could wish to see you prominent in the execution of it. It must be known to be your work. Whether a formal and open nomination should now be made, or whether you should, for the present, by a joint resolution of both Houses of your legislature, congressional caucuses and nominations, you only can judge.*
>
> *One consideration inclines me to hesitate about the policy of a present nomination. It is this: that Jackson ought first to be admonished to be passive, for the moment he shall be announced as a candidate, he will be assailed by the Virginia junta with menaces and with insidious promises of boons and favors. There is danger that Jackson might be wrought upon by such practices.*

Andrew Jackson's bravery and integrity always appealed to Aaron Burr. They had been fast friends from the day he first came to Congress from Tennessee as the single representative of the new commonwealth. Burr was then senator from New York. Jackson, like Burr, had always shown great interest in the West and in all problems looking to its development—particularly the conquest of Texas and the addition of this empire to the United States. Bravery and boundless energy were common attributes of Aaron Burr and Andrew Jackson.

Burr arose at dawn. Breakfast consisted of an egg and a cup of coffee, after which he worked for hours before his clerks and assistants came, one of whom reported that he was a hard task-master; he "kept us on the jump." All day he was dispatching and receiving messages, sending for books and papers, expecting every command to be obeyed with next-to-impossible celerity, inspiring everyone with his zeal, and getting a surprising quantity and quality of work accomplished. "He was business incarnate."

About ten in the evening he would cease work, invite his companions to the sideboard, and take a single glass of wine. Then his spirits would rise, and he would sit for hours telling stories of the past and drawing brief and graphic sketches of celebrated characters with whom he had acted. "At times he was the liveliest fellow in the world, as merry as a boy, never melancholy, never ill-natured."

About midnight, or later, he would lie down on a hard couch in the corner of the office and sleep like a child until morning. In his personal habits he was a thorough-going Spartan—eating little, drinking little, sleeping little, working hard. He was fond of calculating upon how small a sum life could be supported, and used to think he could live on seventy-five cents a week.

His conversation was remarkable for its candor, humor and clarity. He denounced no one—not even Wilkinson, of whom he spoke more severely than anyone else. He asserted in a positive manner that Wilkinson betrayed him. Against Jefferson he never appeared embittered; but his lies disgusted him. He described Jefferson as very agreeable in conversation; a man of no "presence;" a plain, country-looking man; a sincere and thorough "Jacobin" in opinion.

Burr never changed his estimate of Washington: that he was a well-intentioned country gentleman; that he was honest, slow to make up his mind but no great general, not even a great soldier.

The average person was nonplussed by Burr's nonchalance toward his bitter, even degrading experiences, many of which came as the result of his enemies' charges. After more than a century there are still thousands of people ignorant of the facts who still class Burr with Benedict Arnold. Such people will not understand the following incident, nor appreciate it.

As an ambitious young lawyer at Richmond, Winfield Scott followed the proceedings with such anxiety and determination that he climbed up a door and stood with his foot on the lock lest he miss events that were to impress him for life. While the trial was in progress, he departed from Richmond and never again saw Aaron Burr until after his return from Europe. On the evening following Scott's promotion to the rank of general, he was invited to the home of a distinguished politician in Albany, where a dinner was given to celebrate the promotion.

"Have you any objection, General, to being introduced to Colonel Aaron Burr?" inquired the host.

"Any gentleman whom you choose to invite to your house," replied the general, "I shall be glad to know."

The colonel entered, the introduction took place, and he and the party sat down to whist until the dinner was announced. At the table Colonel Burr sat opposite to General Scott; but for a time neither engaged in special conversation. In an endeavor not to embarrass the colonel, Scott avoided any mention of Richmond, or even of Virginia, lest he should excite painful feelings in the mind of the accused of that memorable trial. Suddenly Colonel Burr looked up and said, "General Scott, I have seen you before."

"Have you indeed?" inquired the general, with caution, lest he offend.

"Yes," replied Burr, "I saw you at my trial."

Then, after describing the dress of the young gentleman in the courtroom, he proceeded to converse about the scenes of the trial, Richmond, and the entire event, as if he had been only a spectator, just as Winfield Scott had been. The general was both surprised and relieved.

It was a couple of years after the War of 1812 that this conversation occurred, and after expressing his cordial admiration for General Scott's gallantry and conduct, the old soldier inquired, "Why don't the folks at Washington employ General Jackson?"

After someone had remarked that Jackson had a command in the militia, Colonel Burr observed, "I'll tell you why they don't give him a commission. He is a friend of mine; that's the reason."

After Burr's return to America he wrote to Mrs. Blennerhassett, then in Ireland, asking that she send him the papers and documents in her possession relating to the Bastrop colony and its proposed settlement. She replied, demanding a large sum of money, which was far more than Burr was in position to pay. Considering her destitution, however, he sent her money on two or three occasions.

Concerning Burr's conversations about his duel with Hamilton, James Parton records that:

> *Burr never blamed himself for the duel with Hamilton. He despised the outcry made about the duel, and he would indulge sometimes in a kind of defiant affectation respecting it. "My friend Hamilton, whom I shot" he would say with amazing nonchalance. Usually, however, he alluded to his antagonist with respect, styling him "General Hamilton," and doing particular justice to his merits.*
>
> *"Was Hamilton a gentleman?" inquired a foreigner, once in Burr's hearing. Burr resented the question, and replied with hauteur: "Sir, I met him."*

There appears but one occasion on which Burr returned to the scene of the duel between himself and Hamilton, and this was to oblige a young friend who wished to see the spot made famous. They left their boat at the foot of the heights of Weehawken, just where Burr had left his boat on that fatal morning a quarter of a century before. They climbed over the same rocks and soon reached the spot. Except that the rocks were covered with names and the ground was more overgrown with trees and vines, the place remained unchanged. The companion was placed where Hamilton had stood and Burr on the spot from which he had fired.

As Burr sketched the tragic scene, the old fire seemed rekindled within him; his voice rose and his eyes blazed as he recounted the long catalog of wrongs he'd withstood from Hamilton; how he had remonstrated, and even forgiven, with the understanding that such vile calumnies were to cease. When they were renewed, and there was no choice save to slink out of sight of the wretch degraded and despised, or to meet him on the field and silence him—then, and then only, had occurred the duel.

Burr dwelt much on the meanness of Hamilton; charged that he was malevolent and cowardly, a man who would slander a rival, and not stand to it, unless he was cornered.

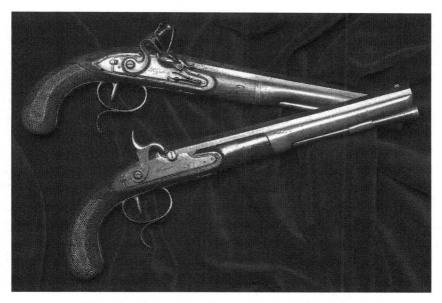

The pistols used in the Burr–Hamilton duel

"When he stood up to fire," said Burr, "he caught my eye, and quailed under it; he looked like a convicted felon. It is not true," he continued, "that Hamilton did not fire at me; Hamilton fired first." Burr heard the ball whistle among the branches and saw the twig severed above his head.

Burr spoke of what Hamilton wrote the evening before the duel with infinite contempt. "It reads," he said, "like the confessions of a penitent monk."

The language of this recital, continued the one who accompanied Burr, gives but feeble expression to the fiery impressiveness of Burr's words, for "they justified all he had done; nay, even applauded it."

Burr had been in bed as the result of a stroke when a newspaper brought the information that his lifetime dream had come true. The gentleman who called that morning found him with the paper in hand, all excitement, his eyes blazing.

"There!" exclaimed the little old man, pointing to the news from Texas.

"You see, I was right. Only I was thirty years too soon. What was treason in me thirty years ago is patriotism for another now."

A phrenologist, ignorant of whom he was examining, reported:

What a head! This is a Van Buren head! What a pity he has lived in obscurity. With many noble traits of character, however, he has some bad ones. He is generous to a fault. He takes pleasure in giving, whether his own or others' property. He is very secretive; relies on his own judgment; is seldom swerved by the judgment of others. He feels he was born to command and as brave as a lion. He would have made a great scholar, a great statesman, a great orator, a great anything, if he had but had the chance. Yet, he can descend to duplicity to gain his ends. As a statesman, he would have been diplomatic and as firm as a rock, whether for good or for evil. A firm friend, without boasting, or presuming. More generous than just. He has little reverence, yet would scarcely be an unbeliever. His head is indeed a study—a strange contradictory head. He is very irritable, and impatient of control. He could look into the souls of men. Gracious! what a lawyer he would have made! He has been fond of the fair sex. His bad qualities are overtopped by his good ones; now pray tell me who the gentleman is?

The answer came: "Colonel Burr."

The phrenologist was amazed and apologized. Colonel Burr whispered, "You have given no offense."

Aaron Burr's life was largely devoted to assisting those about him, especially ambitious students. Possibly the outstanding example of his magnanimous spirit was John Vanderlyn, who was born in Kingston, New York, in 1775 and died in 1852. *New York Magazine* published the following in June 1890:

> *As a country boy in Ulster county Vanderlyn engaged to work for six months for a country blacksmith near Kingston; one morning Aaron Burr's horse cast a shoe and he stopped at the forge to have it replaced; walking about in the vicinity, he was struck with the spirit and truth of a charcoal sketch on a barn door. Turning to young Vanderlyn who stood by, he inquired who was the draftsman?*
>
> *"I did it" was the reply; whereupon Colonel Burr questioned him at length, and recognizing his ability for a higher sphere of activity than the humble occupation he had adopted, he gave him his town address and offered to advise and assist him if he should decide to study and to practice art. "Burr said to me" Vanderlyn afterwards reported "Put a clean shirt in your pocket, come to New York and call upon me."*
>
> *Some weeks later, while sitting at breakfast at his residence called Richmond Hill, a brown paper parcel was handed him with the message that the bearer was at the door. It contained a coarse shirt and the address in the Colonel's handwriting. He called the boy in; invited him to remain with the family, little imagining that Vanderlyn could prove so renowned a protege.*

After studying for sometime in New York, Vanderlyn copied Gilbert Stuart's painting of Burr with such merit that he sent him to Paris, where for five years he enjoyed instruction by the best masters of that capital.

Vanderlyn's first picture to create a stir was his *Marius Amid the Ruins of Carthage*. In 1808 at the Paris Salon it received a gold medal conferred at the behest of Napoleon. There followed seven years of painting in Paris, during which he made copies of Raphael, Titian, and Correggio in the Louvre. In 1812 he painted his nude figure of Ariadne. This created a greater sensation than *Marius*.

Returning to America, Vanderlyn painted portraits of four presidents: Madison, Monroe, Jackson, and Taylor. In 1832 he was commissioned by the House of Representatives to paint a full-length copy of Stuart's Washington. In 1837 he was commissioned by Congress to paint the *Landing of Columbus*. This vast historical panel is a graphic example of great merit of the "Grand Style," mounted on a panel on the domed ceiling of the Capitol in Washington, D.C.

From Roundout, New York, February 11, 1858, Robert Gosman wrote:

> *The twenty letters I have spoken of were written by Burr to Vanderlyn from Holland whilst Burr was endeavoring to get passage to America. Vanderlyn was in Paris, whither he had gone a second time in 1804, and where he remained, save for two years in Rome, until 1816.*
>
> *These letters do not possess any value to a biographer of Colonel Burr, being on matters of business and showing a most scrupulous memory as to some small debts he forwards the money to Vanderlyn to discharge, and a most cheerful and brave spirit under many adverse circumstances.*
>
> *There are some messages to some of his Parisian female friends in some of them, but all couched in the most delicate and respectful language. Without knowing ought of the writer, save to be gleaned from these letters—chirographically as well as their tone—*

one would set him down as a gentleman of education, elegant tastes and pursuits, somewhat a precision in detail, a keen discernment and marked decision. There is nothing to sustain the "vulgar error" of Burr's utter libertinism in the slightest degree, and had this been his characteristic, I am certain from the relation between Burr and Vanderlyn it would have been shown in these confidential communications.

On the occasion of Burr's Parisian sojourn, he assisted Vanderlyn pecuniarily, instead of the latter assisting him. Vanderlyn was always in straitened circumstances. He was generous to a fault, but rarely had a louis that was not mortgaged.

Burr's phenomenal ability to read men's souls was most extraordinary. His characterization of Benedict Arnold is a good example:

He was a perfect madman in the excitement of the battle, and as ready to do deeds of valor; but he has not a particle of moral courage. He is utterly unprincipled, and has no love of country or self respect to guide him. He is not to be trusted anywhere but under the eye of a superior officer.

After a pious old lady had chided him about his sins and his having killed Hamilton, Burr replied "O aunt, don't feel so badly; we shall both meet in heaven yet; meanwhile, may God bless you." She said, "He then tenderly took my hand, and left the house."

Possibly no one else had such opportunity for knowing the true Burr as his intimate associate Doctor Hosack, who was Burr's physician and counselor through the years when most of his intimates had allowed public clamor to lead them to desert the octogenarian. Doctor Hosack inquired, in view of his approaching death, if in the expedition to the Southwest he had designed a separation of the Union. With some impatience Burr replied, "No! I would as soon have thought of taking possession of the moon, and informing my friends that I intended to divide it among them!"

Burr thought the Bible to be by far the most valuable of books, and he greatly admired the Psalms of David. In his opinion the greatest books, after the Bible, were those of Shakespeare, Burns, and Pope. In early life he had been fond of the French authors, but later had asserted that "Rousseau was a self torturing egoist" and that he had lost his interest in Voltaire. Burr said that his grandfather, Jonathan Edwards, "had the clearest head in America."

As was an almost universal practice, a newspaper made a scurrilous attack upon him, concerning which he replied to the one who called it to his attention, "I don't care what they say about me; they may say what they please; I let them alone, I only ask to be left alone."

Burr remained so indifferent to criticism that a lady exclaimed, "Why, Colonel, if they were to accuse you of murder, I don't think you would deny it." His reply was "O, no, my child, why should I? What good would it do? Every man likes his own opinion best."

One day when a gentleman in his office talked of the evils of war, Burr replied, "Slander has slain more than the sword."

Always slow to speak evil of anyone, even to reply to his traducers, Burr was fond of replying to denunciatory language with Burns's "Address to the Unco Guid, or the Rigidly Righteous," stanzas VII and VIII:

Then gently scan your brother man,
Still gentler sister woman;
Tho' they may gang a kennin wrang,
To step aside is human:
One point must still be greatly dark,—
The moving Why they do it;
And just as lamely can ye mark,

How far, perhaps, they rue it.
Who made the heart, 'tis He alone
Decidedly can try us;
He knows each chord, its various tone,
Each spring, its various bias:
Then at the balance let's be mute,
We never can adjust it;
What's done we partly may compute,
But know not what's resisted.

Greatly afflicted, a friend once exclaimed, "O, Colonel, how shall I get through this?"

"Live through it, my dear!" was his emphatic reply.

Still complaining, she said: "This will kill me Colonel, I know I shall not survive this."

"Well," said he, "die, then, Madame: we must all die; but die game, bless me, die game."

One beautiful afternoon, she said, as she arranged his pillows, "O! Colonel, if you were only forty years younger, and we were walking by the side of some pleasant stream with beautiful flowers all around us, how happy we could be."

"Well, my child," he said, "and we shall walk by the side of pleasant streams, and beautiful flowers, if we believe the Book."

Colonel Burr had been ill. Apparently, he anticipated the great adventure. His thoughts were largely of Princeton and college days, of the Revolutionary War and his fellow soldiers and of Theodosia and her son. He talked of his biography, which was sure to be published after he was gone, and appeared much concerned that eventually he should be known as he was.

It has taken a century, however, for the truth to outrun the lies, for men to seek honestly to paint the picture with its faithful lights and shadows. We are quite sure this is all Aaron Burr would desire.

In speaking of death he would often say, "A brave man never fears death," or "Death is only terrible to cowards," or "Death has no terrors for me."

[Burr's] manners were the most courtly of any one of his age. He had not the parade of Morris, nor the gravity of Jay; but he never for a moment forgot himself by assumption or too much familiarity.

– Colonel Knapp
Memoirs of Burr

24
Those Who Knew
Him Personally

After more than half a century of research when every letter, paper, or book concerning Aaron Burr was carefully examined, the sources of information naturally array themselves into two classes: Those who say, and those who saw; or those who recorded from personal knowledge and personal association that they knew. All criticism, calumny, and criminal charges come from the first group. In no case where the speaker had personal knowledge is there anything save commendation and unrestrained admiration.

In his boyhood, Judge John Greenwood spent six years in Burr's office. During this time he says, "I enjoyed peculiar advantages of knowledge of Colonel Burr, having been clerk and student at a period in my life when the strongest impressions were likely to be made upon me." On September 24, 1863, Judge

Greenwood read a paper to the Long Island Historical Society, from which this excerpt is taken:

> *Colonel Burr's diet was very light, a cup of coffee and a roll constituted his breakfast; his dinner in a majority of cases consisted of roasted potatoes seasoned with a little salt and butter, or perhaps thickened with milk, "bony clabber," sweetened with sugar. A cup of black tea with a slice of bread and butter was the last meal. These constituted, as a general rule, his sustenance for twenty-four hours. . . . He never used spirituous liquors. His usual beverage was claret and water sweetened with loaf sugar. His wine he bought by the cask and had it bottled at his residence. The result of his abstemious course of living was that he enjoyed uniform good health.*
>
> *Burr's industry was of the most remarkable character. Indeed, it may be said with truth that he was never idle. He was always employed in some way, and what is more, required everyone under him to be so. Sometimes coming through the office and observing that I was not at work, he would say "Master John, can't you find something to do?" Although it is safe to say that no clerk in an office was ever more constantly worked than I was.*
>
> *He would rise at an early hour in the morning, devote himself to business all day—for he had a large practice—and usually retired to rest no sooner than twelve or half past twelve o'clock at night. In this way he would accomplish a vast amount of work. His perseverance and indefatigability, too, were striking characteristics. No plan or purpose once formed, was abandoned, and no amount of labor discouraged him or caused him to desist. To begin a work was, with him, to finish it. How widely in this respect he differed*

from some professional men of his own and the present day I need hardly say. . . .

But I must say a word of his manner in court. He seemed in the street and everywhere in public strongly conscious that he was a mark of observation—not indeed in the sense in which Hamlet is spoken of as "the observed of all observers"; but as an object, to some curiosity, to others of hostile or suspicious regard. Carrying this feeling into a court-room his manner was somewhat reserved, though never submissive, and he used no unnecessary words. He would present at once the main point of his case, and as his preparation was thorough, would usually be successful. But he was not eloquent. If he thought his dignity assailed in any manner, even inferentially, his rebuke was withering in the cutting sarcasm of its few words, and the lightening glance of his terrible eyes which few could withstand. I may say in this connection that his self-possession, under the most trying circumstances, was wonderful and that he probably never knew what it was to fear a human being.

If there was anything which Burr's proud spirit supremely despised, it was a mean prying curiosity. He early inculcated in me the lesson never to read even an open letter addressed to another which might be lying in my way, and never to look over another who was writing a letter. It was one of my duties to copy his letters, and I shall never forget the indignant and withering look which, on one occasion, he gave to a person in the office who endeavored to see what I was copying. Neither would he tolerate any impertinent staring or gazing at him as if to spy out his secret thoughts and reflections.

You will be glad to hear something of his very fascinating powers in conversation. It may seem strange, if not incredible, that a man who had passed through such vicissitudes as he had, and who must have had such a crowd of early memories on his mind, should be able to preserve a uniform serenity and even cheerfulness; but such is the fact. His manners were courtly and his carriage graceful, and he had a winning smile in moments of pleasant intercourse which seemed almost to charm you. He would laugh, too, sometimes as if his heart was bubbling with joy, and its effect was irresistible. Nobody could tell a story or an anecdote better than he could, and nobody enjoyed it better than he did himself. His maxim was suaviter in modo, fortier in re. Yet, where spirits and a determined manner were required, probably no man ever showed them more effectively. Although comparatively small in person and light in frame, I have seen him rebuke and put to silence men of position in society greatly his superior in physical strength, who were wanting in respect in their language towards him.

Colonel Burr was a social man; that is, he liked the company of a friend and would spend half an hour with him in conversation most agreeably. Occasionally one with whom he had been on intimate terms, and who had shared his adventures, like Samuel Swartwout or William Hosack, would call and have a pleasant time. Dr. W.J. McNevin was also intimate with him. He was very fond of young company. Children delighted him. He not only took an interest in their sports, but conciliated them, and attached them to him by presents. The latter, I may observe, was also one of his modes of pleasing the more mature of the gentler sex.

There are some who suppose Colonel Burr had no virtues. This is a mistake. He was true in his friendships, and would go any length to serve a friend; and he had also the strongest affections. I shall never forget

*the incidents concerning the loss of his daughter Theo-
dosia, the wife of Governor Alston of South Carolina.
Soon after Colonel Burr's return from Europe to New
York, he arranged for her to come and visit him, and
she set out, as is known, from Charlestown in a small
schooner, called the* Patriot. *Timothy Green, a retired
lawyer in New York, a most worthy man and an old
friend of Colonel Burr, went on by land to accompany
her. The fact of the departure of the vessel with his
daughter and Mr. Green on board was communicated
by letter by Governor Alston to Colonel Burr, and he
looked forward with anticipations of joy to the meeting of which, after so many years of separation, was to
take place between himself and his dear child.*

*A full time for the arrival of the vessel in New
York elapsed, but she did not come. As day after day
passed, still nothing was seen or heard of the vessel or
of his daughter, that face, which had before showed
no gloom or sadness, began to exhibit the sign of deep
and deeper concern. Every means was resorted to to
obtain information, but no tidings were ever heard of
the vessel or of the daughter upon whom all the affections of his nature had been bestowed. "Hope de-
ferred" did in this case, indeed, make sick, and nearly
crush the heart.*

*His symbol, which he loved occasionally to
stamp upon the seal of a letter, was rock of the tem-
pest-tossed ocean which neither wind nor wave could
move. But his firm and manly nature, which no danger
or reverse nor any of the previous circumstances of life
had been able to shake, was near giving way. It was
interesting though painful to witness the struggle; but
he did rise superior to his grief and the light once more
shone upon his countenance. But it was afterwards a
subdued light.*

Concerning the gallantries ascribed to Colonel Burr by his critics, Judge Greenwood wrote:

I do not believe Colonel Burr was any worse in this respect than many men of his own and the present day. The difference between them is that he was much less disguised, and that he did not pretend to be what he was not. I think he was quite as much sought after by the other sex as he was a seeker. There seemed indeed to be a charm and fascination about him which continued even to a late period of his life, and which was too powerful for the frail and sometimes for the strong to resist. I know that he has been accused of much in that respect, and it may be the truth.

But I have heard him say, and if it be true, it is certainly much in his favor, that he never deceived or made false promise to a woman in his life. This is much more than many can say who have much better name than he has. His married life with Mrs. Prevost was of the most affectionate character, and his fidelity never questioned. He was a gentleman in his language and his deportment. Nothing of a low, ribauld, indecent or even indelicate character ever escaped his lips.

I must point to you one admirable and strong characteristic of him. He sought with young men, in whom he felt an interest, to graft them as it were with his indomitable will, energy and perseverance. I can truly say, that I thought I was often overtasked beyond my powers, and even to the injury, no doubt, of my health, so that his course seemed to be over-exacting and oppressive; yet that he constantly incited me to progress in all various modes and departments of mental culture, even in music, the influence of which he deemed of great importance, although he had but little taste for, and no knowledge of it himself; and that my success in life, so far as I have succeeded, has been owing to the habits of industry and perseverance which were formed under his training.

As to the character of his mind, it was quick, penetrating and discerning. He was a shrewd planner, and indefatigable and persevering in carrying out his plans. He was a good scholar, acquainted with polite literature, and spoke French and Spanish, the former fluently. I think his heart was not in the profession of the law, but that he followed it principally for its gains. He was, however, a good lawyer, civil and international law; acquainted generally with the reports of adjudicated cases, and in preparing important cases, and in preparing important cases usually traced up the law to its ancient sources. But political and military life seemed to interest him more than anything else, although he never neglected his business. He prided himself probably more on his military qualities than upon any other. If he could have gratified his ambition of becoming king or emperor of Mexico, he would no doubt have been in his glory, but it was not to be. . . .

The fruits of the well known Medcef Eden suits left him a small income. . . . [and] thus terminated the career of one who played so prominent part on the great stage of public life in the days of Washington, Jefferson and Hamilton.

Aaron Burr was blessed with many loyal friends who remained faithful exponents of his virtues ever ready to defend his nobility.

Without exception each one thought Burr superior to his traducers. A benevolent lady, whose lot it became to minister to Burr after he became a paralytic, was quite sure that he possessed one of the best minds and one of the noblest characters that has graced American life. She was Mrs. Joshua Webb, who took him into her home and cared for him in a manner that would have awakened in the heart of Theodosia undying gratitude had she witnessed it.

When Colonel Burr fled from America to escape the wrath of Jefferson, he deposited with Theodosia all the papers that he thought worth preserving. There were, however, others that concerned posterity's interest in his unusual life, and these fell into the hands of Ogden Edwards, who, with Mrs. Webb, carefully examined their contents. Concerning the Burr letters, Mrs. Webb says, "I never saw a letter or document among the papers of Colonel Burr that would bring a blush to the cheek, or a tear to the eye of anyone."

Continuing her defense of the man about whom Matthew L. Davis lied so maliciously—for by destroying the correspondence with women on the grounds that it might be offensive, he inadvertently, and inevitably, maligned Burr's reputation by implying that they were so—Mrs. Webb recorded:

> *All who know Colonel Burr, know him to be a silent, secretive man. Is it likely then, that one that had suffered persecution deeply as he had done, would, even if he had the power, expose others to the tortures he had suffered? As early as the year 1829, the husband of the writer of this statement made preparation, by the examination of documents and frequent consultation with Colonel Burr, for writing his biography. This was long before Mr. Davis was thought of for performing such service. If the circumstances had not prevented the fulfillment of that intention, Colonel Burr would have had, at least, justice done him.*
>
> *The whole life of Colonel Burr contradicts the statement made by Mr. Davis respecting letters & etc. Colonel Burr suffered, but suffered silently. I do not believe that a man exists, or ever did exist, of whom he would have spoken evil, or to whom he would have done injury.*

I do not speak unadvisedly, but from the informa-tion of a dear departed parent, who esteemed Colonel Burr enough to consign his grandson to his care, and his small inheritance to his guardianship—a trust that he faithfully fulfilled. . . .

For all the recollections I have now, or ever had of Colonel Burr, there is not an act of my life, for which I am so grateful as that I was Colonel Burr's Last Friend.

Writing in the *New York Leader*, January 2, 1864, a reporter said:

I knew Colonel Burr personally from my boy-hood, and saw him often in the quiet scenes of domes-tic life in the house of a gentleman who was always his friend.

His personal appearance was peculiar; under me-dium height, his figure was well-proportioned, sinewy, and elastic, appearing in every movement to be gov-erned more by the mental than by mere physical at-tributes. His head was large, but, as phrenologists say, well-proportioned. His forehead was high, protruding, but narrow directly between the eyes, and widening immediately back.

His head was well, even classically poised on the shoulders; his feet and hands were peculiarly small; his nose was rather large, with open, expanding nostrils; and the ears so small as to be a deformity. The feature that gave character and tone to all, and which made his presence felt, was the eye. Perfectly round, large, deep hazel color, it had an expression which no one who had seen it could forget. No man could stand in the presence of Colonel Burr, with his eyes fixed on him, and not feel that they pierced his inmost thoughts.

There was power in his look—a magnetism, if I may be allowed the expression—which few persons could resist In Burr's bearing and presence you felt something beyond other men—I have never seen his peer.

Colonel Knapp wrote:

Burr never courted the mob by mingling with them, and sharing their movements; for it was seldom that they met him. He made no converts by pewter mug stories, and they liked him better for all this abstraction from the great body of democracy; but whenever he came in contact with the humblest of his admirers, it was well known that he treated them so blandly that his manners were remembered when the whole conversations were forgotten. His manner was the most courtly of any of his age. He had not the parade of Morris, nor the gravity of Jay; but he never for a moment forgot himself by assumption of too much familiarity. The self-possession which he always sustained gave him great advantages over other men who are vassals of their passions, and at times cannot hide their weaknesses.

The King of Prussia, whom Burr met at the court of Gotha, had read Burr's farewell to the Senate and had conceived for the speaker high admiration. Possibly, Colonel Burr was accorded greater distinction by the courts of Germany than any other American of his day.

Aaron Burr was well-nigh invincible. Nowhere in the mass of his journals and letters is there a word of repining, repentance, or melancholy. Circumstances often controlled and thwarted but never for a moment subdued him. He lived for five months in Sweden, three in Stockholm, and spent two months traveling about the country. It was the one country in which he escaped the tyranny of Jefferson. Burr liked Sweden and the people of Sweden liked him. Concerning that country and its people, Burr wrote:

> I have never known in any country or at any time, five months of weather so uniformly fine. The excellence of the roads has been a constant subject of admiration to me, much superior to those of England, and free from toll. There is no country in which traveling is so cheap, expeditious and secure. All travelers have borne testimony to Swedish honesty, but no one has attempted to discover the cause of a distinction so honorable. I have sought for it in their laws, in their social and municipal institutions, particularly in their judicial department. There is no country with whose jurisprudence I am acquainted in which personal liberty is so well secured; none in which the violation of it is punished with so much certainty and promptitude; none in which civil justice is administered with so much dispatch and so little expense.
>
> These are strong assertions, but I shall bring with me the proofs. It is surprising, it is unaccountable, that a system differing so essentially from every other in Europe, and so fraught with valuable matter, should have remained to this day locked up in the Swedish and runic tongues, and that not the slightest information on this interesting subject could be found in either English or French. I should have thought national pride, if not philanthropy, would have diffused the knowledge of them through Europe.

Luther Martin, who so masterfully defended Burr at Richmond, took a judgment for twenty thousand dollars for his services. It was evidently in a friendly manner, as he never pressed his claim. On the contrary, Burr took Martin into his home when Burr was hard-pressed for money and cared for him like a brother until Martin's death, which occurred at age 81.

Everyone marveled at Burr's tranquility. Even Charles Biddle wrote:

> *He did not appear to me, nor to my family, much altered. He called several times at my lodging to see me, and was at times cheerful, as usual; but the loss of his daughter and grandson had weaned him away from the world. It was a matter of perfect indifference when he left it. I was sorry to find that some of his old friends did not visit him.*

Politicians considered it political suicide to be intimate with Burr and often avoided him. Henry Clay, to whom Burr paid a handsome fee in Kentucky, thought it impolitic to be seen with Burr in New York and refused to see him.

Colonel Burr's services during the Revolutionary War were regarded as highly efficient. These Washington recognized and approved; the government, however, has refused to recognize that our department of military intelligence is the product of the brain of Aaron Burr. Can there be any doubt that if it had been given birth by anyone else than Burr, proper credit would have been acknowledged years ago?

During the Revolution, Colonel Burr advanced a considerable sum of money to further military efficiency, none of which was ever repaid. Congress even refused him a pension, and it was not until he was very old and feeble that five hundred annually was granted. In youth Burr purchased an annuity of fifty pounds annually from England, and Botts sent him five hundred annually during his declining years.

Between Jackson and Burr personally there existed a warm friendship throughout their lives, yet it was impolitic to even mention the name of Burr—even after he had originated the political movement in New York that resulted in Jackson being nominated for the presidency, Burr was never the beneficiary of Jackson's elevation to the presidency.

Andrew Jackson was the political godfather of Sam Houston during his tortuous path through Tennessee as Indian fighter, as a member of Congress, as governor of Tennessee, as representative of the Cherokee Indians in Indian Territory, and as personal representative of President Jackson to the Indian tribes of Texas, and, finally, it was Jackson who encouraged resistance to the Spanish tyranny in Texas and Houston's final triumph in the Southwest.

Burr blazed this trail that so many were to follow; some with one vision and some with another, but always it was the march of American civilization toward the land of the setting sun. The echoes of that little band of American youth who rode in Burr's houseboats down the Mississippi to Bayou Pierre resounded at the Alamo, only to burst in thunderous tones across the plains of San Jacinto.

Burr's ill-fated expedition had so many imitators who descended as ambitious pioneers of Texas that the Spanish consul reported, "From what I hear and penetrate, it seems that the project of Burr is coming to life."

It was a knowledge of your mind which first inspired me with a respect for that of your sex, and with some regret, I confess, that the ideas which you have often heard me express in favor of female intellectual powers are founded on what I have imagined, more than what I have seen, except in you.

– Aaron Burr
Letter to Mrs. Burr

25
The Spiritually-Minded Burrs

For four generations the Burr family were preachers. Aaron Burr was a teacher, never a preacher. He was the most tolerant man in our public life, unless it be Lincoln. Where else may we find a life that exemplified his declaration that "I never did harm or wished harm to a human being?"

Mental achievement and spirituality at work motivated Burr. In the choice of a wife his selection of Theodosia Prevost aroused speculation. Apparently the three dominant families of the state had taken it for granted that he would choose from their number. Failure to do so started tongues to wagging. Burr's answer was "she had the truest heart, the ripest intellect, and the most winning manners of any woman I ever met." Burr's choice proved the wisest he ever made. Throughout their earthly careers her mind remained the magnet that attracted and the inspiration of his life. The married life of Burr is a poem. The communion of their minds developed a spirituality, a religion concerning which Theodosia wrote, "Worlds should not purchase the little I possess." About a delayed letter she exclaimed, "What language can express the joy, the gratitude of Theodosia! her Aaron safe, mistress of the heart she adores; can she ask more? has heaven more to grant?"

Mind and spirit ruled Aaron Burr; body and heart were servants. He believed that individual liberty and equal justice were the birthright of man; that intellectual and spiritual development was the object of education. Since these were man's supreme endowment, Burr's obsession for those he loved found expression in their training and education. It began with Theodosia and extended to Natalie, the little French girl who was educated with his daughter; it included John Vanderlyn, Charles Burdett, and the two Eden sisters. No person remained long under the roof or in the employ of Aaron Burr who did not respond to his insistent desire for their education. It was his way of expressing his love for humanity.

James Parton wrote:

> To the last Theodosia was a very happy wife, and he an attentive husband. I assert this positively. No one now lives who can, of his own personal knowledge, speak of the domestic life of a lady who died sixty-two years ago. But there are many still living, whose parents were most intimately conversant with the interior of Richmond Hill, and who have heard narrated all the minute incidents of the life led therein.
>
> The last old servants of the family died only a short time ago; and the persons best acquainted with the best part of Burr's character area still walking the streets. His own letters to his wife—all respect, solicitude and affection—I repeat and confirm the positive assertions of these, that Mrs. Burr lived, and died a satisfied, a confiding, a beloved, a trusted wife.

Theodosia the daughter has inspired a number of books. Her love for her father is without parallel in literature, as are her desire to emulate his brilliant mind, her determination to be worthy of his faith and ambition, and her spirit that braved the daggers of his enemies to find contentment and security in his tranquility—even amidst the wrath of the political organizations that combined to seek his life. There she revealed qualities of mind and soul that will live in the hearts of America. The love, the fidelity, and the devotion of Aaron Burr and his daughter will give them immortality. When the critics who spent their lives in persistent calumny in an effort to destroy the good name of Burr are forgotten, still will be told the story of an undying love of this father and daughter. An anonymous author wrote:

> *From her earliest years he had educated her with a care to which we look in vain for a parallel among his contemporaries. She grew up in consequence no ordinary woman. Beautiful beyond most of her sex and accomplished as few females of that day were accomplished, she displayed to her family and friends a fever of affection which not every woman is capable.*
>
> *The character of Theodosia has long been regarded about as we would regard that of a heroine of romance. Her love for her father partook of the purity of the better world; deep, holy and unchanging; it reminds us of the affection which a celestial spirit might be supposed to entertain for a parent, cast down from heaven for sharing the sin of the "Son of the Morning."*
>
> *No sooner did she hear of the arrest of her father, than she fled to his side. There is nothing in history more touching than the hurried letters, blotted with tears, in which she announces her daily progress to Richmond, for she was too weak to travel with rapidity of the mail.*

Even the character of Burr borrows a momentary halo from hers when we peruse his replies, in which forgetting his peril, and relaxing from the stern front he assumes toward his enemies, he labored to quiet only her fears, and inspired her with confidence of his acquittal. He even writes from his prison in a tone of gayety jestingly regretting that his accommodations are not more elegant for her reception. Once, and once only, does he melt, and that is to tell her that in event of the worst, he will die worthy of himself.

Where else may we find in biography, history, or even fiction a family that was so completely dominated by mind—three personalities, each of whom chose to have spirit rule over his every act to become master of his soul?

[T]he hand of malignity may grasp any individual against whom its hate may be directed . . . As [treason] is the most atrocious offense which can be committed against the political body, so it is the charge which is most capable of being employed as the instrument of those malignant and vindictive passions which may rage in the bosoms of contending parties struggling for power.
                                                   – Chief Justice John Marshall

26
The Conspirators in Review

The conspiracy against Aaron Burr brought together three of America's greatest statesmen. It is unfortunate that this portrait may not be painted without portraying the envy and jealousy and other contemptible qualities of Alexander Hamilton and Thomas Jefferson. They possessed many admirable traits. They are among our greatest statesmen. It is doubtful if another American trio was ever thus intimately associated who possessed such talents; certainly none has displayed greater contrasts. However, in holding Hamilton and Jefferson responsible for the deliberate ruin and disgrace of Burr, it is inevitable that their worst traits should appear on the canvas

By birth, environment, and education Thomas Jefferson was a gentleman. His forbears came from Wales. The blood was Irish,

Scotch, and English. Mr. Jefferson's mother was a Randolph—the most distinguished family in Virginia. He and John Marshall were cousins. After enjoying the advantages of some of the best tutors available, Jefferson attended William and Mary College. Always a serious student, he became the greatest scholar to occupy the brilliant presidency until Woodrow Wilson, yet he revealed few of the brilliant qualities that raised Hamilton and Burr to such high esteem in the public mind. Jefferson was an educated country squire who as a boy had been considered dull.

The ancestry of Hamilton challenged the exhaustive research of his son, who became his biographer. It has remained an unsolved riddle, as mysterious as he was brilliant. By common consent he is credited with a Scot for his father and a French Huguenot for his mother. Neither the social handicap of birth nor the environs of the Island of Nevis were to deter his brilliant mind or his ambitious designs; nor should they have. Hamilton became a scholar, an orator, and one of the greatest lawyers of his day. Had he guarded his political speech and displayed an endeavor to stick to the truth, he would not have invited Burr's bullet.

In discussing his plans for the emancipation of Mexico, Judge Workman, a member of the Mexican Association, observed:

> *This had been a favorite object of his for years. When he was a British subject he had proposed it to that government. He "declared upon his honor a separation of the Union was never mentioned or even, as he believed, contemplated by any person associated with him." Colonel Burr was mentioned, as was General Wilkinson and General Dayton.*

Having contributed liberally to Colonel Burr's plans for colonization of the Ouachita, Daniel Clark fully understood them. Clark was the merchant prince of New Orleans. The legislature had just elected him as the delegate to Congress, and a little later the Creole contingent testified that he had advised they "exert their influence to support the Government of the United States, and rally round the Governor."

New Orleans was not the only place in the Union where a bitter political fight was taking place. In the House of Representatives John Randolph had demanded evidence to support the president's charges that Aaron Burr was attempting to divide the Union. Since Mr. Jefferson had no evidence, he avoided a direct reply by saying, "of his guilt there can be no doubt." Then, in an attempt to justify the martial law that was enraging every loyal citizen of New Orleans, the president asserted that by the arrests in that city Wilkinson had forestalled a rebellion.

"The reign of terror," as citizens of New Orleans disgnated Wilkinson's martial law, only partially served its author, as Cowles Mead, the acting governor of Mississippi Territory, quickly perceived. He wrote to Governor Claiborne:

> Burr may come, he is no doubt desperate, but should he pass us your fate will depend on the General, and not on the Colonel. If I can stop Burr this may hold the General in his allegiance to the United States—but if Burr passes this Territory with two thousand men, I have no doubt that the General will be your worst enemy. Be on your guard against the wily General—he is not much better than a Cataline— consider him a traitor and act as if certain thereof— you will say yourself by it.

Governor Mead on December 15 issued a message to the Territorial Legislature of Mississippi, echoing the rumors of a plot to dissever the Union and mustering into service regiments of the state militia. These he ordered to strategic points along the Mississippi River to repel any possible invasion by Burr and his much-magnified mysterious host. To Colonel Woolridge he gave these instructions: "It is apprehended that Colonel Burr may land near Walnut Hills; you are therefore ordered to appoint such number of persons as you think sufficient to act as a guard along the river."

These orders flew as if on the wind, and as they were wafted along they were multiplied, giving monstrous proportions to the approaching horde of Burr. In the midst of this terrible alarm, the outpost sentries who were sent to protect the commonwealth witnessed the approach of the little fleet of less than a dozen houseboats, as they quietly floated into Bayou Pierre.

The fleet was manned by boys just out of school; nearly all were young men, with a few servants, women, and children. The twenty thousand of Wilkinson's imagination had shrunk to fifty-five. They possessed some blunderbusses, squirrel rifles, and old muskets, such as were common to the Western immigrant in quest of game and in defense of his home. There was nothing military about their arms or their attitude. Plainly, to all who wanted to know the truth, they were colonists, going quietly to their new homes, to be hewed out of the forests on the banks of the Ouachita.

Evidence of their innocence of any evil or military intent was seen in the fact that only Burr and one bateau containing twelve men arrived the first evening. The other boats drifted in the next day. These anchored opposite Cole's creek on the Louisiana side.

Colonel Burr sent a skiff across the river and courteously invited Colonel Woolridge and his aides to visit him in camp. Here he declared it the purpose of the party to establish a colony on the Ouachita River, and that they were on their way for this purpose. Colonel Woolridge was baffled at Burr's announcement. While impressed with the evidence of such intention, he was very much put out that he had no boats in which to transport Burr and his party if he arrested them. Upon his return to his camp he declared that there were only about fifty-five men with Burr, and a few women and children, with no stand of arms and no evidence of warlike intent.

Colonel Burr was greatly surprised that his coming should have caused such a tumult. He addressed a letter to the public at Bayou Pierre, then wrote another letter to Governor Mead strongly avowing his innocence of any military intent. He called attention to the contents of his boats as evidence that his party was en route to the banks of the Ouachita for agricultural pursuits.

Governor Mead forwarded this letter to Colonel Fitzpatrick with the comment that:

> *He should be proud to find him as innocent as he there professes himself. . . . If Colonel Burr be disposed to pay due regard to the authority of our Government, you are requested to assure him from me that every security shall be given to private property and every respect paid to him and his associates, which can be done after being assured that his plans are not directed against the United States or its territories. You may further assure him of the particular solicitude I feel for the verification of his professions to me; and, further, if he has been vilified or injured by the rumor, or the "Pensioned," he shall receive all of the benefits of my individual civility, and the full and complete protection of the laws of the Territory.*

With this profession of protection Governor Mead sent his confidential aide-de-camp, Colonel Shields, with an explanatory letter to Burr. But before Shields arrived, Colonel Fitzpatrick had rowed across the river to be graciously received by Burr, who indignantly disclaimed any treasonable intentions. He even expressed willingness to surrender and stand trial on the charges against him, provided such trial would take place in Mississippi territory and nowhere else. By this time Burr had become aware of Wilkinson's betrayal and with good reason feared that he must protect himself against this agent of the president, both of whom were determined to close his mouth forever.

Fitzpatrick agreed to submit his offer to Mead, and started back to Natchez, but on his way learned that Colonel Claiborne (not Governor Claiborne of New Orleans) was on his way up the river to arrest Burr. Consequently he immediately returned to Burr's camp and informed him "under these circumstances that he must submit to civil authorities, or trust to events."

Claiborne arrived January 16 with two hundred and seventy-five men and took position on the Mississippi side of the river, where he captured four unsuspecting members of Burr's party who had just landed from a boat. Natchez was restless and Burr's friends were numerous, so Mead ordered Claiborne to "Seize all malcontents and send them under guard to Judge Rodney, of the Federal Court. Burr's friends require much vigilance and their licentiousness must be curbed."

On the January 16, Shields and United States District Attorney Poindexter, clothed with plenipotentiary powers, conferred with Burr and an agreement was reached. After a further meeting with Mead, Burr offered to surrender to the Mississippi civil authorities and permit his boats to be searched for the rumored munitions of war. The next day he crossed the river with Mead's aides, riding with them to the little village of Washington Town, then the capital of the territory of Mississippi, where he was committed for trial.

Mead reported to the national administration that he had captured Burr and his party and that it consisted of nine boats with one hundred men, the major part of whom:

> *Are boys or young men just from school—many of their depositions have been taken before Judge Rodney, but they bespeak ignorance of the views or designs of the Colonel. I believe them really ignorant and deluded. I believe that they are the dupes of stratagems, if the assertions of Generals Eaton and Wilkinson are to be accredited.*

Burr realized that Wilkinson was in a desperate mood. In proclaiming martial law he had revealed that he was determined to catch Burr. The power usurped in New Orleans was now transferred to gangsters, who were directed to catch and bring him to Wilkinson, even kidnap him or commit murder, if it were necessary.

The territory was aroused. From Pensacola came Governor Vicente Folch, of West Florida, marching at the head of four hundred men who were hastening to Baton Rouge, which was to be protected against the menace of Burr and his mighty host. In contrast with all this military alarm, Burr quietly surrendered to the civil authorities, who assured him that his constitutional rights would be protected by a civil trial. Confident of acquittal, the colonel reassured his associates of their continued peaceful journey to the Ouachita.

On January 18 Burr appeared before Judge Thomas Rodney and was bound over in five thousand dollar bail for the grand jury. This bond was promptly furnished, and once more he was a free man. Two days later President Jefferson appointed Caesar A. Rodney, son of Thomas Rodney, attorney general of the United States.

While this situation made it impossible for Burr to expect justice, his friends were hopeful. Apparently sensing its gravity, Silas Dinsmoor, a U.S. Indian agent, wrote satirically, "We are in a flurry hourly expecting Colonel Burr & all Kentucky & half of Tennessee at his back to punish General Wilkinson, set the negroes free, rob the banks & take Mexico. Come and help me laugh at the fun."

Back in Burr's camp Blennerhassett was in charge. The boys cooked their meals in their little boats during repeated searches for the warlike equipment they were reputed to possess. The few hunting rifles, pistols, and blunderbusses disappointed Colonel Fitzpatrick and his men, who in turn were jeered by the boys. On January 22 one of their number, Comfort Tyler, was removed from camp by a squad of militia and taken to the territorial capital to answer charges with Burr. Enlisted men also were taken and every pressure was brought to make them swear to treasonable purposes. The attempt failed; for all were sincerely devoted to the colonization plans—the homes they were to carve in the forest.

Burr was allowed to return to his camp on January 24 to await the convening of the grand jury in February. Immediately Wilkinson and Claiborne wrote to Mead, urging:

> *The expediency of placing Burr without delay on board of one of our armed vessels in the river with an order to the officers to descend him to this city [New Orleans]. Otherwise, if his followers are as numerous as they are represented to be, it is probable it may not be in your power to bring him to trial.*

Wilkinson was determined to capture Burr. On December 4 he wrote to a friend in Natchez:

> *Plans are laid to cut off the two principal leaders, and it is my wish to have them arrested and carried off from that place, to be delivered to the Executive authority of the Union. If you fail, your expenses shall be paid. If you succeed, I pledge the government to you for five thousand dollars.*

The plan to kidnap Burr failed, but in Burr's camp there was trouble. Mrs. Blennerhassett and her two children, after a perilous trip, were being held prisoners with the other members of the party. Word had come from New Orleans that gunboats were coming to destroy the Burr boats. Burr's drafts were protested, and he found himself without funds with which to pay the men or to supply them with provisions. Naturally they held him responsible for their misfortunes. After filling up with liquor they were mutinous; they refused to police their boats.

The situation was serious. To add to its gravity, Governor Williams returned and assumed the duties that had fallen temporarily to Mead. Immediately Colonel Burr rode over to Washington Town to consult him; he found him professing sympathy for the unfortunate situation into which Burr had been drawn.

Federal Court, the Supreme Territorial Court, convened the first Monday in February, with Judge Rodney presiding. On Tuesday morning United States District Attorney Poindexter moved for a dismissal of the proposed indictment on the grounds that there was no evidence of any criminal acts within the jurisdiction of the court, and on the further grounds that the Supreme Court, being an appellate tribunal, had no jurisdiction over original cases.

Judge Rodney was surprised and angered at this unexpected motion and expressed his resentment. Judge Bruin agreed with the district attorney, and argued that the motion be granted. He also asked that the bail be discharged. Notwithstanding the tie-vote, Judge Rodney insisted that the evidence, consisting chiefly of depositions, be placed before the grand jury. Promptly that body refused to indict Burr.

The temper of the people is reflected by this grand jury. Not content with its declaration that there was no evidence of wrong on the part of Burr, it struck out at the government, Wilkinson, and Claiborne—each in turn was bitterly condemned. The "grievance" of this jury is a remarkable document and a most unusual one. It reveals that the grand jury was convinced there was an organized political effort being made by the president and his agents to hang Burr. Their "grievance" follows:

> The Grand Jury, on due investigation of the evidence brought before them, are of the opinion that Aaron Burr has not been guilty of any crime or misdemeanor against the laws of the United States, or of this Territory; or given any just occasion for alarm or inquietude to the good people of the Territory. To Cowles Mead as acting governor the Grand Jurors present, as a grievance, the late military expedition, unnecessarily, as they conceive, was fitted out against the person and property of the said Aaron Burr, when no resistance had been made to civil authorities. The Grand Jurors also present to General Wilkinson, as a grievance, de-

structive to personal liberty the late military arrest [Adair at New Orleans], made without warrant, and, as they conceive, without lawful authority.

[Finally to President Jefferson] they do sincerely regret that so much cause has been given to the enemies of our glorious Constitution, to rejoice at such measures being adopted, in a neighboring Territory, as, if sanctioned by the Executive of our country, must sap the vitals of our political existence, and crumble the glorious fabric in dust.

Rodney was furious. In his anger he refused to release Burr. On February 4 Burr demanded release; Rodney denied the motion and bound him over to appear before him daily. This was in violation of Burr's constitutional rights. The bail had been set to compel his appearance before the grand jury. That body, after hearing the evidence, had discharged him, but Rodney refused to let him go. Like Wilkinson and in keeping with the desires of the president, he connived to accomplish Burr's destruction and with tyrannical brutality!

Wilkinson sent Dr. Carmichael, a civilian, and Lieutenant Peter, with a party of five, "dressed in citizens clothing" and "armed with dirks and pistols" to assassinate Burr; or, if possible, to seize and bring him to Wilkinson in New Orleans.

Governor Williams was sufficiently impressed with the magnitude of their criminal intentions that he endeavored to dissuade Dr. Carmichael. He protested to Peter, who, after listening to the chief executive, replied that he felt himself "bound to obey the orders of his general like a good soldier." But there was more than obedience to a superior officer in his determination to get Burr. Wilkinson had promised Silas Dinsmoor "five thousand dollars, if he cut off Burr; and if he had resisted arrest we certainly should have used our arms."

These men sent by Wilkinson to kidnap Burr, or "cut him off if necessary," possessed no warrant from any civil authority;

they came from one territory into another territory of the United States. Their orders did not specify any charge of crime against Burr and they were the tools of Wilkinson and Jefferson. While Wilkinson professed to serve Jefferson he was the paid servant of Spain, from whom he received most of his income.

Fortunately Colonel Burr possessed many friends who were in touch with the situation. These friends realized Wilkinson had been joined by Rodney and Williamson, and that these three were conniving with Peter and Carmichael; and that all were guilty in the sight of God and man. Has the military, the presidency, the judiciary, a governorship, and mobocracy ever made a deeper blot upon the pages of the history of the United States?

If Thomas Jefferson inspired "life, liberty and the pursuit of happiness," he also inspired Burr's predicament and the persecution that followed. Every man of authority who was guilty of this crime held office under the direction of the president.

From the shelter of a home of a friend Burr wrote to Governor Williams that the bond was for his appearance before the grand jury, and having been absolved by that body of the charges, that this automatically discharged the bond. The governor ignored Burr's statement of fact and offered two thousands dollars' reward for his apprehension.

Again the colonel reminded the governor that he had come into the territory with a promise that his civil rights would be protected. Since this protection had been withdrawn, it was necessary to avoid assassins who were seeking his life. Burr's letter recorded that, on account of the "vindictive temper and unprincipled conduct of Judge Rodney, it becomes necessary for the present" that he withdraw from the public. Of Rodney's act, Albert Beveridge said, "Rodney out-Wilkinsoned Wilkinson; that the grand jury had refused to indict Burr and that there was no legal charge whatever before the court."

Burr's situation was desperate. Hourly it grew more dangerous. With martial law in New Orleans and Rodney and Williams under the thumb of Jefferson, every legal avenue of escape was blocked. Friends of Burr insisted that he flee for his life, to await an hour when an informed public might possibly be substituted for the subversively organized court and a president who was determined to hang him. Reluctantly, Burr consented.

Probably no other man in our history was calmer in time of storm, especially when his life was at stake and when there was a price over his head that so many were anxious to collect. If he surrendered, the best he could hope for was a court-martial by General Wilkinson, and everyone knew what that meant. If Governor Williams seized him, that executive would probably be rewarded with a crown by the president.

Confronted by this grave situation, Colonel Burr quietly visited his men on their barges, which he told them to keep. He advised them to go to the lands which he had purchased from Baron de Bastrop, and there to settle on the Ouachita and proceed with the development of the colony. If they could not agree to do this, then they could sell the boats and divide the money. As far as he was concerned, he had been tried and acquitted; yet his enemies planned further persecution, hence "he was going to flee from oppression."

The men did as Colonel Burr advised; they sold the houseboats and divided the money. According to Mr. Claiborne, the historian of Mississippi, many of them "dispersed themselves through the territory and supplied it with school masters, singing masters, dancing masters, clerks, tavern keepers and doctors," and a few years later when General Sam Houston called for volunteers, at least three of Burr's boys joined in the fight for freedom.

Burr's stoicism toward his enemies and vulnerability of heart, however, were never better illustrated; under martial law and its bloodthirsty agencies, he had found time to discover the "prettiest maiden in Mississippi," to whom he had paid court. She had encouraged his attentions, even promised to become his wife. While his friends who were planning his escape nervously awaited their tryst, Burr pleaded his love-case and begged that she fly with him; but she would not. "Madaline Price was a miracle of beauty, all that the old masters have painted the Madonna." Tradition has it that she remained true to her plighted troth at Half Way Hill for many years; until the colonel finally wrote to release her, when she married and departed from the scene of one of the strangest romances of record.

John Graham was commissioned special confidential emissary of the government, and sent out to collect information concerning Burr's activities. He followed Burr to Pittsburgh, Marietta, Chillicothe, and Frankfort, and finally he arrived in Washington Town, this being the first place where he was to see and personally interview Burr.

Under the date of November, 28 he wrote to Madison that "at this place they seem to know nothing of the plans of Colonel Burr and I am rather induced to think that he has no one at work for him here. . . . for all is quiet."

Apparently his findings at the other places were not worth reporting. He wrote to Madison from Washington Town on February 8:

> I am sorry to say that since my arrival in this Territory I have met with many people who either openly or indirectly attack the government for not countenancing Colonel Burr in the invasion of Mexico, for it is generally considered here that that was his object. I am well persuaded that most of his followers were of this opinion.

Graham reported from New Orleans, where he became secretary of the Territory of Orleans, that there was an "unpleasant and rebellious attitude toward General Wilkinson and the government, as exercised under military law, which happily had been suspended." Workman and Kerr had been acquitted of General Wilkinson's charges; now they were vigorously protesting against Governor Claiborne's policy in permitting Wilkinson's so called "Reign of Terror."

All through Aaron Burr's tempestuous life men have painted pictures of him. Each painter has seen him under different circumstances from his contemporary and has painted a portrait that has differed slightly from his fellow artists, but all have found him a fascinating subject. While Burr was being arraigned in the Supreme Territorial Court of Mississippi, Judge Adams was an interested spectator, and it is to him that we are indebted for the following portrait:

> *Colonel Burr is a man of erect and dignified deportment—his presence is commanding—his aspect mild, firm, luminous and impressive. . . . The eyebrows are thin, nearly horizontal, and too far from the eye; his nose is inclined to the right side; gently elevated which betrays a degree of haughtiness; too obtuse at the end for a great acuteness of penetration, brilliancy of wit or poignancy of satire, and too small to sustain a capacious and ample forehead. His eyes are of dark hazel, and, from the shade of his projecting eye bones and brows, appear black; they glow. . . . and scintillate with the most tremulous and tearful sensibility—they roll with the celerity and frenzy of poetic fervor, and beam with the most vivid and piercing rays of genius. His mouth is large; his voice is clear, manly and melodious; his lips are thin, extremely flexible, and when silent, gently closed. . . . His chin is rather retreating and voluptuous.*
>
> *In company, Burr is rather taciturn; when he speaks, it is with such animation, with such apparent frankness and negligence as would induce a person to believe he was a man of guileless and ingenuous heart; but in my opinion there is no human more reserved, mysterious and inscrutable. . . . But alas. Burr is an exemplary. . . . instance of the capriciousness of popular admiration, and the mutability of human glory and*

felicity. . . . The circumstance that has contributed to blast the popularity and poison the peace and happiness of this unfortunate man is lamentable indeed; but he who will presume to ascribe it to a corruption or a depravity of heart rather than the fallibility of man, and the frailty of human passions, must be blinded by his own venom. . . . Yes, even Aaron Burr, the inimitable, the incomparable Burr, is disturbed, is unhappy! Often did I mark the perturbation of his mind, the agonizing sensations which rung his too susceptible heart, and which wrote themselves in the darkest shades of his countenance; and when I beheld the melancholy, the Saturn clouds which often enveloped his bleeding, his magnanimous soul, my feelings were melted with a thrilling, a sublime sympathy. . . .

27
The Final Summons

In the twilight of life, when most men are leaning on a cane, Aaron Burr found the richest woman in New York, a client of his, who for many years had been enamored by the gentility of his name and the fact that he had been vice president of the United States. For these she was willing to trade some of the comforts of her wealth.

If Aaron Burr had enjoyed every height of fame and endured every depth of despair, this was little less true of Madam Jumel. She was born the daughter of a prostitute to become the vagrant child of the street, purportedly madam of a house of assignation in Providence, Rhode Island. She had trod the primrose path through New England to become the mistress of a New York sea captain. She gave birth to a son, who as an old man laid claim to a share of her estate and alleged that George Washington was his father. In the records of that legal battle Madam Jumel's name is indelibly written.

This remarkable woman was noted for her beauty, her charming personality, and her power to command—qualities, had she been a man, that would have made her a general. As the wife of Stephen Jumel, a wealthy wine merchant in Manhattan, she spent his money in an endeavor to gain entree to New York society, and failing in this, she went to Paris, with Jumel, who came from France and had connections with Napoleon, to be more successful.

In an endeavor to induce society to forget her past, Madam Jumel furnished the Roger Morris House (now the Morris-Jumel Mansion in Harlem Heights in Manhattan and at one time Washington's headquarters in the Battle of Harlem Heights) in such good taste and in such lavish manner that it became the showplace of New York. Aside from accidental birth and her inevitable environment, this remarkable female of the species was clever, a woman who commanded a degree of respect in spite of her social background.

Notwithstanding the avalanche of criticism concerning this mating, it is quite likely that the most caustic pen would have been stilled by the presence of either of the principals.

If it be said that Burr stooped to conquer, he at least was elevated socially by this marital mating; yet who should object that this old man, whose life after fifty had been an incessant round of turmoil and desperate fighting for its preservation, should lay his tired head upon the downy pillow of a rich widow. Both were weary with fighting for political favor and social justice; each had made a strenuous effort for things that looked glamorous and inviting.

It required only a few months to demonstrate that each was too much an individualist and too determined to have their way for harmony. Thereafter they lived apart. She aired her troubles in court until the very day of Burr's death, September 14, 1836, when the court of earth gave her a divorce and the court of heaven gave Burr a summons eternal.

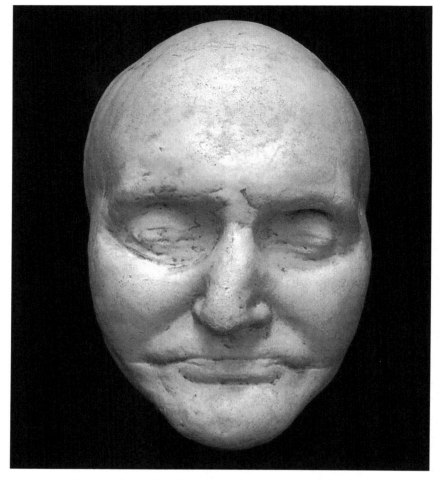

The death mask of Aaron Burr (note crooked nose)

Two days later Burr's body rested in the chapel "within the walls where his own novitiate was passed, and where his sire and grandsire were wont to offer prayer to God." Here Dr. Carnahan, president of Princeton College, delivered a memorial portraying this scholar, militarist, statesman, and humanitarian who, while wrongfully accused and little understood, had demonstrated patriotism unparalleled in the Union. The address was listened to by the student body, citizens of Princeton, friends from far and near, relatives, and a few notables.

Burr's burial was near the graves of his father and grandfather. Both had served as presidents of Princeton—three lives that typify great learning, divine spirituality, and persecuted patriotism. Many years ago while engaged in retrospection near this shrine, the author of this work was joined by a notable figure who appeared as quietly as though a spirit. It was Woodrow Wilson. Together we paid homage to the only man in the United States ever to be offered the presidency who declined it: Aaron Burr. This casual meeting with Woodrow Wilson revealed that he, too, recognized that Burr was crucified on the altar of politics, and that Burr was one of America's noblest patriots.

For twenty years Burr's grave remained unmarked. Alfred Edwards, a relative, erected a simple marker on which was inscribed "Colonel of the American Revolution and Vice-President of the United States from 1801 to 1805," but, as in life, this was to suffer at the hands of a common vandal. Persecution of Burr followed to his grave. It is another example of how prejudice and partisanship finds outlet for expression.

Burr was an enigma that his closest friends never fully fathomed. His mind was so brilliant that it either quickened the pulse of admiration or aroused a spirit of conflict. Burr was born to command. His reorganization of the voluntary espionage system resulted in the organization of our military intelligence. It is doubtful if the Revolution produced another such organizer, disciplinarian, and leader.

Nor was Burr less successful as a political organizer. Out of his ward organization of New York in 1800 came the defeat of the Federalists and the hostility of Hamilton. After failing to induce Governor Jay to join in an attempt to steal the electoral vote, Hamilton induced the House of Representatives to elect Jefferson, his outstanding political enemy for twelve years—not that he loved Jefferson; rather, he hated Burr even more. The records of Hamilton and Jefferson during those two political contests make Hamilton a thief and Jefferson a prevaricator—Hamilton tried to steal the electoral vote; Jefferson falsified the terms of his election in his Anas. Hamilton continued his fight against Burr until Weehawken; Jefferson persisted through the trial to impeach Justice Samuel Chase, through seven attempts to convict Burr, and through an endeavor to impeach John Marshall when the chief justice refused to allow Jefferson to convict Burr without evidence to support his charges.

Hamilton and Jefferson, however, succeeded in convincing the public that Burr was guilty of their accusations, but unhappily for both, the archives of America and Europe completely exonerate Burr from their charges. Burr was a greater patriot than either of his traducers!

Of this fight to destroy Burr, Henry Adams has painted a graphic picture:

> *Never in the history of the United States did so powerful a combination of politicians unite to break down a single man as did that which arrayed itself against Burr; for as the hostile circle gathers about him he could plainly see not only Jefferson, Madison and the whole Virginia legion; but strangest of all companions—Alexander Hamilton.*

In capturing the electoral vote of New York, Burr displayed amazing political talents. Jefferson became president as a result of Burr's political acumen and energy, and now that Burr was vice president, he was sure to succeed Jefferson, unless he was stopped. As vice president John Adams had been elevated to the presidency. As vice president, Thomas Jefferson also was elected president. This must not be repeated, not if the Virginia legion and Alexander Hamilton could prevent it. They did, but at what cost!

After John Marshall had considered the accusations of Jefferson and the lies of Eaton and Wilkinson, he said:

> *The hand of malignity may grasp the individual against whom its hate is directed; and since treason is the most atrocious offense which can be committed*

against the political body, so it is the charge which is most capable of being employed as the instrument of those malignant and vindictive passions which range in the bosoms of contending parties struggling for power.

After more than a century the archives are unlocked. The evidence is available to all. The fires of political prejudice and passion are burned low. Out of the ashes of misinformation and from years of unrelenting toil comes evidence convincing and reassuring. From the records it is plain that Burr was not without guile and not without the tricks of the politician, but he was never a shrewd, calculating businessman. He was prone to error; his greatest weakness was an inherent faith in his fellow man, whom he loved and trusted. Burr's greatest misfortune was in having encountered in politics Alexander Hamilton and Thomas Jefferson.

Aaron Burr was fundamentally democratic. He believed in the rule of the masses. Alexander Hamilton was his exact antithesis. He was a natural autocrat. He believed in the rule of the few and insisted that he was chosen to select the few. To Washington he said, "I have long since learned to hold public opinion of no value." During the Revolution Hamilton was pen to Washington. During the years that Washington was president, Hamilton was leaned upon heavily, but the president admitted that he did not approve of many of Hamilton's methods.

While secretary of the treasury, Hamilton often assumed the position of prime minister, to the embarrassment of Washington and the disgust of Jefferson and the other members of the cabinet.

In the campaign of 1804, Hamilton placed himself directly across the path of Burr in a manner no gentleman could endure and maintain his self-respect. In removing Hamilton, Burr won the plaudits of the West and the South, where Hamilton's punishment was regarded as just, except for the reward of a crown as a martyr!

Washington was chosen from Virginia; Adams was from Massachusetts; but for the interference of Hamilton, the third president would have been from New York. Out of the political machinations of the House of Representatives, Hamilton and Jefferson emerged obsessed with a common ambition to kill Aaron Burr politically. Hamilton's part cost him his life; Jefferson suffered a cantankerous taint from which he never recovered. Eventually the sins of both have caught up with them. In the light of the records, each of this trio must be reappraised. The archives of America and of Europe are filled with the concepts and deeds of these three illustrious Americans, and these are the source of *The Conspiracy Against Aaron Burr*. The student of biography and history is invited to investigate; he is urged to carefully consider the credibility of the witnesses.

The youth of America is on the march. The future of the republic is in his hands. His greatest single weapon for the defense of Liberty, Freedom, and Justice is Truth.

Aaron Burr inherited an ancestry that walked with God. He was wed to grace and wisdom. In the law no man of his day was more successful, and only one has been deemed worthy of comparison. As father and teacher, his companionship with his daughter has immortalized both. Until soiled by political association, he enjoyed the favor of the gods and the plaudits of his fellow men, "a record high above the ranks of ordinary mortals."

It was six years after the death of his wife that his political troubles began in earnest; when, as heir apparent to the presidency, he was marked for destruction by politicians whose lies had poisoned the public mind with defamation and treachery. Then was hatched the episode known as the conspiracy, which was not of Burr's creation but was concocted by his enemies.

The trial at Richmond was a political plot created by Eaton, Wilkinson, and Jefferson, where the lies of Eaton, the treachery of Wilkinson, and venom of Jefferson manufactured political odium such as was never before revealed. It so misled the public that neither biographer nor historian has dared tell the truth. Concerning this state of the public mind, John Marshall wrote, "It would be difficult or dangerous for a jury to acquit Burr, however innocent they might think him."

Burr escaped with his life only to be driven from home to an alien land, where he wandered for four years as an outcast, persistently dogged by hunger, poverty, and Jefferson's sleuths. If the picture is unbelievable, examine the records. In being forced from public life and in withstanding obloquy, Burr became a heroic figure.

To men Burr was a natural leader; he was prepossessing and inspiring. To women he was irresistible. To those seeking the truth concerning this gallery of faces, here are some new lights with a shifting of the rays, where are revealed both men and devils. In common with all honorable men, Burr asked only a fair appraisal in life; he would ask no more in eternity.

[So ends Oliver Perry Sturm's biography of Aaron Burr, the manuscript of which, after Sturm's death at Fayetteville, Arkansas, in 1944, was inexplicably acquired by the Aaron Burr Association and is in its collection of Burr memorabilia in Special Collections at the library of Rutgers University.]

End Papers

Researched and edited by ABA member
Henry H. Anderson, Jr.

Reproduction of the lost John Pierre Burr portrait, which originally hung in Lori Cornish's ancestral home for generations, but has since disappeared.

#1
John Pierre Burr

Members of ABA—primarily Phyllis Arm Morales, Louella Mitchell Allen, Lyman B. Coddington, and Henry H. Anderson, Jr. (all of whom are collateral descendants of Aaron Burr), assisted by Kay Freeman, have over several years attempted to verify, via vital statistics in churches, published works, county and city records, City of Philadelphia Archives, etc., the information in the family history collected by Louella Burr Mitchell Allen recording that Burr had a second family in Philadelphia. Here is a digest of the records kept by the family and the results of the research. The story of the loving care and support that Aaron Burr devoted to these heretofore unrecognized offspring reinforces the picture of him presented by Oliver Perry Sturm in The Conspiracy Against Aaron Burr *as a family man, an educator, an abolitionist, and an advocate for women suffrage.*

Philadelphia, as the site of the annual meeting in 2005 of the Aaron Burr Association, coincided with the culmination of the research on aspects of Colonel Aaron Burr's life while in Philadelphia that have either been slighted by, or were unknown to, his foremost biographers.

First is the story, gleaned from family records, of Burr's second marriage to Mary Emmons, who was a person of color in Philadelphia, and their daughter, Louisa Charlotte, born 1788, and son, John Pierre Burr (hereinafter JPB), born 1792.

The course of JPB's life from manhood onwards as a resident of Philadelphia, a leader of the abolitionist movement, and a person of letters is amply reported in contemporary publications, whereas the circumstances of his birth and ancestry can only be deduced from a combination of family records and tales told to and put to pen by his descendants.

For the preponderance of his life one can rely on records collected by the family, periodicals, newspapers, records of organizations, and a variety of other objective documentation, including the

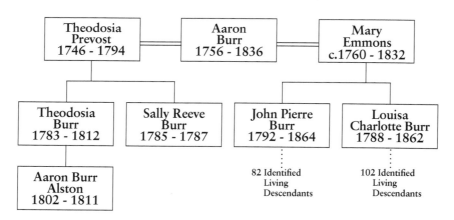

Aaron Burr's lineage with his first wife Theodosia ended prematurely with her death in 1794, along with the early deaths of his two daughters and his beloved grandson. It is a different story entirely with his second family with Mary Emmons. To date, members have identified approximately 184 living descendants, but that number could be much higher as several family lineages have yet to be researched.

authors of several books. These include the recording of his death, dated April 7, 1864, with an age consistent with the year of his birth, and residence on Lombard Street above 13th, albeit the misspelling of his last name as "Barr," as well as a death notice in the *Philadel-*

phia Public Ledger of the same date with correct spelling of "Burr" and residence at 1309 Lombard Street and a contemporary portrait in sepia confirming that he was a light-skinned person of color, befitting someone with one parent being white and the other of color. Further clinching that "Barr" actually was "Burr" is the form at the City of Philadelphia Archives combining the "Physician's Certificate" and "Undertaker's Certificate" from which his death was recorded; the "u" in "Burr" is distinguishable from an "a" only by comparing the physician's handwriting of "a" in the word "year" and in the abbreviation of his first name. Periodicals describe his role as an officer of Chairman of the Board of Managers of the American Moral Reform Society (a politically safe moniker for "pro abolitionism"); as a founder of the Demosthenian Institute (a literary society formed at his home for the purpose of elevating the morality of its members through lectures, a small library, etc.); as a barber for whites operating out of his home at 113 South 5th Street, below Prune (the name of the street has been changed to Locust but appears clearly as Prune on a 1790s map), along with the service of his wife, Hester (Hetty, 1796–1862); as an officer and co-founder of the Olive Cemetery (currently Eden Cemetery Company), America's oldest African-American public cemetery company; and as a trustee of the Women's Association of Philadelphia (for the benefit of slaves).

Vital statistics confirming the date and location of his birth, however, are lacking. One is left, therefore, relying on a combination of family history and circumstantial evidence to confirm his parentage. Herewith is a recapitulation of the sources which the researchers have used and which constitute (in the judgment of the editors) the irreducible minimum essential to back up the family oral history that was committed to writing by successive generations. Thanks to the great-great-granddaughter of JPB, Louella Burr Mitchell Allen, these have been compiled and preserved in a series of binders.

A. Allen B. Ballard, Professor of History in African Studies at SUNY–Albany, in *One More Day's Journey: The Story of a Family and a People*, claims JPB as an ancestor and relates that

Ballard's great-aunt, Elizabeth (Doll) Durham, witnessed the destruction of the marriage certificate for JPB's parents, Aaron Burr and Mary Emmons. (It was the practice after the ceremony to give the marriage certificate to the newlyweds to store in the family Bible.) Dr. Charles L. Blockson, curator at Temple University for the Afro-American Collection, containing the most comprehensive collection extant of artifacts from St. Domingue, in his *The Underground Railway in Pennsylvania*, 1987, refers to JPB as Aaron Burr's "illegitimate son." The recent Malcolm Bell, Jr., director of the Georgia Historical Society, in *Major Butler's Legacy: Five Generations of a Slave-Holding Family*, 1987, under "Personae" states "The Vice-President's natural son, John Pierre Burr, a mulatto, became a successful Philadelphia barber and an active participant in the underground railroad." Of the four books cited as sources for the material related to Burr in "Personae," the pages referred to in three make no mention of JPB.

B.   Family oral and written history assembled by JPB's descendants, such as Mabel Burr Cornish's (1879–1955) notebook History of Our Family Tracing Back to Aaron Burr and the Beginning of St. Thomas Episcopal Church in Philadelphia; data collected by her niece, Louella Burr Mitchell Allen; and research of public and Latter Day Saints archives by Louella and an Arizona D.A.R. associate, such as City of Philadelphia Directories and U.S. Censes, add substance and reality to JPB's life.

C.   Louella's aunt Mabel is a source for JPB having been "born at sea between the USA and Haiti," then St. Domingue. Family oral history identifies JPB's mother, Mary Emmons, as an East Indian who moved to the West Indies and that she made several trips with the two children to and from St. Domingue, whereas Prof. Ballard designates her as a West Indian. Colonel Burr moved to Philadelphia October 24, 1791, to take his seat in the U.S. Senate. According to family recollection Mary Emmons was a member of his household. Based again on family recollection, she and their daughter, Louisa Charlotte Mary, sailed in 1792 to St. Domingue, so JPB could have been born either en route to the island or on return from there. Aunt Mabel, as quoted by Prof. Ballard, identifies Mary Emmons as an East Indian (perhaps born in India?) who moved to the West Indies. Customary sources of vital family statistics (e.g., churches, town and county repositories, and historical societies) for verification have in the interim been destroyed by fire, thwarting attempts to corroborate.

D. Louella Burr Mitchell Allen meticulously collected and filed accounts of her ancestors passed down through generations, in particular memories written by her aunt Mabel. They constitute several binders but lack an index. It was with some reluctance that Louella made the family records available, since she felt that in a sense this was abrogating a family tradition of not publicizing its Aaron Burr ancestry—a tradition no doubt with diplomatic roots based on the climate of the times in the early 1800s and perpetuated from generation to generation. As she further observed, the linkage needed no heralding, as it was widely recognized within the family and community. Note that whereas JPB and his elder sister were born while Burr's wife, Theodosia, was still alive, the marriage of Aaron and Mary occurred after her demise. If there had been family records at, for example, the St. Thomas African-American Church in Philadelphia, with which JPB and his family were closely affiliated, he as a member of the vestry, they might have indicated when he was baptized and the names of his parents; unfortunately the records of the church were destroyed when it burned at its second location. A bronze marker mounted on the sidewalk on the west side of South Fifth Street north of Locust Street (formerly Prune) commemorates the church. JPB's home at 113 South Fifth was on the east side, below Prune.

E. Family history mistakenly refers to an 1817 deed involving Aaron Burr and property at No. 113 South Fifth Street in the Old City of Philadelphia, claiming that Burr purchased as a home

Fans of Aaron Burr Find Unlikely Ally In a 'New' Relative

* * *

Retired Black Nurse Tells Story of His Other Family; 'An Upstanding Citizen'

By Greg Ip

PHILADELPHIA—For years, Stuart Fisk Johnson, a white criminal-defense attorney, has doggedly researched the life of his distant ancestor Aaron Burr in hopes of restoring Burr's good name. Recently, Mr. Johnson found an unlikely ally here: an 86-year-old retired black nurse who says she is Burr's great-great-great-granddaughter, the descendant of Burr's illegitimate, mixed-race son.

Louella Burr Mitchell Allen

The nation's third vice president, Burr hasn't been treated kindly by history. He is chiefly remembered for killing his rival Alexander Hamilton in a duel in 1804. Thomas Jefferson suspected Burr of trying to take the presidency from him in the disputed election of 1800. Years later, Jefferson had him arrested for treason for allegedly trying to start a war with Spain and separate the western territories from the United States. Though Burr was acquitted, his reputation was ruined. It has more or less stayed that way, in part because of the great esteem in which Hamilton and Jefferson are still held.

Lately some historians have painted a more benign picture. They note that Burr, unlike Jefferson, actively opposed slavery (though he may have owned a few slaves himself). He introduced a bill in the New York Legislature to abolish slavery. He courted the political support of New York's black leaders. And his purported illegitimate son, Philadelphia barber John Pierre Burr, was a prominent abolitionist.

Since this article was published in the *Wall Street Journal* on October 5, 2005 the Aaron Burr Association's location of family birth, marriage, and death certificates, media articles, property deeds *et alia* conclusively link John Pierre Burr to Aaron Burr.

At its annual [meeting] in King of Prussia, near Philadelphia, this week, the Aaron Burr Association, a small group of Burr devotees headed by Mr. Johnson, plans to share a trove of family documents, pictures and oral history owned by Louella Burr Mitchell Allen, the nurse who traces her lineage to John Pierre Burr. Mrs. Allen, who lives in a Philadelphia retirement home, will speak at the meeting about Burr's family of color.

Aaron Burr

The documents and oral history aren't conclusive; there is no birth, death or marriage certificate linking Aaron Burr to John Pierre Burr. And DNA testing hasn't been done. Still, Mr. Johnson and his association are embracing Mrs. Allen and her relatives as long lost kin. "Even though it hasn't been proven yet, we're very conscious [Mrs. Allen] is getting up in years and we want to learn about her and this family before it's too late," says Mr. Johnson, 62 years old, who runs the association from his home in Upper Marlboro, Md.

His sister, Phyllis Morales, says there's no question that Mrs. Allen "is my relative," adding that she "looks just like us—her mannerisms, her voice," Mr. Johnson and Ms. Morales trace their family tree back to a cousin of Burr's.

The Burr group's embrace of Mrs. Allen contrasts with the cool reception many of Thomas Jefferson's white descendants have given descendants of Jefferson slave Sally Hemings. In 1998, DNA testing demonstrated that Jeffer-

Please Turn to Page A14, Column 5

II

Aaron Burr Supporters Find Ally

Continued From First Page

son was probably the father of one of her sons. Nonetheless, the Monticello Association, which controls burial rights at the Jefferson family cemetery near Charlottesville, Va., says the DNA evidence is not conclusive. So far the association has declined to permit Hemings descendants to be buried at the cemetery, which is restricted to Jefferson's direct descendants.

Many of the details of Burr's life are well-known. In 1782, he married a woman 10 years his senior, Theodosia Prevost, the widow of a British army officer. They had at least two children, but only one survived to adulthood, a girl also named Theodosia. Burr was rumored to have fathered illegitimate white children, but Mr. Johnson says he knows of no living descendants of them and no descendants of Burr's daughter.

Much of what the Aaron Burr Association now knows of Mr. Burr's mixed-race family was collected and written down by Mabel Burr Cornish, the great granddaughter of John Pierre Burr. After Mrs. Cornish died in 1955, her notes were given to Mrs. Allen, her niece. Mrs. Allen displays a thick scrapbook of documents and handwritten remembrances in her retirement suite. "We are proud of the fact [Burr] was an upstanding citizen and not a dirty politician," she said. She opened the book to a picture of John Pierre Burr that, she says, hung in his Philadelphia barber shop. It shows a handsome, grave man with a distinctive narrow nose that resembles Aaron Burr's and Mrs. Allen's.

The history collected by Mrs. Cornish and Mrs. Allen suggests that Aaron Burr had two children with Mary Emmons, who was a servant but not a slave in Burr's household in Philadelphia while he was married to Theodosia. Mary Emmons was born in Calcutta and lived in Haiti before coming to the U.S. The couple had a daughter, Louisa Charlotte, in 1788. They had a son, John Pierre, in 1792.

Allen Ballard, a distant cousin of Mrs. Allen who counts himself as a Burr descendant, says that some of his own, older relatives felt ambivalent about being descended from Burr. "This traitor thing still hung on him," he says. "There hadn't been all this revisionist history" of recent years that portrays Burr as victimized by the malice of Hamilton and Jefferson. Mr. Ballard, who teaches history and African-American studies at the State University of New York at Albany, says his mother's aunt had a marriage certificate showing that Burr and Emmons were married after Theodosia's death but that the aunt tore it up out of frustration with the family's lack of interest.

Though his mother may have been East Indian, John Pierre Burr considered himself an African American. A free man, he turned his barber shop into a station in the underground railroad. He hid slaves in the backyard and attic, according to Mrs. Cornish's writings.

Mrs. Allen thinks Aaron Burr may have quietly supported John Pierre Burr in his abolitionist activities although there's no proof of that.

After serving as an officer in George Washington's army, Burr became prominent in New York state politics. In 1800, Jefferson chose him as his vice-presidential running mate. The two tied in the Electoral College, which in those days did not cast separate ballots for president and vice president, so the decision was thrown to the House of Representatives. Whether Burr actively tried to become president is unclear but Jefferson, who eventually prevailed, suspected that he had, and hated him for it. Burr later ran for governor of New York, incurring the wrath of Alexander Hamilton, who tried to undermine Burr's candidacy. Hamilton's alleged slanders—precisely what he said is unclear—led to the fatal duel, fought on the New Jersey cliffs overlooking Manhattan.

Burr then traveled west to explore turning Spanish territory, and possibly some of the newly acquired U.S. western territory, into a separate country. Jefferson learned of the plan and had him tried for treason in 1807. He was acquitted thanks to the interventions of Chief Justice John Marshall, a Jefferson antagonist, who presided over the trial. Burr, his reputation ruined nonetheless, left for Europe. He returned in 1812. He married a wealthy widow in 1833; they were divorced the day Burr died in 1836.

The new evidence of Burr's family of color gets mixed reactions from historians. Thomas Fleming, author of "Duel: Alexander Hamilton, Aaron Burr and the Future of America," is skeptical, arguing that Burr's enemies would almost certainly have learned of such a family's existence and "played it up very big." But Roger Kennedy, author of "Burr, Hamilton and Jefferson: a Study in Character," calls the story "plausible." He notes Burr, in a letter to his daughter Theodosia, briefly mentioned a woman in Philadelphia about whom he seemed to feel both affection and guilt. Mr. Kennedy speculates it may have been a woman of color.

The Aaron Burr Association has explored DNA testing to verify the link. But the test is generally on the male Y chromosome, which changes little between generations, and the association has not found a suitable male descendant of John Pierre Burr from whom to take a sample.

Mrs. Allen has no doubts. "Since the beginning of time, the races all meshed," she says. "And you know what? You get quality from this combination."

for JPB. As mentioned above, an abundance of anecdotal evidence, which is supported by accounts in publications, establishes this as the location where JPB lived, operated his barbershop, and conducted a stage of the Underground Railway for refugee slaves—an activity that complemented Aaron Burr's pro-abolitionist advocacy. Although the 1817 deed, which was located at the City of Philadelphia Archives, turned out to apply to distant property on the road to Lancaster, the lack of any deed tends to confirm Louella's recalling that there was no deed on record for John Pierre's residing at 113 South Fifth Street, implying that neither Colonel Burr nor JPB ever held title to the residence. JPB moved from there in 1849, eventually to Lombard Street, until his demise.

F.   Most recently fifth and sixth generation members of Aaron Burr's family of color including Karla Ballard (Allen B. Ballard's niece), Sherri Burr, William Young, Lori Cornish, Dolly Marshall, and Anita H. Trotman have applied modern Online ancestory services, and positive DNA matching with collateral white descendants, to expand and validate the Burr family tree into the present time. As they are the first to acknowledge, this is still very much a work in progress and the results are often not conclusive, but a picture of Burr's second bloodline is slowly coming into focus.

In summation, the family oral and recorded history in combination with a plethora of circumstantial evidence builds a convincing case for substantiating the existence of Aaron Burr's second family. Lacking is correspondence between Burr and the family, and records of transactions dealing with real estate, finances, etc. It is essential, therefore, to corroborate the relationships via both additional original sources and DNA testing. Otherwise historians and special-interest groups, who are inherently defensive of the terrain that they have staked out, will be prone to contest the conclusions and discredit the Aaron Burr Association presentation on the grounds of its being hypothetical. In refutation of critics, as Dr. Blockson observes, there is a wealth of history in family records that has been, and continues to be, overlooked by historians who, paradoxically, do not hesitate to accept as history evidence that has been chronicled in sagas and ballads until recorded often centuries later.

In the 1800s the story of the family was folklore in the community. The incredible detail with which Mabel Burr Cornish describes the use of JPB's home as part of the Underground Railroad and other verbal legacies from ancestors are too realistic and interlocking to have been figments of the imagination; they add convincing credibility to the reliability of the family history.

What solace it must have been for Aaron Burr to have a second bloodline with an heir apparent in the person of John Pierre fulfilling the role of perpetuating Burr's lifelong commitment to society—a trust that he had hoped grandson Tad would carry on. JPB and his son, Walter Harris Burr, took up the mantle from James Reston, founder and leader of the abolitionist movement in Philadelphia.

The new John Pierre Burr headstone, produced under the direction of Aaron Burr Association member and Burr descendant Sherri Burr, and erected by the ABA in 2019 at the Historic Eden Cemetery in Collingdale, PA. There is no documentation for the use of "(Jean)" on the headstone. John Pierre Burr and his wife, Hetty, had initially been buried in Olive Cemetery in Philadelphia. They were moved to Eden Cemetery in 1902 after city officials condemned Olive Cemetery. Their headstones at Eden disintegrated over time, leaving an unmarked plot.

#2
Leonora (Hassall) Sansay

Aaron Burr's uncanny capacity to identify individuals of talent inspired him to nurture and support persons whose distinguished careers often fulfilled his expectations of them.

The second aspect of the ABA research on Aaron Burr's life and associations in Philadelphia (as revealed at the ABA annual meeting in 2005) addresses his longtime connection with, and support of, America's first recognized woman novelist, Leonora (née Hassall) Sansay.

Collateral research to explore the possibility of Leonora Sansay and Mary Emmons Burr (JPB's mother) being the same person refutes the theory. The dates and travels of Leonora compared with those of Mary are far too mismatched for this being the case. In addition, Mary was a person of color, and Leonora, in her second novel, *Laura*, states that her parents were William and Rosina Hassall, the former being from a Dutch family and proprietor of the tavern, The Sign of the Half Moon, located opposite the State House . (They could have migrated via the West Indies, like another Hassell family (the Dutch spelling), who emigrated from Holland to the island of Saba and remain in the shipping industry.)

Leonora's letters to Aaron from St. Domingue during the uprising are a combination of the reportorial and autobiographical, and those during the episodes of the revolution that formed the basis for her novels, along with his purchases of several properties from her, personally or as agent, on the eve of her departure with her husband Louis for St. Domingue, all confirm their close (and probable romantic) relationship. Inspection of the locations of the properties might indicate a pattern revealing more about their association in Philadelphia and perhaps a transaction involving 113 South Fifth, but every avenue pursued has led to naught.

Among additional clues to the relationship are: a letter from Burr on her behalf to a diplomat requesting an introduction to someone of influence in St. Domingue; her presence in New Orleans under the disguise of Mme. D'Auvergne with Burr's cohorts, Dr. Erich Bollman and Samuel Swartwout during the period when General Wilkinson sought to imprison and indict Burr; mention of her in a letter containing instructions about his estate; and an 1815 letter from Bollman when in London to Burr inquiring about her: "I would give much to know how Leonora is doing— all what occurs to me good, springs from. . . . I remember her daily with gratitude and affection—no European beauty has made the least impression on me since I left the U. States. Tell her so, and I shall truly rejoice in the pleasure of seeing her again."

Bollman became one of her partners in a factory one mile west of Philadelphia that manufactured artificial flowers designed by her.

Leonora was the archetype of the women of talent and intellect who intrigued Burr and stimulated his impulse to inculcate and educate as he did with daughter Theodosia and other young wards. In effect Burr served as an early militant for women's emancipation, a movement the momentum of which, ironically, would come to fruition before the abolitionist movement for which he was unique in his time as an activist and so appropriately succeeded in by son JPB and grandson Walter Harris Burr (1825–1912), who resided in Norwich, CT—a transfer station in the Underground Railroad at the tidewater of the Thames River.

Facilitating the marriage of Leonora and Louis Sansay, expediting their move to St. Domingue, and becoming the sounding board for her letters that became the fountainhead for three or more novels was typical of his penchant to foster education for the welfare of the nation. It echoed his financing the education in France of protégés such as the landscape-portrait painter John Vanderlyn and godson Aaron Columbus Burr.

For more on Leonora's life and novels see Secret History: or, The Horrors of St. Domingo and Laura *by Professor Michael J. Drexler, See also* Afro-Americana: Rediscovering Leonora Sansay *by Philip S. Lapsansky, Chief of Reference, the Library Company of Philadelphia.*

#3
John Vanderlyn

Aaron Burr Association members Henry H. Anderson, Jr.
and Dennis E. Lauchman were made privy at the Senate House
Museum, the original capitol building of New York, in Kingston,
New York, to The Unpublished Biography of the Life and Works
of John Vanderlyn, *written by Marius Schoonmaker, bequeathed*
by Edward Coykendall in 1949 and deciphered by Mary Black
Terwilliger. Courtesy of the author and the museum, a copy is in
the Aaron Burr Association Collection at Rutgers University. It is
a story of Burr's uncanny capacity to spot talent and seek to edu-
cate and elevate his fellow man. He virtually became Vanderlyn's
mentor, and by the time Vanderlyn reached his thirties he was
considered by many a finer portrait painter than Gilbert Stuart;
as a landscape painter he had few equals. The following com-
prises excerpts from the biography dealing with the relationship
between Burr and Vanderlyn, edited by Anderson.

Gilbert Stuart formed acquaintance with young John Vanderlyn; "his opinion of him was so favorable that he granted him
the privilege to copy two of his portraits, one that was of Col.
Aaron Burr." Vanderlyn at the time lived in Kingston and could
not afford to live in New York City. The Burr portrait was purchased by Hon. Peter Van Gaasbeek of Kingston (there is a heavy
Dutch presence still in Kingston)—the location of the portrait is
unknown.

When Burr heard of the superior character of the portraits
he wrote to a friend in Kingston:

> *Philad. 21 June 1795: My Dear Sir: I understand*
> *that a young Mr. VanderLyn, who lived a short time*
> *with Stuart the Painter, left him for want of means of*
> *suitable support . . . I . . . shall be infinitely flattered*

*by an opportunity of rescuing genius from obscurity.
He may draw on J. B. Provost New York, for any sum
which may be necessary for his outfit, and on his arrival in this city . . . he will find a letter from me . . . pointing out the channel of his future supplies. The source
of which never will be known except to himself. . . .
This arrangement is intended to continue as long as it
may be necessary for Mr. V.D.L. to cultivate his genius
to the highest point of perfection. Your aff'ct., A. Burr*

Burr, of course, was singular in his capacity for detecting
genius and nurturing talent, but in later life his generosity for
helping the bright and the broke kept him perpetually in debt.

When J. V. arrived at his NYC lodgings he found a note directing him to call at the corner of Church and Fulton Streets,
where he found the office of Col. Burr and his stepson J. B. Provost. "Every necessary arrangement was at once made and Vanderlyn departed for Philadelphia, where he became an inmate of
the family and took his place in the studio of Gilbert Stuart who
had removed to that city."

The author disposes of the libel often contradicted by Vanderlyn (which has been given currency by James Parton in his *Life
of Aaron Burr*, 1848):

*Alleging that Vanderlyn at the time came to Col.
Burr's house, "a rough country boy" who "fairly forced
his way into the breakfast room" "walked straight up
to the table where Burr was breakfasting, pulled a
coarse clean shirt out of his pocket and silently laid
it down before him," and one version further stating
that "he was apprentice to a wagon maker, another to
a Blacksmith and in his employment remained until
nearly twenty-one."*

*How flatly the above libel is repudiated by indis-
putable evidence—that Vanderlyn was then a young*

man of about twenty years of age, blessed with an academical education, had passed three years of his life in one of the most celebrated stores in the City of New York. . . . The writer has a paper of Mr. Vanderlyn, written by him a few years before his death referring to that old story. . . . "scurrilous statement of his early life and introduction to Col. Burr evidently from unworthy and malicious motives."

In the fall of 1796 Col. Burr sent J. V. with liberal provisions to Paris, whose schools were then in high repute:

He then paid special attention to accuracy and skill in drawing and to the anatomy of the human frame. His anatomical accuracy and beautiful delineation of the human form is one of the great distinguishing and triumphant features of his pencil. He spent four years in Paris bringing a few sketches from Correggio's works and of other masters evoking Col. Burr to write to a friend, "he is pronounced to be the first painter that now is or ever has been in America."

He returned in the summer of 1801 with the intention, under the advice of his patron Col. Burr, to take sketches of some prominent places of interest in the country, especially Niagara Falls (the Great Cataract), with a view of making copies and engravings for the purpose of disposal in Europe. Some of his paintings of Niagara Falls are in the Senate House. Quoted is a letter from Col. Burr to Thomas Morris at Niagara requesting him to assist J. V.

While members of the ABA know J. V. best as a portrait painter by reason of his portraits of the Col. Burr and Theodosia:

The truth is that his tastes never run in the line of portrait painting, but as has been well and truly said by another "his studies had been directed to classical or historical subjects and the contemplation of grace and beauty in its most engaging forms, which were then the all engrossing object of the schools at which he studied."

Time and again in the biography, both at home and abroad, J. V. perforce turned to portrait painting in order to earn the wherewithal to survive while undertaking landscape and classical subjects.

Col. Burr wrote to Theodosia in a letter Dec. 6, 1802, "Vanderlyn has finished your picture in the most beautiful style imaginable. When it was done he exclaimed with enthusiasm 'There is the best work I have ever done in America.'"

On his return to Paris he was well connected and traveled to many cities, and in 1804 to '05 traveled to Switzerland and Rome. In 1803 he had painted his first historic picture, *The Death of Miss McCrea*, from Barlow's poem of the vision of Columbus (now in the Hartford Athenaeum).

In a letter Jan. 25, 1807, he observed, "I have long discovered that painting is not the road to wealth. This discovery does not alarm me, for my ambition of wishes has long been absorbed by that of fame." At that time he was working on a painting that was to make him famous, *Marius Amid of Carthage*. This work carried on into 1807, preparing it for an exhibition in the Louvre. It won in 1807 the gold medal presented by Napoleon for the "best original picture," which Napoleon himself selected ("the Emperor Napoleon pointing his finger to . . . "). Quoted from the jury: "the historical style especially this 'beaux-ideal.'" Of almost equal fame was his copy of Correggio's *Antiope*.

Prevented from returning to America by the War of 1812, he finally did so in 1816, by which time "he lost the assistance of his patron Burr," who was in sore financial straits. In fact, while Burr had been in exile in London and Paris:

Vanderlyn of course was ready to divide his last crust with Burr, and assume the role of patron, and with his scanty earnings they lived in obscure and cheap lodgings.

Of that little is known, and Vanderlyn would not talk or allude to it. And whenever it was broached was irritated.

In a letter to Col. Gibbs of Boston, J. V. alludes to his anxiety to come home, and complains of a want of sufficient encouragement and friendship among his countrymen and thus alludes to Col. Burr:

> *I think I may with just grounds attribute the reserve and shyness of some of my countrymen here to my connection and intimacy with Col. Burr when in Paris. The idea grieves me to find so little liberality and independence in the world. . . . I shall not only ever feel the liveliest sentiments of gratitude towards him, but a high esteem and admiration for his qualities of heart and mind. . . . To my knowledge there has been much calumny and direct falsehood circulated against him here among Americans.*

"In 1837 he received the commission from Congress to paint a picture of the landing of Columbus to fill one of the panels of the Rotunda in the Capitol." He went to Paris to do so via the West Indies, where he "Studied the foliage and scenery to make his picture as true to nature as possible, and the probable appearance of the landing place in its native garb." He went to Madrid to procure "the best authenticated likeness of Columbus."

"Vanderlyn was without doubt in his prime the finest artistic and historic painter that ever was born in this country."

He finally returned to his home town of Kingston, and one morning in 1852 was found a corpse in his room at the hotel, "with his hands raised and in position as if holding the brush in the very act of transferring to canvas one of his fine artistic touches with his pencil." His works at the Senate House include *Flight from Pompeii, Mark Anthony and Cleopatra,* a *Madonna and Child,* the original study of the *Landing of Columbus,* the model for *Columbus* and others, and sketches for the *Panoramic View of the Palace* and *Gardens of Versailles.*

#4
Aaron Columbus Burr
and Charles Burdett

Best known for his contributions to the nation as a statesman and warrior, Aaron Burr has not been portrayed to the same extent as a humanitarian. In the latter role he influenced the lives of numerous wards adopted intentionally or by happenstance, e.g., legacies such as Prevost stepsons, children of clients, offspring of indigent friends, and the young whose potential he sought to elevate.

Aaron Columbus Burr and Charles Burdett fit the last category, but historians have differed on their precise relationship to Burr. Contemporary comment such as obituaries in newspapers tend to confirm what was common knowledge at the time.

The *New York Times* of July 28, 1882, in an obit on page five, characterizes Aaron C. Burr as "an adopted son of Col. Aaron Burr. . . . a son of Count Verdi de Liste of Paris, France, where he was born. In 1816"—recall that Burr returned from self-exile in 1816—"he left his own country, under the guardianship of Col. Burr for the purpose of completing his education in this country, and at the death of his father was adopted by his guardian." The obit continues, "Mr. Burr [Aaron Columbus] had in his possession a great deal of the private and diplomatic correspondence of his foster father." In correspondence with Col. Burr, Columbus closes with "A. B. Columbus" or "A. Burr Columbus" and "godson." An obit in the *New York Herald* for Columbus's son, Hippolyte, refers to Hippolyte as "an adopted son of the anti-federalist."

According to the *New-York Tribune* of Sept. 26, 1862, Charles Burdett was also "an adopted son of the celebrated Aaron Burr" and that "In early life obtained, through the influence of his foster father, a commission in the navy." His legacy to Burr was *Margaret Moncrieffe, the First Love of Aaron Burr: A Romance in the Revolution*, with an appendix containing a letter from Leonora to Burr.

Sources of Research

As a boy just entering my teens, I was told by my paternal grandmother that she was a descendant of Aaron Burr. Appalled by what appeared to be a family skeleton in my closet, I consulted my history and then scanned every available book. All said he was a traitor.

Curiously enough, I did not believe it. Like the average Missourian, I had to be shown. Then was begun this research for evidence that, as Thomas Jefferson declared, "Burr had formed the no less daring projects than to reduce New Orleans, subjugate Mexico, and divide the Union."

Soon my research became the hobby of a journalist, where every vacation was planned with a view to learning something about the charges—something new about Aaron Burr. The first comprehensive source of information was the trial at Richmond, where the court reporter's record filled two large volumes. Then I examined court records from New York to New Orleans, after which the research was extended to England, France, and Spain.

No evidence was found that Burr even contemplated an act of treachery toward his native land. The records fairly teem with charges by Thomas Jefferson and his associates. These were first presented to grand juries in Kentucky and Mississippi. In refusing to indict Burr, these juries turned upon Jefferson and his political agents and reported in most vehement language that the charges were political, that those who instigated them were the agents of a political tyrant. The evidence all proved hearsay, or just the charges of politicians who, as ex-President John Adams said, "had no more regard to Truth than the Devil." Perhaps two thousand original sources were scanned, consisting of letters, diaries, court papers, deeds, contracts, posters, maps, cartoons, manuscripts, newspapers, magazines, and pamphlets. More than three hundred books have been read or consulted as secondary sources.

The institutions at which this research was pursued were: the Library of Congress, Princeton University, the New York Historical Society, the New York Public Library, the New Jersey Historical Society, the Historical Society of Delaware, the Virginia Historical Society, the Tennessee Historical Society, the Oklahoma Historical Society, the Library of the University of Arkansas, the Archives and History of Mississippi, the Library of the University of Texas, the Texas State Archives, Yale University, and the Carnegie Library at Tulsa, Oklahoma.

Similar research was done by James Parton, Henry Adams, Walter F. McCaleb, Nat Schachner, Samuel Wandell, and Meade Minnigerode. Parton enjoyed the advantage of being able to consult contemporaries of Hamilton, Jefferson, and Burr.

The list of those who have rendered service for which I am under obligation is too large to print. The reader of *The Conspiracy Against Aaron Burr* who desires additional information will find the bibliography most helpful; its compilation required more than fifty years. The preparation of the manuscript has occupied my entire time for five years. It was, however, a happy task—the fruition of a lifetime hobby.

The association with Alexander Hamilton, Thomas Jefferson, and Aaron Burr has been a rare experience—rich in memories of three contrasting personalities, with never a dull moment. Hamilton was a natural autocrat; Jefferson was a great scholar and philosopher; while Burr's obsession was man and his social and intellectual improvement. If this volume arouses in the students of America a desire to know more about these three men, and the causes that led to their estrangement, it will have served the purposes of the author.

– Oliver Perry Sturm, 1943

The Conspiracy Against Aaron Burr *manuscript by Oliver Perry Sturm contained no formal bibliography other than the references appearing in the text. Except for published court records, the editors have been unable to locate numerous originals in order to verify the accuracy of their precise wording. However, a partial bibliography of recently verified sources appears on the next page.*

Partial Bibliography

A Man Without a Country, Edward Everett Hale

Aaron Burr, Volume I, by Samuel H. Wandell and Meade Minnigerode

Aaron Burr: A Biography, by Nathan Schachner

Afro-Americana: Rediscovering Leonora Sansay, Philip S. Lapsansky

Biography, by Philip Brooks

Five American Politicians: Study in the Evolution of American Politics, by Samuel P. Orth

History of the Presidency, by Edward Stanwood

Life of Joseph Brant, by William L. Stone

Major Butler's Legacy: Five Generations of a Slave-Holding Family, Malcolm Bell, Jr.

Margaret Moncrieffe, the First Love of Aaron Burr: A Romance in the Revolution, Burdett, Charles

Memoirs of Burr, Colonel Knapp

One More Day's Journey: The Story of a Family and a People, Allen B. Ballard

Portrait of a Prodigy, by David Roth

Secret History: The Horrors of St. Domingo and Laura, Michael J. Drexler

The Aaron Burr Conspiracy, by Walter F. McCaleb

The Burr Conspiracy, Thomas Perkins Abernethy

The History of the United States of America 1801–1817, by Henry Adams

The Life and Times of Aaron Burr, by James Parton

The Life and Times of Jefferson, by Thomas Edward Watson

The Trial of Aaron Burr for High Treason, J. J. Coombs

The Trial of Aaron Burr, Silas Carpenter

The Underground Railway in Pennsylvania, Charles L. Blockson

The Unpublished Biography of the Life and Works of John Vanderlyn, Marius Schoonmaker Third Annual Report of the Director of the Department of Archives and History of the State of Mississippi from October 1, 1903, to October 1, 1904, With Accompanying Historical Documents Concerning the Aaron Burr Conspiracy, by Dunbar Rowland

Two Letters of Andrew Brown, Dennis Lauchman

Index